THE
FASHODA INCI[...]
OF 1898

THE
FASHODA INCIDENT
OF 1898

Encounter on the Nile

DARRELL BATES

OXFORD UNIVERSITY PRESS
1984

Oxford University Press, Walton Street, Oxford OX2 6DP

London Glasgow New York Toronto
Delhi Bombay Calcutta Madras Karachi
Kuala Lumpur Singapore Hong Kong Tokyo
Nairobi Dar es Salaam Cape Town
Melbourne Auckland
and associates in
Beirut Berlin Ibadan Mexico City Nicosia

Oxford is a trade mark of Oxford University Press

British Library Cataloguing in Publication Data

Bates, Darrell
The Fashoda Incident of 1898.
1. Fashoda Crisis, 1898
I. Title
962.9'3 DT156.6
ISBN 0-19-211771-8

Library of Congress Cataloging in Publication Data

Bates, Darrell, Sir.
The Fashoda incident of 1898.
Bibliography: p.
Includes index.
1. Fashoda Crisis, 1898. I. Title.
DT156.6.B38 1983 962.4'03 83-8176
ISBN 0-19-211771-8

Set by Rowland Phototypesetting Ltd
Printed in Great Britain by
The Thetford Press Ltd,
Thetford, Norfolk

For Susan

Contents

Acknowledgements

I am indebted to Sir Patrick Reilly, lately HM Ambassador in Paris, for his introductions to the Director General of the *Archives nationales* in Paris and to the Director of the British Institute in Paris. I also wish to thank the Keeper of Oriental Books at Durham University Library for the facilities given to me to use the Wingate papers in the Sudan Archive, and the Librarian and Archivist to the Marquess of Salisbury for facilities to use the papers of the third Marquess at Hatfield House. My thanks are also due to Dr Ronald Seaton of the Liverpool School of Tropical Medicine for once again supplying suitably laconic answers to my diffuse medical enquiries, and to Maître Marc Michel of the University of Paris for his scholarly researches in the French national archives and for permission to draw on his comprehensive list of French sources. I must also express my thanks to the Director and the staff of London House in Mecklenburgh Square for providing me with such an amiable base while engaged on my researches in London. Finally I am indebted to Mr Richard Hill, the distinguished Sudan historian, for reading through the typescript and for his helpful suggestions and comments.

List of Illustrations

Maps

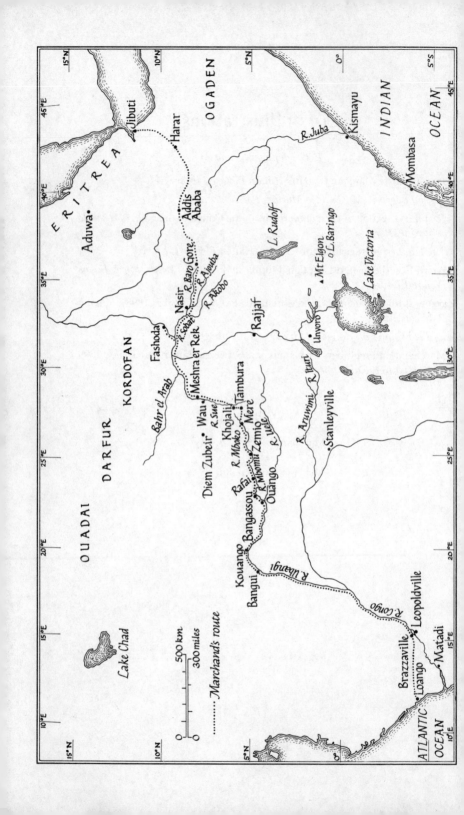

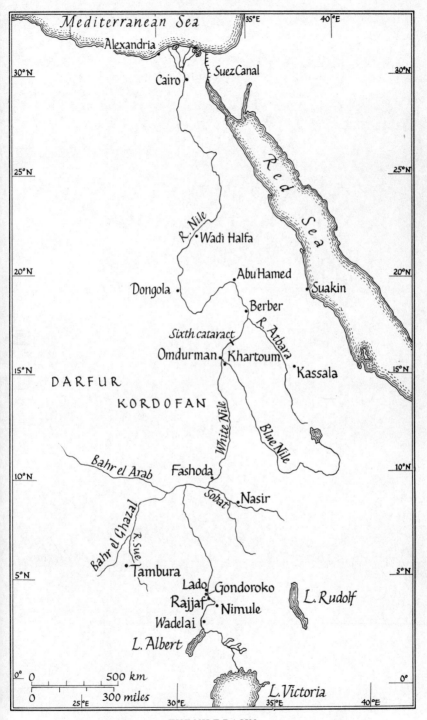

THE NILE BASIN

CHAPTER I

The Vision of Victor Prompt

AT three o'clock on the afternoon of 20 January 1893 a gathering of Frenchmen and French-speaking Egyptians met at the *Institut égyptien* in Cairo to listen to a lecture. The speaker, Victor Prompt, was a distinguished hydraulic engineer whose special interest was in the waters of the river Nile. The audience must have sensed that something unusual was in store for them. The meeting had been advertised as an extraordinary meeting; the president of the Institute, His Excellency Yacoub Pasha Artin, was himself in the chair, and in the audience were two of the most important members of the French community in Egypt – Le Chevalier, the French Commissioner for the Public Debt, and Prunières, the President of the Mixed Courts.[1] By the time the speaker rose to his feet his French listeners were in a good mood; in the streets outside on their way to the lecture they had encountered crowds engaged in a noisy public demonstration which was unmistakably anti-British.

The situation in Egypt at that time was described by *The Times* in London as 'very strained', and the popular agitation as 'widespread and vociferous'. A crucial trial of strength was taking place between the British presence, personified by Lord Cromer,[2] and the new

[1] In 1876 the Khedive Ismail of Egypt, after many years of living and ruling beyond his means on borrowed money, was obliged by his creditors in Austria, Britain, France, and Italy to accept the supervision of four commissioners of the public debt in order to ensure that he reduced his expenditure and repaid his debts. In the same year special mixed courts, largely staffed by European judges, were established to adjudicate in cases in which Europeans were involved.

[2] Evelyn Baring, born at Cromer in 1841; created Baron Cromer in 1892 and Earl in 1901. Although he was commissioned into the Royal Artillery, his inclinations, talents and family connections soon opened up other opportunities. He went to India in 1872 as ADC to the viceroy, and five years later became the first British commissioner for the public debt in Egypt. In 1883 when he was 42 he was made Agent and Consul-General at Cairo, a post which he held with awesome distinction and authority for 34 years. During this period Egypt was virtually a British protectorate, and he its *de facto* ruler. It was a Frenchman who said of his long period of stewardship that 'it was no good having right on your side if Lord Cromer is against you'.

Khedive, Abbas II, a youthful and volatile ruler whose education and experience on the continent had left him with independent views, expensive tastes, and an aversion to most things British. These tastes and feelings were shared by many other Egyptians. Although *The Times* spoke scathingly of 'the Cairene rabble, ready to demonstrate upon any side on the most reasonable terms', and hinted that their feelings had been deliberately 'fanned by the French local Press and the native papers enjoying French patronage', there was little doubt that in the early part of 1893 popular feelings in Cairo were decidedly anti-British. Rivalry between France and England[3] for prestige, influence, and commercial advantage in Egypt was at that time at one of its periodic peaks of intensity. Anti-British demonstrations were therefore more than usually welcome to the French-speaking members of the *Institut égyptien*, and helped to put them all into the right frame of mind to hear what Monsieur Prompt had to say to them.[4]

As Victor Prompt warmed to his subject and emerged from his humdrum recital of statistics of cubic metres of water per second, he explained that, whereas in the rainy season the flood waters of the Nile came more from the Blue Nile than the White, during the dry season the level of the river in Egypt depended mainly on the White Nile and reservoirs provided by the great lakes. He went on to show that the benefits which the Nile brought every year to Egypt could equally be transformed into disasters, if, for example, the flow of water were reduced in the dry season to a mere trickle, or if it were increased in the time of the rains to a flood. These situations could be caused, he said, in three ways. They could be caused by what he called *accidents météreologiques*, that is to say by too much rain in the wet season or too little in the dry. They could also be caused if undue amounts of water were drawn from the upper reaches of the Nile for irrigation or for storage. Finally, Prompt told his fascinated listeners, situations of both drought and of flood could be caused artificially by what he delicately referred to as 'opérations dues à la malveillance'. He did not mince his words. A dam constructed at strategic points on the White Nile could be deliberately and mis-

---

[3] It was common practice at this time both in London and in Paris to speak and write of England and the English where now we would say Britain and the British.

[4] It was not only the French who tried to tease and discomfort the British. Cromer told Lord Rosebery in a personal letter that 'during the crisis I played tennis every day. It gave confidence to the English and it annoyed the French'.

chievously manipulated both to reduce the flow of the Nile in the dry season to a level which would cause 'la ruine la plus complète pour l'Égypte', or to add to the normal flood waters to the point where 'the towns, the canals and the dykes would be destroyed and most of the inhabitants would perish either from flooding or from lack of food'.

The idea of regulating the flow of the Nile by artificial means was not new. The Director of Public Works in Egypt was a civil engineer named Scott-Moncrieff with considerable experience of dams and irrigation in India, and he and others had been advocating the construction of a dam at or near Aswan for years. What was new was the concept of malevolence, the idea of building a dam, not for Egypt's good, but for its ruin. Egypt had for centuries lived in the shadow of a fear that the most important flood-season sources of the Nile lay in Abyssinia and could somehow be held up or even diverted into the Red Sea. Prompt showed that, for practical reasons, these fears were groundless. The dams which he had in mind were on the White Nile south of Khartoum where, he calculated, the terrain was such that they could be built for not much more than half a million Egyptian pounds.[5] Two of the possible sites were in the region of the great lakes, the Victoria Nyanza and Lake Albert. They were a long way away and in the hands of the British, but there was a third site which was closer and in an area still unoccupied by any European power. It was at a point some four hundred miles south of Khartoum, near where the White Nile was joined from the east by the river Sobat. No towns or villages were named by the speaker but anyone could work out from the map that it was in the vicinity of a small, smelly, abandoned mud-flat fort called Fashoda.

Despite its dramatic conclusion Victor Prompt's speech does not seem to have aroused any widespread interest in Cairo at the time. Although there was an Englishman named Cope Whitehouse at the lecture who is recorded in the minutes as 'having exchanged observations with the speaker', no mention of the speech was made either in the English papers or in Cromer's official reports. One place where it did not go unnoticed however was Paris. Copies of the text of Prompt's speech were sent to a number of French government departments, and personal copies seem to have been

[5] The Egyptian pound, like most essentials of power and commerce in Egypt, was firmly linked to London and was then worth one pound sterling and sixpence.

sent both to Delcassé, the minister for the colonies, and to Sadi Carnot, the President of the Republic.

Prompt's speech reached Paris at a particularly opportune moment. Delcassé had been made minister for the colonies only two days before the speech was delivered in Cairo but he was already on the look out for a cause to call his own, one which would satisfy his consuming personal ambition. It was an ambition whose cutting edge had been sharpened over the years by his small stature, his unprepossessing appearance and his awkwardness with women. Théophile Delcassé had grown up from being an ugly, undersized, solitary, secretive, and immensely clever boy into a squat, swarthy, solitary, secretive, industrious, and immensely clever man who wore built-up heels to bolster his ego. In 1887, when he was 35, he married a shy, solitary but well-to-do widow who gave him the emotional and physical companionship he had lacked, as well as the self-confidence engendered by a private income of £12,000 a year. His wife was not a good hostess[6] but the stream of letters which Delcassé wrote to her show that she became the mainspring and motivation of almost everything he did.

Delcassé had become interested in colonial affairs as a young journalist and when he entered politics in 1889 he made them his speciality. He was particularly concerned with the decline of French influence in Egypt which he attributed as much to the weakness of successive French governments as to the perfidy of successive administrations in England. He was, as someone put it, 'tormented by Egypt'. By 1893 he had almost given up hope that any British government would honour its repeated promises to get out of Egypt, and he was looking for means of obliging her to do so. He was already involved in the expansion of France's colonial empire elsewhere, and he soon acquired a reputation for combining a romantic belief in France's sacred duty to extend the blessings of French civilisation with a hard-headed appreciation of the material benefits. 'Europe', he wrote, 'is stifling within her present boundaries with production everywhere outstripping demand. Its peoples are therefore driven by necessity to seek new markets far away, and what more secure markets can a nation have than the countries placed under her own influence?'

[6] Lord Bertie, the British ambassador in Paris, told Lord Lansdowne in a private letter after one of Madame Delcassé's parties, 'the food was foul beyond description and I had a bowl of soup on my return home'.

Delcassé's interest in colonial affairs attracted the attention of an organization called the *Comité de l'Afrique française*. It had been founded in 1890 by a journalist named Hippolyte Percher, who wrote under the easier pen-name of Harry Alis, and by a rich, land-owning member of the Chamber of Deputies called Prince d'Arenburg. Percher may have been an unscrupulous journalist on the make, and the Prince a rich man who wanted to be richer, but both seem to have been fired also with a patriotic zeal which gave the organization an appealing blend of passion and profit. One of its aims was to ensure that in the scramble for Africa France should get the major share which her clearly superior moral and material assets demanded. Although Eugene Étienne, the then colonial minister, was cautiously sympathetic, Harry Alis was soon complaining that 'the government seems to view the work of the *Comité* with indifference'. It was at this point that Delcassé's help was sought to form a *groupe colonial* in parliament made up of members of all parties who shared a common desire to extend France's overseas possessions. The help which Delcassé gave them was not over-looked when the government fell and the post of minister for the colonies became vacant in January 1893 as a result of one of France's periodic public scandals.[7] It was largely because of press-ure from the *Comité* and the *groupe colonial* that Delcassé was appointed.

From its inception the *Comité de l'Afrique française* had made a point of promoting and subsidizing expeditions and ventures de-signed to extend French influence and markets in West Africa and the region of Lake Chad. In 1892 however it shifted its main interest eastwards to the Bahr el Ghazal and the basin of the Nile. It had as its ultimate objective a vision of a continuous belt of French territory across Africa from Dakar to Jibuti; its more immediate and commercially attractive aim was to secure a river port on the Nile which could serve existing French possessions in equatorial Africa. The King of the Belgians had let it be known that he would support and even pay for a venture of this nature. He hoped both that concerted French and Belgian advances towards the main stream of the Nile might stop the British from pushing up the river from Uganda, and that a French move into the Bahr el Ghazal would

---

[7] The failure of a French company set up to cut a Panama canal was followed by allegations of bribery and corruption by various deputies and ministers.

divert them from the areas of the Ubangi and Mbomu rivers which he wanted for his own Congo Free State.

Thus it was that soon after Delcassé assumed office at the beginning of 1893 the Comité sought his support for an expedition into the Bahr el Ghazal and the valley of the Nile.[8] On 10 February he gave his official approval, but the secret instructions which he sent ten days later to the French governor at Libreville made it clear that he had ideas of his own and was determined that the expedition should be paid for and controlled by his own department, serving French and not Belgian interests. His telegram laid down that the expedition's first task was to support Liotard, a French colonial officer who was engaged in fighting the Belgians for control of the Ubangi and Mbomu rivers. Thereafter it was to cross into the basin of the Nile and establish a French presence in the untenanted expanse of territory to the east of the watershed between the Congo and the Nile.

For a venture of such wide-ranging objectives and potentially provocative consequences Delcassé needed more authority and more money than he could command on his own. He was a new and very junior under-minister, and his department had for years been no more than an appendage of various more important ministries like the Ministry of the Marine, the Ministry of Commerce and the Ministry of Foreign Affairs. The only improvement which Delcassé had been able to get when he took office was the right to sit in the Council of Ministers, and bigger and better offices in a wing of the Louvre known as the Pavillon de Flore.[9] He knew that his plan to send an expedition to help Liotard on the Mbomu and to penetrate into the basin of the Nile would upset not only the King of the Belgians but also the British, who already behaved as if the whole of the Nile basin belonged to them. He knew too that the Quai d'Orsay, where the Ministry of Foreign Affairs had its offices on the other side of the river, would disapprove of anything which was likely to disturb good relations with Britain or Belgium at a time

---

[8] It was said that Harry Alis was secretly in the pay of King Leopold, and that this was one reason why the Comité and its bulletin were active in support of this expedition.

[9] Describing the colonial ministry's earlier quarters at the Ministry of Marine, a speaker in the Chamber of Deputies said that 'he had to go up three floors by a staircase whose like it would be hard to find in the darkest hovels in the poorest quarters of Paris'.

when France was badly in need of allies in Europe. Delcassé's answer to this was that he neither consulted the Ministry of Foreign Affairs nor told them what he had in mind.

Apart from the weakness of his own personal standing Delcassé had to contend with a fundamental division of opinion among ministers and officials of the French government. On the one hand there were the continentalists who believed, with passionate intensity and logic, that after the defeat and humiliation sustained by France at the hands of the Germans in 1870 all the resources and energies of the French nation should be concentrated on building up the armed forces and the country's industrial strength. On the other hand were the colonialists who believed, with equal passion and logic, that the national interest would be better served by a rapid expansion of the political and economic power of France in the world as a whole. The differences between these two factions were sharply drawn and deeply felt.

There was also another reason why Delcassé was in need of a powerful ally. In March and again in April he had approached a young but already distinguished French officer named Major Monteil to take command of his projected expedition.[10] Monteil had just returned from an arduous spell of exploration and fighting in West Africa, and he had twice declined the invitation. It was important to have a man of Monteil's established reputation to take charge of such a venture, and Delcassé needed the help therefore of someone of commanding authority who might persuade Monteil to change his mind. He eventually found the ideal ally in the shape of Sadi Carnot, the President of the Republic. Carnot was ideal not only because he was the President and a well-known sympathizer with the colonialist point of view. He was also a civil engineer who had been at the polytechnic with Victor Prompt. He had seen what Prompt had said to the *Institut égyptien* in Cairo on 20 January, and he had been impressed by the opportunities which Prompt and others had exposed as open to France if she were now to step in and occupy a strategic position in the valley of the upper Nile.

Monteil was a brave and resourceful soldier but he was not, as Samuel Johnson once unkindly said of the explorer James Bruce, 'an exact relater'. His account of his meeting with President Carnot is colourful and dramatic but there were those, then and later, who

---

[10] Parfait-Louis Monteil (1855–1925), soldier, explorer and writer.

doubted if it were entirely true. According to him he was summoned by a *pneumatique*[11] on 3 May to meet Delcassé in the street. There he was inveigled into Delcassé's carriage by what he described as *un guet-arpens*, a stratagem, and whisked off to Carnot's office in order, as Delcassé blandly informed him, to see if he would give the President of the Republic the same refusal which he had given to him. When Carnot asked if he would command the expedition, Monteil is said to have replied: 'You are head of the army, the head of the navy. Give me an order and I will obey it!'

If Monteil had any doubts about the scope of the proposed expedition they were dispelled as soon as he saw the maps which were spread out on the President's table. They covered not only the areas of the Ubangi and the Mbomu rivers but the Bahr el Ghazal and the whole of the basin of the White Nile. M. Carnot proceeded to explain that the project which they had in mind stemmed from what he called the realities of the situation in the valley of the Nile. It was an area which in international law had the status of *res nullius*, that is to say it was an area which had been abandoned by Egypt and was temporarily occupied by the rebel forces of the Mahdi. 'It behoves us', the President continued, 'to take advantage of this situation to try and give our establishments in the Upper Ubangi an outlet on the Nile through the Bahr el Ghazal. The point chosen has been designated for us by Monsieur Prompt, *un de mes camarades de Polytechnique*,[12] who is now head of Hydraulic Works in Cairo. In a paper which I ask you to treat with discretion M. Prompt pin-points as a suitable place for a settlement the small locality of Fashoda.' When Monteil asked whether it was to be a question of exploration or of occupation, President Carnot is said to have replied: 'Il faut occuper Fachoda!'[13]

By 10 June Monteil's preparations were sufficiently advanced for him to send his second-in-command to Dakar to recruit 250 Senegalese soldiers for the expedition. In July Monteil was in Holland

[11] An express letter transmitted by a complicated system of pneumatic tubes in Paris.

[12] President Carnot had been a successful civil engineer but when he became a candidate for the presidency Clemenceau is said to have supported him on the grounds that, when in doubt, always vote for the least brilliant.

[13] In all texts in French, French spelling of African names has been used, e.g. Fachoda. Otherwise commonly accepted English spellings, like Fashoda, have been adopted.

arranging with a Dutch transport company to have river craft ready to carry his men and materials up the Congo and the Ubangi. By the end of August he had already despatched the bulk of his stores, and a month later he said that he had completed the rest of his arrangements. On 10 October he consigned his personal baggage to Bordeaux, and was ready to follow and embark for Africa. After this impressive beginning it came as a disappointment to some, and a scandal to others, that nine months later Monteil was still in Paris.

In his memoirs Monteil said that the reason why he did not leave at this point was that, just when he was ready to depart, a cable reached him from de Brazza, the French high commissioner in the French Congo, urging that the expedition should be put off as the Belgians in the Congo Free State were threatening to use force to stop it. No trace of any such cable has been found in the French archives, and the evidence now available from other sources suggests that the real reason was that Monteil thought it would be more prudent to wait, in the hope that the French and Belgian governments would settle their differences by negotiation. He may also have wondered, supposing he had to use force against the Belgians on the Mbomu, or against the English in the Nile basin, whether he would in practice be supported by his government, or whether he had already been cast in the convenient role of a scapegoat. A year in the corridors of civilian power in Paris and Brussels had taught Monteil a measure of unsoldierly caution.

The attitude of the French Ministry of Foreign Affairs to the venture was not improved by the fact that Develle, the then foreign minister, first learnt of Monteil's appointment through the newspapers and that as late as July he had to write and complain to Delcassé that he had still not been informed officially of 'the composition and objectives' of Monteil's expedition. When Develle discovered that Monteil's orders were to penetrate the upper Ubangi and other areas claimed by the Belgians, and that Delcassé had gone on to suggest occupying the disputed areas first and negotiating afterwards, he replied with frigid, foreign office formality that 'this was a pleasantry whose humour was not appreciated by the ministry of foreign affairs'.

Both the British and the Belgian governments were disturbed by the rumours and the reports from clandestine sources which they both received of the preparations being made for Monteil's expedition. The Foreign Office sent young Captain Lugard[14] to Paris in March 1894 with instructions to 'pose as an officer out of place and with rather a grievance' in the hope of inducing Monteil to reveal his objectives and his state of readiness. It was a surprising choice for such a delicate mission. Lugard, on his own admission, 'didn't speak a word of French', and he was also in bad odour in Paris because of somewhat drastic steps he had recently felt obliged to take against some French missionaries in Uganda. However, in a relaxing ambience of wine, women and whispers at the Moulin Rouge, he was able to elicit and report that 'Monteil means to march on Lado or Fashoda with an exceptionally well-organised expedition'.

It was Sir Percy Anderson[15] who had sent Lugard to Paris and proposed his dubious disguise.[16] Two days after he had received Lugard's report he sent one of his own officials to Brussels to see what could be gleaned there, and to talk to the Belgians. A month later a secret Anglo-Congolese Treaty was signed in London. When, under public and parliamentary pressure, the details of this treaty were finally revealed on 21 May, it turned out to be a distinctly unusual and provocative arrangement, and its publication caused an uproar in almost every capital in Europe.

[14] Frederick Dealtry Lugard, later Lord Lugard of Abinger (1858–1945), started his adventurous and varied career as a regular soldier but in 1897 he left the army and joined the colonial service in Africa. Thereafter he had a very distinguished career both as an administrator and a writer, and was made a peer in 1928.

[15] Sir Percy Anderson (1831–96), a Foreign Office official who specialized in African affairs and became head of the African Department. The FO records give one the impression that between 1885 and 1896, when there were seven changes of minister, it was Anderson who really made and directed British policy in Africa.

[16] When Lugard put in a modest claim for 4s. 2d. a night for the time he was in Paris Anderson told him that he could not really ask for less than a pound a day. 'So', Lugard told his brother, 'I did, and my bill will pretty nearly pay for all my follies in Paris.'

CHAPTER II

The Expedition of Major Monteil

IN any other period of history it would be hard to believe that an agreement concluded between the British government and the King of the Belgians over a remote and little-known part of Africa would have caused an uproar in the capitals of Europe. At the end of the nineteenth century, however, most of the European nations were busily and competitively engaged in expanding their overseas possessions and trade, and by 1894 the partition of Africa had reached the point where there were few areas which had not been occupied or ear-marked by one or other of the great powers. Apart from independent Abyssinia, almost the only part of Africa which had escaped these processes was the basin of the White Nile. One reason for this was that it was, for the most part, flat, featureless country, unprepossessing to look at, unhealthy to live in and, in the summer, almost unbearably hot. It was inhabited by attractive but not very productive peoples like the Azande, the Nuer, the Dinka, and the Shilluk. For generations its main marketable products had been ivory, conscripts, and slaves.

It was largely to exploit these assets that the Egyptians extended their dominions southwards into the basin of the White Nile in the first half of the nineteenth century. It was in protest against the cruelties and corruptions of this administration that the people of the northern Sudan rallied in the 1880s to the potent blend of patriotic fervour and religious fanaticism preached by Muhammad Ahmed, the son of a Nile boatman who became known as the Mahdi. Having expelled or exterminated the Egyptians, along with their British and other foreign agents, the Mahdi's predominantly Arab and Muslim forces proceeded to invade and dominate the largely Nilotic and pagan peoples of the southern Sudan. During the period of their dominance they virtually closed most of the Upper Nile to the outside world, as much perhaps by their failure to keep the vital waterways clear of weed as by their active hostility to strangers.

The attitude of the British government to this area was summed up by Lord Salisbury in the statement that 'any European power established on the Upper Nile would have Egypt in its grip'. Because of its interests in India and other places east of Suez it was a basic premise of British policy then that there should be a stable, efficient, and amenable government in Egypt. As it was generally believed in Victorian England that foreigners and natives were not as a rule to be relied upon in such matters, it followed that these conditions could only be secured by British control. It was mainly for this reason that Britain occupied Egypt by force in 1882. Although successive British governments repeatedly assured their critics both at home and abroad that this was merely 'a temporary response to an awkward situation and would be terminated as soon as possible' no moves in this direction were actually made.

When Salisbury spoke of the danger of allowing any European power to become established on the Upper Nile he really meant Germany or France, with Italy and Belgium as lesser hazards. The forces of the Mahdi and his successor had occupied the upper Nile area since 1885, and for the time being the British government was content that they should stay there. The Mahdists had neither the resources nor the expertise to interfere with the flow of the Nile or to threaten the borders of Egypt. So long as they were in control of this vast and unproductive area there was therefore no need for Her Majesty's Government to go to the trouble or the expense of re-conquest. There was always the danger however that one of the European powers might try to take advantage of the situation and move in. In 1890 and 1891 the British government had therefore been at pains to negotiate treaties with both Germany and Italy whereby, in exchange for concessions elsewhere, they recognized that the whole of the basin of the White Nile was in the British sphere of influence.

The agreements with Germany and Italy were concluded by a Conservative government under Lord Salisbury.[1] At that time Salisbury was not only prime minister but his own foreign secretary as well. He believed as a general proposition that foreign affairs were too important and too complex to be left to popularly elected

---

[1] Robert Arthur Talbot Gascoyne Cecil, third Marquess of Salisbury (1830–1903), was educated at Eton and Christ Church, Oxford where he got a fourth class degree in mathematics but still managed to become a Fellow of All Souls at the age of 23. He was prime minister and foreign secretary from 1885–6, 1887–92, and 1895–1900.

members of parliament or to public opinion, and he conducted the foreign relations of his country with the same care and devoted attention which he gave to the administration of his estates at Hatfield. In 1892 however his government gave way to a Liberal administration in which the ageing Gladstone was soon replaced as prime minister by the Earl of Rosebery,[2] while Rosebery's post as foreign secretary went to the Earl of Kimberley,[3] an elderly, garrulous, muddle-headed peer with little experience of foreign affairs. The change of government had less effect on the conduct of foreign affairs than might have been expected from the radical, anti-imperialist statements made by many members of the Liberal party when it was able to indulge in the customary irresponsibilities of opposition. Rosebery himself however was an unabashed imperialist, and British policy as far as Egypt and the Nile were concerned seems to have continued under the influence of Sir Percy Anderson as if no change of government had occurred.

It was during this period of Liberal government that two fresh challenges emerged to threaten the situation in the valley of the Nile. One came from the Congo, whence an expedition under van Kerckhoven had been despatched by King Leopold to take possession of the west bank of the Nile between Lake Albert and Lado. The other was the French expedition under Major Monteil with the Bahr el Ghazal and Fashoda as its objectives. It was to deal with the situation posed by these two operations that the Anglo-Congolese Agreement was negotiated in the spring of 1894. The negotiations were conducted in secret, partly to keep them from the French and

---

[2] Archibald Primrose, fifth Earl of Rosebery (1847–1927); also educated at Eton and Christ Church where he bought his first racehorse, and, when the college authorities objected, left Oxford without a degree rather than give up racing. In 1870 he was elected to the Jockey Club and made his maiden speech as a Liberal in the House of Lords. In 1878 he married the daughter and heiress of Baron Rothschild and thereby acquired Mentmore and all its treasures. Although he was foreign secretary 1892–4 and prime minister 1894–5 he is better remembered, as he would probably have wished, as the man who won the Derby twice running.

[3] John Wodehouse, first Earl of Kimberley in Norfolk (1826–1902). Like Salisbury and Rosebery, and many other members of both the Conservative and Liberal governments of this era, he was at Eton and Christ Church. He, however, was rated 'one of the cleverest boys' at Eton, and at Oxford he got a First in Greats. Academic success did not bring him the success in politics which he had hoped for, and it was not until 1894, when he was close on 70, that he at last realized a life-long ambition to be foreign secretary. Kimberley in South Africa was named after him when he was minister at the Colonial Office.

the Germans, and partly so that they did not become known to the press or to parliament either in London or in Brussels.

It was an ingenious and unscrupulous agreement of which Machiavelli himself could have been proud. To begin with, Leopold, in his capacity both as King of the Belgians and as sovereign of the Congo Free State, followed the Germans and the Italians in recognizing that the whole of the basin of the White Nile was in the British sphere of influence; for the sake of appearances and the largely academic advantages of international legality, what were referred to as 'the contingent rights' of Egypt and the Sultan of Turkey in this area were declared 'not to have been overlooked'.[4] In return for this act of recognition King Leopold, and in this case his successors, were granted a perpetual lease over the Bahr el Ghazal. As often happened in treaties of partition concluded in Europe during this period some of the boundaries of this little-known area were simply drawn for convenience along straight lines of latitude and longitude, taking little or no account of tribal limits, traditional rights, or the wishes of the inhabitants. The eastern boundary stopped well short of the main stream of the White Nile, and the intervening strip, from Lake Albert in the south to Fashoda in the north, was leased to King Leopold personally and not to his successors, and only so long as he remained sovereign of the Congo Free State.[5] Another part of the agreement provided that, in exchange for the lease of a narrow corridor of Uganda territory which gave the Congo an outlet on Lake Albert, the King gave Britain a lease of a strip of Congo territory which connected Uganda with the northern end of Lake Tanganyika, and so preserved the possibility of a continuous line of British communications from the Cape to Cairo. Cecil Rhodes had been in London propagating his wealth and his visions.

It was an agreement which suited both sides. Installing the Belgians as permanent tenants in the Bahr el Ghazal, which the British did not then want, was a cheap and effective way of denying it to the French and of blocking their route to the Nile and Fashoda. Installing King Leopold temporarily on the west bank of the Nile served to protect this stretch of the river and the northern

---

[4] When it had first occupied the Bahr el Ghazal and other parts of the upper Nile in the 1820s Egypt was a province of the Ottoman Empire.

[5] The Foreign Office knew that King Leopold's rule in the Congo was the subject of much criticism both at home and abroad and was unlikely to last long. It was in fact terminated in 1908.

approaches to Uganda both from the Mahdists and from the French but on terms which allowed the British to occupy it herself, if the need arose, in the not too distant future. King Leopold for his part had the satisfaction of extending his Congo dominions into the basin of the Nile and of gaining access to the river for the produce of the Congo; it also put him in a position in the Bahr el Ghazal in which he could offer the French the use of a port on the Nile river system in exchange for further concessions in the disputed areas of the Mbomu and the Ubangi.

The agreement between Britain and King Leopold of the Belgians which was signed on 12 April 1894 provided that it would be kept secret by both parties for a period of three months. Partly for reasons of secrecy, and partly because Rosebery knew that there would be strong objections from some of his more radical Liberal colleagues, he did not even submit the treaty to the Cabinet. The Belgians, for their part, knew that a French delegation was due in Brussels on 16 April to resume negotiations about the Ubangi and the Mbomu, and the last thing King Leopold wanted was for them to discover that he had just signed a secret agreement with the British. To avoid any impression of bad faith Leopold eventually persuaded the British to sign a fresh agreement in almost identical terms but with the date altered to 12 May. On this basis the agreement was made public but the secret was so well kept by both sides that the existence of the original agreement signed on 12 April was not revealed until the official archives became available thirty years later.

When the agreement was made public the French were not surprisingly the first to object. In a spirited speech to the Chamber of Deputies on 7 June Gabriel Hanotaux, the new foreign minister,[6] argued with Gallic logic that if the upper Nile belonged legally to Egypt or Turkey the British had no right to lease it. If it did not belong to them, then France had as much right to it as anyone else. 'No country', he urged, 'could claim to exercise influence and authority over a region which it did not actually occupy and possess', and he reiterated President Carnot's view that in international law the upper Nile was *res nullius*, that it belonged to no one

---

[6] Gabriel Hanotaux (1853–1944) was foreign minister for many years but when he came to write his memoirs he preferred to describe himself simply as 'a member of the *académie française*'. He was a scholar of 16th and 17th century French history, and his best-known work was a study of Cardinal Richlieu. It was Hanotaux who penned the untranslatable epigram 'La négotiateur français veut convaincre tandis que le négotiateur anglais se contente de vaincre'.

and would become the property of whoever got there first. On this basis he had, as he dramatically put it, ordered Monteil 'to return to his post immediately'. Hanotaux ended his speech in the Chamber of Deputies with a flow of pungent statements which satisfied both the literary taste and the patriotic emotions of his listeners. 'The first detachments of his mission have arrived on the scene. They will be re-inforced without delay. The head of the mission will leave shortly by steamer. The Chamber will allow me to say no more on this subject.'

It was not only in France that there were protests. The German government objected strongly to Leopold's lease to the British of a strip of Congo territory on the western borders of its new colony in East Africa. They protested in such threatening terms that the king's ministers in Brussels became so alarmed that they pressed Leopold to revoke this part of the agreement. A parallel German protest to the British government was couched in language which Rosebery described to the Queen as 'insufferable'. Ripples of indignation reached other capitals in Europe as Austria, Italy, Russia, Turkey, and Egypt were approached in turn for diplomatic support. None seem to have responded with any enthusiasm, and a spokesman for the Austrian government expressed the general feeling of astonishment that any great power should think of quarrelling over 'a strip of wilderness in darkest Africa'. French attempts to wring some drip of support from its traditional alliance with Russia met with the usual baffling blend of silence and exquisitely phrased expressions of regret.

For all his brave words in the Chamber of Deputies Hanotaux, sensing France's growing isolation in Europe and her need of allies, did not want to provoke a clash with either Britain or Belgium at that juncture. The British government had reacted strongly to the despatch of Monteil's expedition and Lord Dufferin, the Ambassador in Paris, had warned Hanotaux that 'the deliberate and unprovoked irruption of French troops into a territory over which our jurisdiction has been proclaimed would naturally exasperate public opinion at home and produce a situation fraught with danger to the peaceable relations between the two countries.[7] Hanotaux took the

[7] The draft which Dufferin sent to the FO for approval bluntly said 'it would mean war between the two countries'. The archives show that these words were sidelined with three exclamation marks in red pencil in the FO and that they were hurriedly replaced by the more diplomatic wording quoted above.

point, and before Monteil left told him privately that he was on no account to send 'a force or even a man into the basin of the Nile'. Monteil's new instructions also made it clear that he was only to occupy those parts of the upper Ubangi which had 'not yet been infiltrated by the Congolese forces'. Hanotaux hoped in this way not only to appease the British but to facilitate his own secret negotiations with King Leopold. He was rewarded when on 14 August 1894 these negotiations bore fruit in a Franco-Congolese Agreement. Under this treaty King Leopold, in return for a generous settlement of his claims on the Ubangi, now surrendered all the leases he had obtained from the British in the area of the White Nile. Although this was a clear breach of the Anglo-Congolese Agreement and opened the way once more to a French advance to the Nile it was finally decided in London at a cabinet meeting, at which Rosebery was overruled by the more radical members of his government, to overlook the breach and take no action.

Once the Franco-Congolese Agreement had been signed and the differences in the upper Ubangi had been settled, Hanotaux had a telegram sent to Monteil in Africa saying that, in view of the Agreement his expedition had 'lost much of its purpose'. Major Monteil himself and the bulk of his troops were soon afterwards diverted to the Ivory Coast where they gradually disintegrated under the dual pressures of military reverses and official neglect. So, after a flurry of great hopes, fine words, and abrupt changes of course, ended the first French attempt to penetrate into the basin of the Nile and reach Fashoda.

CHAPTER III

The Mission of Victor Liotard

WITH the threat of a French expedition to the Nile out of the way, or, as Hanotaux preferred to put it, in suspense, the French and British governments embarked, like middle-aged lovers after a tiff, on a matter-of-fact discussion of their differences. This was made easier by the protracted absence on leave of the British ambassador. Lord Dufferin was a capable and conscientious ambassador but he lacked warmth.[1] His absence left negotiations in the hands of his deputy, Edmund Phipps.[2] Phipps developed such an admiration for Hanotaux's scholarly charm that his superiors in London thought that he sometimes projected the French point of view with more enthusiasm than their own. The relationship between Phipps and Hanotaux may have helped the two governments to understand one another's feelings, but there were those, like the cynical Sir William Harcourt, the Liberal Chancellor of the Exchequer, who thought that it was more like a relationship between a cat and a mouse, with Phipps as the mouse.

Their exchanges continued through the summer and into the autumn of 1894, and moved cautiously towards a standstill arrangement, *un désistement réciproque*, whereby both parties agreed not to make any move into the basin of the upper Nile for the time being. In the end, however, this came to nothing. The French felt, with some reason, that they were much better placed to make an incursion than were the British from either Egypt or Uganda, and that they were therefore doing more than a fair share of desisting. The British, for their part, refused to agree to anything which implied that anyone except themselves had any rights, dormant or otherwise, in the valley of the Nile.

Having failed to persuade their governments to reach agreement

[1] Frederick Blackwood, 1st Earl of Dufferin and Ava, was descended on his mother's side from Sheridan. After an adventurous youth, he served successively as high commissioner in Canada, viceroy in India, ambassador in Rome and Paris and finally as leader of the Liberals in the House of Lords.

[2] E. C. H. Phipps (1840–1911), later Sir Edmund Phipps, and minister in Brazil and Brussels.

on this basis Hanotaux and the patient and persistent Phipps started to explore the possibilities of doing a deal whereby France recognized the British claim to the upper Nile in exchange for concessions elsewhere. As Anderson noted in a confidential minute on the file, 'to keep France entirely off the Nile would be a triumph for British diplomacy and might justify a surrender elsewhere'. Hanotaux at first seemed to like this idea, and despite Dufferin's return to his post at Paris, hours of detailed discussion and a host of telegrams and despatches were devoted to seeking an agreement on these lines. But once more they came to nothing, with the *parti colonial* in France, and their counterparts in the city and the west end of London[3] putting pressures on their governments not to offer too much nor take too little. On 7 November 1894 a meeting took place between Dufferin and Hanotaux which showed that for the time being there was no more to be said. When Hanotaux was asked if he would promise 'in the name of France' not to proceed beyond the basin of the Congo Hanotaux shook his head, and Dufferin for his part refused to commit his government to any form of standstill agreement however elegantly or ambiguously phrased.[4] Ten days later on 17 November the French council of ministers directed Hanotaux to break off negotiations, and authorized a new expedition to the Nile.

The decision to send the new expedition was taken on the initiative of Delcassé as minister for the colonies. Although he had been obliged to terminate Monteil's expedition in the summer, he still believed that such a venture would not only bring France great rewards, such as an outlet on the Nile through which the produce of French equatorial Africa could be shipped down the river to the Mediterranean, but would also put her in a strong position to apply pressure on the British in Egypt. Delcassé had therefore taken advantage of the presence in Paris in September of Victor Liotard to discuss the idea. Liotard knew the area well. He had been employed for some years by de Brazza, the governor of the French Congo, in extending French control in the upper reaches of the Ubangi and Mbomu rivers. With this idea of a new venture into the basin of the Nile in mind Delcassé now nominated Liotard to take charge as

---

[3] Part of the pressure in London came from the headquarters of the Royal Geographical Society in Kensington Gore, close to the Albert Hall.

[4] Among the variations tried were: *proposition de désinteressement* and *désistement provisoire réciproque*.

civilian governor of a new French province called Upper Ubangi
whose eastern boundaries were purposely left undefined.

Delcassé waited for an opportune moment before he sought
authority to launch his new expedition. By November it had become
clear that negotiations with the British had reached an impasse, and
he could argue that, diplomacy having failed, the time had come for
action. This argument was reinforced by reports and rumours that a
British expedition into the basin of the upper Nile from Uganda was
being prepared by Colonel Colvile. These reports and rumours
were generally exaggerated, and often quite untrue, but they
provided Delcassé with useful ammunition. His position was also
helped by other events which had nothing to do with the Nile. At the
end of September the intelligence department of the French army
received information which suggested that a well-to-do Jewish army
officer named Captain Dreyfus had been selling French military
secrets to the Germans. When the question whether or not he
should be prosecuted was discussed in the council of ministers,
Hanotaux, as foreign minister, argued against prosecution because
it might damage relations with Germany. Delcassé took the oppo-
site view. 'If these are the facts, and unfortunately they most
probably are, there is no place for pity, and we must apply the full
rigour of the law.' This was also the view of Casimir-Périer, the new
President of the Republic, and this in the end was the view which
prevailed.[5]

Delcassé had judged his moment well. When the Liotard expedition came up for discussion in the council of ministers on 17
November Delcassé provided the details but it was Casimir-Périer
himself who pressed for approval. Hanotaux opposed it as provocative and likely to upset relations with England but, for the second
time in two weeks, was outvoted. The council authorized Delcassé
to instruct Liotard to occupy as much of the Nile basin as he could
before Colvile could get there from Uganda. In reply Delcassé
assured his colleagues that Liotard would be on the Nile 'within a
year'. The following day the *Comité de l'Afrique française* and the
colonial group in the Chamber of Deputies joined forces to present
Delcassé with a piece of sculpture 'as a tribute to the services
rendered by him in the cause of colonial expansion'. The sculpture

---

[5] Jean Casimir-Périer (1847–1907) was elected president of the republic after
Carnot had been killed by an anarchist bomb in June 1894. He resigned six months
later on the grounds that as president he had too little power.

was called 'The Explorer', and to quote from the *Comité*'s bulletin 'showed a white man raising his hand in a gesture of hope and pride to point out the heavens to a young black kneeling before him'.

*   *   *

Although on this occasion it was the French who broke off negotiations and launched an expedition there was no lack of aggressive attitudes on the other side of the Channel. A few days after the French government's decision, the chargé d'affaires in London, d'Estournelles de Constant, reported Cecil Rhodes as saying that any French trespass into the upper Nile would be the flashpoint, *le point noir*, as he put it, which would produce an explosion. Despite this unpropitious atmosphere Hanotaux continued his efforts to reach agreement. In December he sent the able and amiable Baron de Courcel to London as ambassador to try and arrest the deterioration in Anglo-French relations. With the British government determined to prevent the French entering the upper Nile in any circumstances, and France as determined to reserve and exercise its right to do so, the chances of agreement were slight. But Kimberley and de Courcel got on well together, and Kimberley did his best to soften the uncompromising policies imposed on him by Rosebery, and by Anderson at the Foreign Office, with indecisive answers and occasional indiscretions. When he had to reject de Courcel's suggestion that the British should promise not to enter the disputed area for a fixed period, such as ten years, he added off the record that it was unlikely that 'we shall be led to enter the territory concerned for a long time. We have quite enough to do in Unyoro'.[6]

Again these negotiations came to nothing, and again failure to reach agreement played into the hands of those on both sides of the Channel who did not want any compromise. Although Harry Alis was killed in a duel early in 1895 while defending his honour against well-founded allegations that he was in King Leopold's pocket, the *Comité de l'Afrique française* continued to urge the government to occupy the upper reaches of the Nile before the British got there, and supported its case by further exaggerated reports of Colonel Colvile's advance. Their outbursts and pressures were matched in England. In March *The Times* and a number of Conservative members of Parliament asked what the Liberal government was

---

[6] Unyoro was a troublesome part of Uganda (see Chapter VI).

doing about the various French expeditions which were said to be encroaching on British spheres of influence in west and middle Africa. Matters came to a head on 28 March when Sir Ellis Ashmead-Bartlett[7] asked two questions in the House of Commons about reported French advances on both the Nile and the Niger. With the foreign secretary Lord Kimberley in the Lords, it fell to the junior minister Sir Edward Grey[8] to answer them. The answers given were, as usual, drafted in the Foreign Office and, as is often the case with answers to parliamentary questions, were correct, precise, and uninformative. On the Niger, the answer was that enquiries were being made in Paris. On the Nile, it was simply that 'we do not know that any French expedition has left for the Nile waterway'. As the British government had not received any official notification of Liotard's mission this was strictly true but when a few days later Rosebery sent a note to the Queen on the subject he admitted that the French were 'trying to occupy some place on the Nile in our sphere of influence'. Rosebery was by no means the only person who knew that, and it soon became clear that the opposition intended to use a routine debate on the Foreign Office Vote in the House of Commons that evening to raise the whole question of French incursions in Africa. Thus it was that Ashmead-Bartlett and other Conservative imperialists like Joseph Chamberlain pressed the government again to make its position plain in regard both to the Niger and the Nile, and to take action, if need be, with gunboats. These demands were made at such length that it was half-past nine before Grey rose and made what was then and for many years afterwards regarded as a major statement of British foreign policy.

It was not in truth a distinguished speech, either in content or in style. Grey claimed afterwards that he had worked it out impromptu while he sat on the Treasury bench 'as carefully', he explained, 'as the brief time and the obligation to give at least one ear to the speeches would allow'. The early part of the speech, with its imprecision and its woolliness, suggests that this may indeed have been the case:

---

[7] Member of Parliament for Eye in Suffolk. His younger brother William was proposed to and married by the immensely rich Baroness Angela Burdett-Coutts in 1881 when he was 27 and she 66.

[8] Sir Edward Grey, later Earl Grey of Fallodon (1862–1933): educated at Winchester and Balliol College, Oxford; under-secretary for foreign affairs 1892–5; secretary of state 1905–16.

The Honourable Member for Sheffield said that the policy of the Agreement has been to try and shove forward the Congo State to occupy British territory. No description of that Agreement, of the motives and the policy of it could be more inaccurate. The Government did not try to shove the Congo State forward at all. When we came into office we found a large force had already shoved itself forward, and was in part of that territory at any rate. There was no anxiety on her part to be shoved forward . . . I am asked whether or not it is the case that a French expedition is coming from the west of Africa with the intention of entering the Nile valley. I will ask the Committee to be careful in giving credence to the rumours of movements of expeditions in Africa. Even places in Africa are apt to shift about, and it is sometimes found that some place, supposed to occupy a particular position, does not in fact occupy that position . . .

The wording of the declaration itself however was clear and concise, and it seems likely that it was carefully prepared by the Foreign Office beforehand:

The advance of a French expedition under secret instructions right from the other side of Africa into a territory over which our claims have been known for so long, would not be merely an inconsistent and unexpected act, but it must be perfectly well known by the French government that it would be an unfriendly act and would be so viewed in England.

Many years later when old men forget and write their memoirs Earl Grey of Falloden said that it was about French incursions in West Africa that he expected to be questioned that evening. On this assumption he had asked Lord Kimberley what he should say. He had found, not it seems for the first time, that when asked to deal quickly and briefly with a political question Kimberley was apt to talk about the managements of country estates or such like rural matters. The most, it seems, that Grey could get from him on this occasion was: 'You must do the best you can but I think you should use pretty firm language.' To his surprise Grey found when he got to the House that the speakers in the debate were more concerned with French activities on the Nile than on the Niger. So, to use his own words, 'I therefore transferred to the subject of the Nile the firmness I had been authorized to show about competing claims in West Africa'.

Whatever the background to Grey's famous declaration the effect was explosive. At home the objections flared as soon as Grey had finished his speech. They came not from the Conservative opposition, which welcomed it, but from his own party. They were most voiced by a backbencher, Henry Labouchere[9] who described it as 'a speech of menace' and accused Grey of behaving as if 'the Nile was as much our property as the Thames'. If, he concluded, we had left Egypt as we should and had repeatedly said we would, the upper Nile would be of no use to us. So why stop the French going there?[10], Rosebery and Kimberley had to face similar objections inside the Cabinet, particularly from Sir William Harcourt who complained that Grey's declaration was 'contrary to the view of the Cabinet and a deliberate departure from the prepared statement which he himself had approved'.

Equally vociferous objections came from the French. To say that something would be regarded as an unfriendly act was about as near as a nation could get in the diplomatic language of the day to saying that it would go to war; direct threats and gunboat language were, as a rule, only used to those beyond the diplomatic fringe like the Chinese, the King of Dahomey, or the Americans. It was not so much that Grey's declaration contained anything that had not been said before in exchanges between foreign ministers and ambassadors. What was new, and insupportable, was to say it in public, to be reported and commented upon in *The Times* and in other countries' journals, and discussed in the salons and boudoirs of every capital in Europe. Although both sides felt obliged to keep up a façade of stiffness and invective, behind the scenes in Paris and London statesmen and officials were busy pouring diplomatic oil on the troubled waters of Anglo-French relations. As de Courcel told Hanotaux, his task in London was to make a fuss and be indignant, *faire la grosse voix*, so that Hanotaux could play a conciliatory role in Paris. Kimberley responded so readily to these tactics that de Courcel was soon able to report him as saying that Grey's words were really of little account – 'celles d'un simple sous-secrétaire d'état'. Kimberley even suggested, according to de Courcel, that they might consider partitioning the Bahr el Ghazal in order to give the French some outlet on the Nile.

---

[9] Labouchere's record in the Liberal party merited his inclusion in the Cabinet but, by a surprising survival of the royal prerogative, he was excluded at the Queen's request from any position in which they would be likely to meet. This was partly because Labouchere owned a radical periodical, *Truth*, which was given to scurrilous criticism of the royal family, and partly perhaps because he had married an actress.

[10] In a private letter to Cromer, Rosebery said, 'Here we are in a country in which every minister (except myself) has pledged himself to evacuate.'

For all these fair words and conciliatory gestures both sides privately suspected that the other was still secretly engaged in trying to get there first. Colonel Colvile did not help matters by saying publicly in April that Britain could advance into the southern Sudan from Uganda whenever she liked, but the fact remained that throughout the spring and summer of 1895 both Kimberley and Dufferin were honestly able to assure the French that Britain was not engaged in entering the upper Nile and that 'the status quo had not been disturbed'. To be on the safe side orders were sent to Uganda saying that whatever may have been said or implied in the past no advance north of Unyoro was now to be made.

The position of the French representatives was more difficult. They knew that Liotard had been instructed to go 'towards the Nile' but they did not know how far he had got. De Courcel told Kimberley in April that 'no news had been received of the expedition to these parts with which communication was extremely tardy and difficult, and that he did not see therefore how it would be possible for the French government to give assurances while they were in ignorance of the facts'. When Rosebery saw the report of the ambassador's remarks he put the following tart minute on the file:

It appears from this conversation that the French do not profess to have any knowledge of the position or objectives of the large armed parties that they appear to launch at hazard in Africa. No wonder there are complications. I wish de Courcel's attention could be called to this strange and perilous state of affairs.[11]

Hanotaux became so worried that Liotard might spoil things by suddenly appearing on the Nile that he instructed de Courcel to call on Lord Kimberley at his house to ask if, to prevent misunderstandings, it could be agreed that 'expeditions in Africa not having a military character should be regarded as not raising political questions between the two governments'. Kimberley knew, of course, that Liotard was technically a civilian administrator and not a soldier, and he replied that he could not give an answer off-hand but that it would be considered if it were put officially. This does not seem to have been done but soon afterwards Hanotaux went out of his way to assure the British ambassador in Paris that Liotard only

---

[11] The minute was written in pencil. When the time came to publish the relevant papers in a White paper the minute was crossed out and marked 'Not to be copied'.

had fifty men available for exploration, and that these small numbers were surely enough to guarantee their peaceful conduct.

Nevertheless the *mission Liotard* hung like a shadow over Anglo-French relations for more than a year. In fact the venture, so bravely and brashly proclaimed and launched, was never a serious threat to the Nile basin. The main reason for this was that, as explained earlier, Liotard had not only been instructed to extend French control towards the Nile but had also been put in charge of the amorphous and largely undeveloped French territory of Upper Ubangi. Liotard's task, as he saw it, was to complete the occupation of the area and set up the framework of a civil administration, and to tap, develop, and if need be to exploit its resources in order to make it an economically viable proposition. This was a slow and painstaking process of exploration, mapping and making roads; of inducing local chiefs to make treaties of friendship and trade by means of presents or of threats, and if necessary by force; of establishing administrative stations in out-of-the-way places and police or military posts. It left Liotard and his officials little time or energy to extend French control eastwards into the basin of the Nile. In the event the furthest he got was Tambura, a few miles beyond the watershed line. It was surprising indeed that he got so far. Almost from the start Liotard was ill-provided with men, means, and money, and when he pleaded for reinforcements they did not arrive. The whole enterprise appears to have been so neglected that one wonders whether it was ever seriously intended, even by Delcassé, as more than a gesture to appease the *parti colonial* and to put pressure on the British.

It was in any case soon doomed to failure. Two months after it was launched Delcassé lost his office in a government re-shuffle. He was succeeded by Chautemps, a hard-headed radical who had no time for colonial adventures. With Hanotaux's encouragement, he allowed the venture to wither away, like a previous tenant's seedlings, for want of water, manure, and cultivation.

CHAPTER IV

Jean-Baptiste Marchand

A month later Hanotaux had a visitor at the Quai d'Orsay. His name was Jean-Baptiste Marchand, and when he saw the minister for foreign affairs on 14 June 1895 he was thirty-one years of age. He stalked through the cool corridors of the ministry with the disdain and arrogance and physical appearance of a desert nomad, lean and taut in face and figure, his skin burnt and weathered by the sun and the wind. Dressed like a man of the Sahara he could easily pass as one and march or ride on a camel all day without food or water.

Marchand was at that time a captain in the marines, an arm of the French forces popularly known and respected and feared as *les marsouins*, the porpoises. His father was a carpenter in the village of Thoissy in Burgundy, and Marchand joined the army as a private soldier to see the world and escape from the predictable, humdrum life of a clerk in a small country town. He soon found his way into the marines and there rose from the ranks to become an officer. He then went through one of the hardest and most exacting of military initiations, the *engrenage des soudanais*, as it was called, the mill-hopper of service in the élite corps of men who served in the Sahara and the French Sudan. These *officiers soudanais* were dedicated to the cause of colonial adventure and expansion, and prided themselves on a reputation for acting on their own initiative, ignoring civilian orders to keep within their allocation of funds and, on occasions, of deliberately putting their governments into positions from which they could not in honour retreat. Many were drawn, like Marchand himself, from the marines, and were for the most part courageous, resourceful, without pity either for themselves or for others, and addicted in roughly equal measure to love of France and all things French, and to scorn of foreigners and all their works. Their philosophy was simple: 'As soldiers we only know that there are territories in Africa which could belong to us. The English and the Germans are in the process of annexing them. We are trying to beat them to it.' It was in this spirit that Marchand went to see Hanotaux with his plan of campaign.

The plan which Marchand put to Hanotaux was not new. It was to do what both Monteil and Liotard had hoped to do but had never been given the authority or the resources to achieve: to establish France firmly on the banks of the White Nile. Marchand's idea was to take a light, mobile column of seasoned officers and men to proceed at speed and in secret to reach and occupy Fashoda before anyone else could get there. What was new about his plan was the spirit and style with which it was presented, and the engaging and compelling personality of the man who presented it. Captain Marchand had by then already built up a formidable reputation as a man of action and imagination, and he had a charismatic ability to invest his project with vision and passion, and to give it almost the character of a crusade.

Marchand had taken his proposition to Hanotaux because he was personally known to be an admirer of the *Soudanais* and sympathetic to their aims, but as minister for foreign affairs all he could do was to advise Marchand to put his proposals in writing and submit them to the minister for the colonies, in whose province such matters clearly lay. Marchand submitted his written report on 11 September. It was long and detailed, with a map and twenty-one closely written pages of manuscript. Although Marchand left school when he was thirteen, he was far from being an illiterate soldier, and he expressed himself on paper freely and often at considerable length. The tone of Marchand's report was set by the map. It was a map of Africa scored by two thick lines in black. One ran from the Cape to Cairo, the other in an arc from Lagos in West Africa to Mombasa in the east. They were drawn to form a cross with its point of intersection in the valley of the upper Nile. Marchand labelled it 'The English theory of the cross'. His plan in essence was to frustrate both of these English designs by planting the French flag at Fashoda. It was like taking the central position in a giant game of noughts and crosses; it not only stopped the British but it opened the way for a continuous belt of French territory from Dakar to Jibuti. To complete the line it was assumed that Abyssinia would be made a protectorate either by France herself or by 'one of our allies', by which he meant the Russians who were even then showing a lively interest in Abyssinia and the Red Sea. There was no suggestion in Marchand's report that a simultaneous expedition should set out from that quarter, but it was taken for granted that the Mahdist regime in the Sudan would welcome the French in the common struggle with the English and would give them every assistance. For this reason Marchand proposed that, instead of following in the footsteps of Monteil and Liotard, his expedition should strike north from the Ubangi and the Mbomu, and enter the basin of the Nile by the Bahr el Arab.

It was typical of Marchand that he made no attempt to argue or to pretend that there would be any economic benefits. There is no mention of trade in his proposals, nor of mineral wealth or raw materials. It is essentially a soldier's project designed partly, no doubt, for the honour and glory and accelerated promotion of Captain Marchand and his chosen companions but mainly, it would seem, for the honour and glory of France. His plan would enable her to insist that French interests in the whole of the Nile valley should be respected, and would ensure that France's 'eternal rival' would not be able to exclude her from a dominant position in Africa as she had done in the eighteenth century in India and North America. He accepted that England would regard the venture as a hostile act and that there was therefore the risk of some kind of international incident; but, he concluded, in terms calculated to appeal to most Frenchmen, 'will we allow ourselves to be intimidated?'

Although Marchand's proposals had a political and patriotic core, he knew from his experience in the army, that it was no use putting up a scheme of this nature unless it was supported by down-to-earth facts and figures. The last part of the report was therefore devoted to detailed specifications and estimates of numbers, duration, and costs. It was to be a small expedition of seven officers, four NCOs, five technicians and 150 Senegalese soldiers. The total cost was estimated at 580,000 francs,[1] and was based on the payment of wages and salaries and other expenses for 30 months.

Chautemps was still the minister for the colonies when Marchand submitted his proposals. It did not take him long to see the implications and the likely consequences of adopting Marchand's plan,[2] and it was with relief and a determination not to burn his fingers that he passed the report, like a hot potato, to Hanotaux at the Quai d'Orsay on the grounds that it dealt 'more with general foreign policy than with purely colonial interests'. Hanotaux was

[1] About £60,000.
[2] Marchand's report bears numerous caustic comments and exclamation marks written in the margins in pencil when it was examined in the ministry for the colonies.

sympathetic to the idea but as a politician he preferred to have neither the responsibility of saying Yes nor the odium of saying No. He suggested therefore that Marchand's proposals should be considered by an inter-departmental committee. This allowed him to continue reserving his position without running the risk either of making a wrong decision or of incurring the blame for inaction. At the end of October the government fell in yet another mid-term convulsion.[3] In the reshuffle of the ministerial pack which followed Hanotaux was succeeded by Marcelin Bertholet, a distinguished chemist, while Chautemps's post went to Guiyesse, an equally distinguished Egyptologist.

Marchand and his sponsors were quick to take advantage of this situation to press the two new ministers to approve the proposals without any more delay. To help the ministers make up their minds Marchand seems to have been advised by experienced civil servants in the colonial ministry to condense his original detailed report into a simpler and shorter note two-and-a-half pages long. It was not only simpler and shorter; it was a revised version calculated to allay the suspicions and hesitations of a pair of inexperienced left-wing academics. Although the possibility of some kind of international incident was still admitted, the aims of the expedition were now defined as the effective occupation of recently acquired territory north of the Mbomu river, and the extension of French influence from there to the west bank of the Nile. It was stressed that these Nile regions belonged as of right not to the English but to Egypt and its nominal overlord the Sultan of Turkey, and would merely be held in trust for them. For this reason the expedition, 'casting off any military character and appearance', would only occupy land in these parts with the consent of its inhabitants or with the agreement of the Mahdist regime. Marchand's expedition would thus be no more than 'a visit by a group of anonymous European travellers without a national flag or government instructions'. The French flag would only be displayed, and the expedition's real objectives revealed, if they encountered 'representatives of another European power seeking to violate Egyptian rights and legitimate French aspirations'. In no circumstances, the note blandly concluded, could such an encounter give rise to a conflict. Both parties would calmly stand on their dignity and their rights, and await instructions from

---

[3] The French government changed seven times between 1893 and 1898.

their governments. It was predicted that by such correct and peaceful means England would be obliged to submit the whole question of Egypt and the upper Nile to an international conference, at which, it was hinted, France would not lack friends.

Faced by the unaccustomed pressures and responsibilities of public office, and prostrated by the death of his daughter, Bertholet seems to have had a nervous breakdown. Félix Faure, the President of the Republic, noted privately that at meetings of the council of ministers Bertholet 'limited himself to listening and making notes on scraps of paper that he could not decipher next day', and that during this period he had become as easy to persuade 'as a schoolboy'. Within three weeks of taking office Bertholet had agreed to Marchand's plan, and on 30 November 1895 he confirmed this in writing. As this was the first and indeed the only time that Marchand's expedition was formally approved in writing by any minister it is surprising that Bertholet did not refer it first to the council of ministers. All he did was attempt to cover himself with the reservation that he was only approving the expedition in the form it had been presented to him, and that no authority had been given for Marchand to occupy territory or to conclude treaties. He did add however that the expedition nevertheless had 'his entire adherence'. When it came to allotting praise and blame it was of course these words rather than the reservations that were remembered.

Bertholet may have been easy to persuade but there seems little doubt that he was purposely confused, even misled, by those who advised him both inside and outside his own office. They did so from what they believed to be the best and most self-evident of motives. They believed that the extension of French influence in Africa and elsewhere was in the best interests not merely of France but of the indigenous people of the country concerned. They felt, and knew with a Cartesian certainty, that France and all things French – French culture, French institutions, the French language, French law, French cooking – were the best in the world. Therefore, they argued, it was France's plain duty to confer, and if need be, to impose these benefits on less fortunate peoples. Marchand himself held these views with particular fervour. It was said that the words *La France* and *le drapeau* had a hypnotic effect on him. Anything done in their name was not only permissible; it was right.

Although Marchand himself wasted no time in choosing his companions and ordering his stores and equipment, it was more than six months before he was able to make a start. Like other army officers of his time his admiration for France and all things French did not as a rule extend to politicians and government officials, and he attributed the delay to 'bureaucratic inertia'. In this case however there were also other reasons. There were long drawn-out arguments about policy, and nagging conflicts of personality. In both cases the real clash was between those who wanted the venture to be under political control, and those, like Marchand, who thought that more positive results would be achieved if it were treated as a military operation. These differences were reflected in the revised instructions which were issued by Guiyesse on 24 February. Several controversial matters, such as the route to be followed, and the question of overall command, were left unresolved in the hope that they would be settled later between Marchand as military commander of the expedition and Liotard as the civilian governor of the Upper Ubangi. For the first time however Fashoda was put down in writing as the ultimate objective, and an element of urgency was introduced by stressing once more the need to get there before Colvile. And what had before been described as 'la mission Marchand' was now called 'un raid' after Dr Jameson's recent dashing exploit in South Africa.

All seemed ready for the expedition to start when, in April, the various left-wing alliances that had made up the government fell apart, and it was succeeded by a more conservative amalgam with Hanotaux back at the Quai d'Orsay and the more experienced and down-to-earth André Lebon at the Pavilion de Flor. Although Hanotaux still managed to avoid committing himself to the expedition in writing he did nothing to discourage it, and Marchand claimed that in an interview before he left France Hanotaux told him: 'You are going to fire a pistol shot on the Nile; we accept all the consequences!'

Marchand finally left Marseilles for Africa on 25 June 1896. He believed that, despite the delays, there was still time for him to reach Fashoda before the end of 1897, and that he could and would beat Colonel Colvile or anyone else in the race to the Nile.

CHAPTER V

The Beginnings of the Expedition

WHEN Marchand finally arrived on the coast of the French Congo in July 1896 he expected to find everything ready for him to start on his long, three thousand mile journey across Africa. He had been assured that all the resources of the local French administration would be at his disposal, and to avoid delay he had sent the other members of the expedition and its stores on ahead in accordance with a carefully prepared plan of campaign. Marchand himself was the last to leave France.

He had been given a free hand in composing his expedition, and he had chosen with care. The key figures, Germain, his second-in-command, Baratier, Largeau, Mangin, and Dr Emily the medical officer, were all men who had served together in various parts of West Africa, and were known to one another as men of proven endurance and courage. They formed a nucleus of old friends and comrades in arms to whose habits and convictions the other members of the party were expected to conform. As one was a civilian artist named Castellani, who came from quite a different background on the left bank of the river in Paris, this presented problems. There were also four French non-commissioned officers – Bernard, Dat, Prat, and Venail – but they all had the same background of service in the marines and in West Africa as the officers. The military escort consisted of a company of a hundred and fifty smart, campaign-hardened, smiling, indefatigable and pitiless African soldiers recruited, like the best of France's overseas soldiers, in the Senegal and the French Sudan.

The average age of the officers was twenty-nine, with Marchand at thirty-two the eldest, and Lieutenant Dyé, a naval officer, the youngest at twenty-two.[1] Apart from Largeau, who like Marchand had risen from the ranks, they came from conventional and well-

---

[1] Dyé had attracted attention with a scheme to chart the waters on either side of the watershed between the Nile and Lake Chad. He was an engaging and outspoken young man given to teasing his army companions by making unfavourable comparisons with the way they did things in the navy.

connected military backgrounds, and both Mangin and Baratier were products of the military academy of Saint-Cyr. They were professional soldiers but, in intelligent conversation and other forms of social intercourse, they displayed a sophistication and fluency which made most of their British counterparts from Woolwich or Sandhurst seem callow. While Marchand was the unquestioned leader, he was, of all the band, the one with the fewest advantages of birth and education.

Marchand was equally careful over the selection, ordering, and transport of the expedition's stores and equipment. Within the limits of his budget he seems to have been allowed to buy where and what he wanted. The expedition's very detailed records and accounts show that they took more than sixteen tons of coloured beads and 70,000 metres of cloth for use as currency in Africa. The beads and the cloth had to be exactly right in colour and texture. Marchand found that the French industrial machine had not adapted itself to these specialized requirements, and that he had to go abroad for his needs – to Venice for the beads, and for the cloth to Manchester and Liverpool where the tastes of the indigenous peoples of Asia and Africa had been more carefully and profitably studied. Most of the other purchases however were made in France. There were large quantities of what were described in the lists as *articles de Paris*, fancy goods and bric-a-brac intended as presents and rewards for services rendered – mirrors, embroidered slippers, scarves, gold braid, parasols, muslins, silks and gauze, handbells, musical boxes, and scent. For presents to chiefs and potentates they took lengths of better materials, glamorous uniforms, and weapons. They took provisions for six months – ten tons of rice, five tons of corned beef, one ton of coffee, 1,600 kilos of biscuits, 50 kilos of tea, 1,300 litres of red Bordeaux wine[2] and 525 litres of toddy. Marchand himself placed the orders for specialities such as *paté de foie gras*, galantine laced with truffles, *tripes à la mode de Caen*, 25 bottles of cognac, 50 of Pernod, and an unspecified amount of Champagne. Also ordered were 170 muskets of the latest model, and 100,000 cartridges. In all 90 tons of stores for the expedition were despatched to Loango made up, at Marchand's direction, into three thousand porters' loads of 30 kilos each. He also paid a special visit

[2] Further supplies of this wine were sent out to them in glass containers holding 16 litres but Marchand later sent a note from Africa asking if in future they could be sent out in 26 litre barrels 'as supplied to missionaries, at 12 francs a barrel'.

to Rotterdam before he left Europe to negotiate and sign a contract with the Dutch transport firm which dealt with the transport of goods on the Congo.

Although the Congo is one of the biggest rivers in the world it cannot be used by sea-going ships because of cataracts, once known as the Livingstone Falls, which bar the river a hundred miles from its mouth. But unlike the other great African rivers such as the Nile and the Niger, which spill out into shallow deltas, the mouth of the Congo has a single stream which is deep and clear of obstructions. To take advantage of this the Belgians had already built a port at Matadi, on the seaward side of the falls, and were in the process of connecting it by rail with the main river port of Leopoldville. Despite this advantage Marchand chose Loango on the coast as his starting point. He did so largely because it was in territory under French control. He did not want to be dependent on the Belgians, nor did he wish to disclose the details of his expedition to the Congo authorities whom he suspected of having rival ventures of their own in mind. Loango was also the terminus of the caravan route which had for generations carried the produce of the Congo from Brazzaville to the coast. It had few other advantages. There were no facilities for unloading stores from ship to shore or for warehousing them on land. Ships had to anchor a long way out in the bay, and once landed in bumboats through the surf, stores were generally left to lie unprotected on the beach.

Although Marchand said in a letter three days after he had arrived that he still hoped to be in Brazzaville by the middle of October, he was soon disillusioned. It was 525 km or about 300 miles across country from Loango to Brazzaville; except for one difficult four-day stretch of thick mountain forest described as sweltering, sombre and steamy, it was not usually difficult going. Porters starting at five in the morning and carrying loads of sixty pounds could do the journey in 25 days. But Marchand found that despite the arrangements he had made in Holland most of his 3,000 loads of stores were still lying on the beach, together with some 25,000 other loads belonging to the French Congo administration, to religious missions, and to various traders and shops in the interior. Some, he found, had been there for weeks, even months. The Dutch transport company pleaded *force majeure* in not being able to fulfil their contract. The situation in the interior was said to be very disturbed. Porters were throwing down their loads and deserting, and men were refusing to work. There were reports of villagers refusing to supply food and water to passing caravans, of travellers waylaid and robbed. There were stories of inter-tribal fighting, of whole tribes in revolt against the government, and of itinerant bands of marauders from the north taking advantage of the confusion to rampage and rape.

As he and his companions waited in the hot-house atmosphere of Loango, and watched the situation get worse and worse, Marchand came close to despair, fearing, as he put it in one of his letters home, that his precious mission was finished before it had begun. He had pleaded with de Brazza, the civilian governor of the French Congo, to restore law and order and to provide him with porters, and he and the others complained bitterly in their letters and reports that de Brazza and his officials would or could not do either. They were dismissed as 'un mélange hétéroclite', a medley of misfits, who drank every night into the early hours and only stopped to go in search of the convent-educated, French-speaking, Gabonese prostitutes who roamed the streets in high-heeled shoes. De Brazza himself was described as 'not even a proper Frenchman, Italian to his finger-tips, and a Neapolitan at that'. As a distinguished early explorer and pioneer, de Brazza had in fact been largely responsible for extending French influence into the rich forests and rivers on the north side of the Congo. He also had a rare understanding and feeling for the problems and needs of the people who lived there. They possessed few heroic qualities; years of slave-trading, disease, and cheap liquor had demoralized both the men and the women, and made them particularly susceptible to exploitation both by Europeans and by their fellow Africans. De Brazza had gradually and patiently induced them to place themselves more or less willingly under French protection. But such qualities and achievements had little appeal to soldiers in a hurry like Marchand and Mangin and Baratier, whose only concern at that point was to get themselves and their stores through to Brazzaville as quickly as possible. They had no time for what Marchand called de Brazza's 'politique négrophile dans toute sa prestigieuse pureté'. Where Marchand wanted to force people to carry his loads, de Brazza was inclined to argue that they had suffered compulsion enough; and when Mangin wanted to use force to make the route safe, de Brazza preferred to listen to the grievances which had first caused the people to revolt.

Marchand was a determined and single-minded man, and he was not prepared to be held up in this way. He demanded that de Brazza should give him a free hand to pacify the country and re-open the caravan route. When de Brazza hesitated, Marchand threatened to take the next boat back to France and expose the unhelpfulness and the shortcomings of his administration. In the end de Brazza gave way. He knew the importance which the French government attached to Marchand's expedition, and throwing up his hands in chagrin and despair he told Marchand on 18 August to write out his own instructions.

Marchand entrusted the task of pacification to Baratier and Mangin who was in charge of the company of Senegalese soldiers. The Senegalese looked on the primitive Congo tribesmen as savages, and had few qualms about doing whatever was necessary to cow and coerce them. There was little actual fighting. The Congo tribes had no military cohesion and few firearms. Apart from refusing to provide porters or supply food, their revolt against authority took the form of guerrilla activities. They ambushed and robbed; they picked off small parties and stragglers with spears and poisoned arrows; they attacked lonely outposts; they hit and ran. When confronted, they slipped away and vanished in the labyrinth of forest and rivers which made up a large part of what Marchand called 'le marécage puant', the stinking bog of the French Congo. He told his men only to do what was absolutely necessary to open up the caravan route and ensure a supply of porters but he soon found that the only way to get things done was to take hostages, and that the only punishments which were effective were to burn villages and crops. The climax of the operations came two months later with the pursuit of the leading figure in the insurrection, known to the French as Mabiala, the witchdoctor. Part of his popular appeal lay in his having once killed a French official, and as the revolt spread and flourished he emerged as a formidable opponent. In desperation Marchand gave orders for him to be taken, dead or alive. Baratier eventually cornered him in a network of caves in the hills, where he and his followers fought so stoutly and inflicted so many casualties on the French that in the end Baratier had to smoke them out. He used what he called a *saucisson*, an incendiary bomb made of melanite, an inflammable mixture of picric acid, gun cotton, and gum arabic much favoured by the French army in operations of this nature. When the flames had died down and the smoke had cleared the corpses of Mabiala and his men were found in the caves. Mabiala became a legend and a national hero as a result of his defiance, and in the long term his death probably caused more problems for the French than it solved.

Marchand and his companions were not concerned with the long term. They had been entrusted with a mission, and they were determined to carry it out, however difficult and hazardous it was for them, or for others. 'Nous ne sommes pas du Congo', Marchand told Mangin. 'What happens there is no concern of ours. We can leave that to the glory boys in gold braid.' With this philosophy behind him Marchand and a handful of French officers and NCOs, with a company of Senegalese and some 200 locally recruited militia, succeeded in pacifying an area the size of Italy with a population of half a million, and in making it safe for the caravans of porters on which the interior of the French Congo and its hinterland depended. His treatment of de Brazza and his civilian officials was often high-handed, and the methods he used were sometimes harsh but it is doubtful whether he would otherwise have got his expedition up from the coast. To save time during the six months which it took to complete this operation Marchand had swallowed his original objections and made arrangements for some stores to be re-embarked at Loango and despatched by sea to Matadi, to be taken from there by rail to the railhead, some 150 km short of Leopoldville. As a result of this foresight and his single-minded ruthlessness he and his expedition were by the end of 1896 firmly established at Brazzaville or elsewhere on the navigable part of the Congo, and were ready to begin the next phase of their mission.

CHAPTER VI

The Other Runners in the Race

THE orders given to Captain Marchand on 24 February 1896 had stressed the need for haste in order to forestall Colonel Colvile. At that time Marchand was confident that he could reach Fashoda before Colvile or anyone else, but the six months he had lost made him anxious to know how far Colvile had got. Although he was constantly asking Paris for news, and making local enquiries of his own, the information he received was meagre and misleading. At the end of 1896, when he was ready to travel up the main stream of the Congo, he still did not know where Colvile was or what orders he had received.

Colonel Colvile had first gone out to Uganda in 1893 when it, or parts of it, were still administered by the British East Africa Company. The company was a commercial concern although, as *The Times* put it, 'it would hardly be fair just to describe it as a purely commercial body, for it is notorious that the majority of, if not all, the subscribers are actuated rather by philanthropic motives than by expectation of receiving any adequate return for their outlay'. The directors of the company had their offices at 2, Pall Mall, conveniently close to the official sanctums of the Athenaeum and the Travellers' Club, and not far from Exeter Hall in the Strand where, on a site now occupied by the Strand Palace Hotel, missionaries and merchants met and discussed the possibilities of combining philanthropy and five per cent. In the case of Uganda the prospects were poor, and the company had intimated that it proposed to withdraw. Colvile had gone out as a military member of an official mission to advise whether the government should take over responsibility for the territory from the company. With Gladstone still at the helm the Liberal government of the day was reluctant to do so on principle, but a recent White Paper on the 'Proposed Railway from Mombasa to Lake Victoria Nyanza' had recommended that making Uganda a Protectorate and building a railway would, in the long run, 'provide the cheapest and most effective way of stopping the slave trade'. Existing arrangements, based on keeping a squadron of five cruisers operating in the Indian Ocean, were costing the taxpayer £100,000 a year which, it was noted, 'presents a field of saving which would justify a considerable outlay'. This mixture of philanthropy and parsimony had a strong appeal to Gladstone and most of his Liberal colleagues but when Rosebery who was then foreign secretary sat down to draft secret instructions to Portal who was in charge of the mission, he and the officials at the Foreign Office had other less radical considerations in mind. They believed that it was important for Britain to control the headwaters of the Nile, and they suspected with good reason that both the French and the Belgians were trying to get there before them. So, he wrote in August 1893:

It has therefore become necessary for Her Majesty's Government to take such steps as may be within their power to protect the important interests of this country in the Upper Nile. I have therefore to instruct you, should the means at your disposal and the interests with which you are temporarily charged in Uganda permit, to send emissaries into the district of the Nile Basin in order to ascertain the state of affairs in that portion of the British sphere. They should further be authorised to negotiate any treaties that may be necessary for its protection . . .[1]

It took five months for these instructions to reach Uganda, and by that time Portal had gone, leaving Colvile in charge. In pursuance of Rosebery's instructions Colvile sent one of his officers down the Nile. The furthest he got was Wadelai, north of Lake Albert. He only stayed there for 24 hours but during that time he made a treaty, hoisted union jacks on both sides of the river and left a small garrison with two months' pay in advance. Three months later a visitor could find no trace of the flags or the garrison. Colvile sent another party to the north in August 1894 to reconnoitre 'down the Nile to its furthest navigable point'. It was at Nimule, a hundred miles beyond Wadelai, that they found their way blocked by floating vegetation. Colvile's only other activities in northern Uganda were in Unyoro. The British government had taken over responsibility for Uganda in April of 1894 but Kabarega, the sixteenth king of Unyoro, resisted attempts to include his territory in this arrangement with such spirit and determination that it took most of

---

[1] To make sure that these secret instructions did not become known to his more radical colleagues or get published later in a White Paper Rosebery marked the despatch 'Not to be printed'.

Colvile's time and resources to subdue him.[2] Colvile left Uganda early in 1895, and was thus never a threat to the French in the upper Nile. Nevertheless the 'mission Colvile' was for years regarded by them as a serious rival in the race to the Nile, and continued to be so regarded by Marchand long after Colvile had left Uganda.

This however was not the end of what the French regarded as perfidious British plots to advance into the upper Nile from Uganda. Salisbury had taken over as head of a Conservative government in the middle of 1895, and he shared Rosebery's conviction that the best way of gaining control over the headwaters of the Nile, and of preventing anyone else from doing so, was from the south. He believed, however, that this could not be done effectively until good communications had been secured by building a railway up from the coast. When he returned to office he did his best therefore to push ahead with this project, and finally succeeded in getting enough funds from parliament to start work in 1896. Meanwhile Salisbury resisted army proposals to advance from the north on the grounds that it would only spur the French 'into a forward movement on the Nile' which HMG would be unable to counter 'till our railway has reached the lake'. A year later he was still telling the Queen that there is 'no remedy for the Upper Nile until the Uganda railway is completed'.

The Uganda railway soon ran into formidable difficulties of construction and climate, and in the end it was to take seven years to complete. In the early part of 1897 reports reaching Salisbury from military intelligence convinced him that Captain Marchand really was 'going in' from the west and that he was probably acting in conjunction with Belgian advances from the Congo and with another French expedition from Abyssinia in the east. He thought the situation was sufficiently serious to take the matter to the Cabinet, but he met with so many political and financial objections and received so much contradictory advice that in the end he decided to act on his own. All he wanted was, as he put it in one of his distinctive notes in red ink, 'an inexpensive, unobtrusive scheme which would not arouse the Opposition or the Treasury or get to the ears of the French'. With this as his objective he approached a Captain J. A. L. Macdonald of the Royal Engineers. Macdonald

---

[2] When Kabarega was finally subdued he was sent into comfortable and prolific exile in the Seychelles until, at the age of 80, he was allowed to return on the grounds that he was no longer a threat to law and order.

knew East Africa from a preliminary survey for the Uganda railway
which he had carried out some years before. As Salisbury was at this
stage acting without reference to the Cabinet negotiations with
Macdonald were discreetly conducted by his private secretary.
Macdonald's first plan, 'detailing the way in which I would carry out
Lord Salisbury's bold conception', was set out in a letter dated 27
March 1897. The plan was to send an expedition to Fashoda from
Uganda immediately so as to get there before anyone else. It would
start from Kismayu on the east African coast north of Mombasa and
follow the course of the Juba river to its source in the Abyssinian
highlands. From there it would go across country to the source of
the river Sobat and follow it downstream to its junction with the Nile
near Fashoda. He calculated that, using camels for transport, he
would get to Fashoda within a year. 'I think', he concluded, 'there is
every reason to anticipate success.'

The plan did not please the Foreign Office, largely because it
involved crossing territory recently conquered and claimed by
Menelik of Abyssinia. Macdonald then suggested sailing straight
down the Nile from Lake Albert but the attractions of simplicity,
speed, and low cost were offset by the report that the river at Nimule
was blocked by masses of floating vegetation. This plan too was
therefore rejected. His next proposal was to strike north from Lake
Baringo in Kenya to the area of Lake Rudolf, and from there to go
north again through the ill-defined borderlands of south-western
Abyssinia to the Nile at Fashoda by way of the rivers Akobo and
Sobat. To conceal his real objective, and as an explanation of why
he was carrying portable boats, he proposed to say that his plan was
to go east from Lake Rudolf to explore the upper reaches of the
river Juba.

Salisbury liked this idea, not least for the advantages it offered of
deceiving both the French and the more cautious members of his
own Cabinet.[3] On 25 April he wrote in confidence to Hicks Beach,
the Chancellor of the Exchequer, asking for £35,000 for 'sending an
expedition to the east bank of the Nile to make friends with the
tribes before the French get there from the west . . . the ostensible

---

[3] As part of the deception a special folder was opened in the Foreign Office
marked 'Special Mission to the Juba river'. It shows the care taken not to reveal the
real purpose of the expedition to the Cabinet or to offer any more information about
its composition or objectives than was absolutely necessary to persuade the Treasury
to meet the expenses.

reason for despatch will be to explore the sources of the Juba'. This high-level deception made it necessary to issue two separate sets of instructions. The 'cover' instruction, which gave the expedition's objective as the sources of the Juba, were shown to the Cabinet. Macdonald's real instructions were not. Although his activities were confined to the east bank of the Nile, and to the latitude of Fashoda in the north, he was directed to 'secure the allegiance of the Chiefs by presents and the grant of the British flag', and 'effectually to secure the territories against other powers'. He was also instructed, in terms which suggest that they were drafted by Salisbury himself, that if he met any other European expedition he should continue with his own operation and disregard 'any claims or pretensions which may be advanced on the ground of prior treaties or occupation'.

Armed with these instructions, and set on what could well have been a collision course, Macdonald wasted no time. Within a month of receiving his orders on 9 June 1897 he had assembled his forces at Baringo and was ready to leave for the north.

*   *   *

One of the reasons why Marchand was so keen to press on, and why Salisbury decided to send Macdonald in from the south, was that King Leopold of the Belgians was also reported to be sending an expedition from the north east of the Congo into the Nile basin. Its aim was said to be to secure for the products of the eastern Congo an outlet on the Nile from which they could be transported quickly and cheaply by water to the Mediterranean and the markets of Europe. The king himself had boasted: 'The edifice which I am raising in central Africa will have three frontages; one on the Atlantic; the second on the Nile, and a third on the Zambezi.' Having failed to get his frontage on the Nile by diplomatic means he decided to send an expedition to take what he wanted by force.

In the end he sent two expeditions. One, led by Captain Chaltin, set out in April 1896 from Stanleyville to march up the valley of the river Uele and make for the Nile in the region of Gondoroko. The other and much larger expedition under Baron Dhanis set out a few months later by a more southerly route for the same destination. It was a particularly hazardous route through tropical rain forest inhabited by hostile tribes of pygmies, but it was chosen for reasons of secrecy to keep news of it from both the French and the British.

The plan was for these two expeditions to join forces and then, despite a promise by King Leopold to the French that he would not go beyond Lado, to continue as far north as they could, towards Fashoda and even beyond to Khartoum. By the end of the year, as Marchand was starting to move up the Congo, both expeditions were within striking distance of the Nile.

*   *   *

In addition to the reports of Belgian expeditions to the Nile there were rumours of other expeditions being plotted and planned in Abyssinia. Abyssinia was at that time a little-known country, and the information which reached the headquarters of British military intelligence at 18, Queen Anne's Gate about happenings there was often surprising. In 1891 when the European powers were still engaged in the scramble for the remaining bits of Africa, Menelik II, Lion of Judah and King of all the Kings of Ethiopia had issued a proclamation which opened with an undiplomatic directness:

Ethiopia has for fourteen centuries been a Christian island in a sea of pagans. If powers from a distance come forward to partition Africa between them I do not intend to be a spectator . . .

Menelik went on to claim as his dominions not only the areas he had conquered himself, like the Muslim sultanate of Harar and the mainly Somali Ogaden, but what he called the ancient lands of his ancestors, extending to the Red Sea and the Gulf of Aden on one side, and on the other to the White Nile from Lake Victoria in the south to Khartoum in the north. When the British representative in Addis Ababa expressed surprise at the extent of these claims Menelik retorted that 'as a Christian power in Africa his claim was better founded than those of powers whose seat of government was in another continent'. Menelik's claims were not taken very seriously at the time because it was known that his people were only at ease in their cool highlands, and had no liking or tolerance for the fiendishly hot Red Sea coast or for the humid unhealthiness of the upper Nile. But when Delcassé and President Carnot were planning the first expedition to Fashoda under Major Monteil they saw how Menelik's ambitions might be used to propose a joint Franco-Ethiopian venture which would both support Monteil's mission and establish Menelik's claim to the east bank of the Nile. To make the bargain more attractive the French secretly offered Menelik facilities to import arms and ammunition through Jibuti for use against the Italians who were encroaching from the north. They also undertook to build a railway connecting Jibuti with Menelik's new capital at Addis Ababa, and eventually to extend it westwards to the White Nile. In return Menelik promised to allow a French expedition from Jibuti to cross Abyssinian territory to join forces with Monteil at Fashoda and to give it every assistance. In the end nothing came of these proposals but the germ of the idea was sown both in Addis Ababa and in Paris.

The idea was revived in 1896 as part of the planning for Marchand's expedition. Although the concept of concerted expeditions from the east and the west did not form part of Marchand's original plan, he claimed later that he would never have embarked on his mission to Fashoda if he had not been assured that a parallel expedition would be mounted from Jibuti. Negotiations were initiated by Lagarde, the French representative in Addis Ababa, and eventually bore fruit in a *Convention pour le Nil blanc* which formally recognized the White Nile as the boundary between the French and Abyssinian spheres of influence. The French promised to help Menelik to establish his authority on the east bank of the river while Menelik for his part undertook to support 'to the best of his ability' Marchand's expedition from the west.

On this basis the French government proceeded to launch two expeditions at the end of 1896 to join forces with Marchand at Fashoda. One was organized in Jibuti by a former army officer named Clochette. With two other officials from Jibuti who knew the country he set off from Jibuti equipped with 40,000 Maria Theresa thalers and little else. The other expedition was organized in Paris. To keep its real destination and purpose a secret it was put under the auspices of the ministry of education as a project for scientific research, and thus included an entomologist, a geologist, and an artist. It was commanded by an explorer named Charles Bonvolet, assisted by another explorer, Christian de Bonchamps.

*   *   *

By the spring of 1896, when the French government issued its first instructions for Marchand's expedition to the Nile, eleven years had passed since General Gordon had been killed at Khartoum and the Sudan had been abandoned to the Mahdi. There were those in Britain and in Egypt who, for a variety of reasons, wanted to avenge

Gordon's death and reoccupy the Sudan but the prevailing view of a succession of both Conservative and Liberal governments was that it would be wiser, and also cheaper, to do nothing. This point of view was shared by Sir Evelyn Baring, and during the twenty-four years that he was in Egypt little was done in the middle east without his approval. His attitude to the reconquest of the Sudan reflected the conflict between the proconsular and diplomatic sides of his duties. As a proconsul he followed the traditions of the Indian Civil Service and identified himself with the interests of Egypt and its people, even to the point of championing their causes against difficult or niggling Whitehall departments like the Treasury or the War Office. In this capacity he opposed the reconquest of the Sudan until the finances of Egypt had been restored to health. When this had been done he continued to oppose military action because it would cost money that could be better spent on hospitals and schools, and the construction of dams and other useful public works. As Britain's chief diplomatic representative in the middle east, on the other hand, he was primarily concerned with British interests, and paid no more attention to other people's needs or sensibilities than was absolutely necessary. In this capacity he believed that, whether the people of Egypt liked it or not, Britain should stay in Egypt to ensure that the Suez Canal would remain open for communications with India, and provide a link between the two main pillars of British imperial power – the Mediterranean Fleet and the Indian Army. While it was essential to the British position in Egypt that no other European power should control the headwaters of the Nile, he shared the view that occupation of the Sudan was unnecessary so long as it was effectively closed to the outside world by the Mahdi and his successor, the Khalifa Abdullah. Many years later Cromer confessed that, if anyone had asked him in 1886 how long this situation would last, his answer would have been 25 years.

There were those who took a different view. There were the military men who saw Gordon's death and the evacuation of the Sudan as shameful episodes that must be avenged. There were the philanthropists and the merchants who regretted that, as Cromer put it, 'certain provinces which had before been open to trade, and which might have been subjected to the influences of civilisation, had been allowed to relapse into barbarism'. There were the Cape-to-Cairo enthusiasts and others who wanted to paint the map red. Although the Conservatives liked to brand the Liberals as advocates of 'scuttle' in Egypt and the Sudan, it was Rosebery who took the first steps in the other direction in the spring of 1895 when reports of a French expedition to the Nile had stirred public interest and evoked Grey's famous declaration. In this, as indeed on other matters, he was often out of tune with many of his Liberal colleagues. This meant that, particularly in foreign affairs, he was inclined to act on his own. 'Pray remember very carefully', he told Cromer, 'the distinction between telegrams – it is only those marked Private that I consider personal to me – all the others go into the hands of my sixteen colleagues. There are many nuances of the situation that, without any disloyalty to them, are better only seen by me . . .'. So it was that on 5 April 1895 he wrote a private letter to Cromer. He was in failing health and his letter began 'A rather feeble pen must confine this letter to interrogatories in which I am interested . . .'. He went on to list four questions. The first two were:

1. Is the Egyptian government at all interested in, or disquieted by the threatened advance of France towards the Upper Nile?
2. Has the Egyptian Government of late shown any desire to move towards Dongola?

Cromer's reply came a week later. His answers to the questions made the point that, while little importance need be attached to what the Khedive or his ministers thought, it would be wiser from the political and international aspects if, in referring to the Sudan and the Upper Nile in the future, 'we speak less of the British sphere of influence', and more of recovering 'Egyptian territory'. He went on to argue that while evacuation of the Sudan had been unavoidable in the 1880s, and its re-conquest unnecessary and undesirable in the early '90s, 'the presence of the French on or near the Upper Nile entirely alters the situation. If they are allowed to establish themselves in these regions, there is an end of all ideas of Egyptian reconquest. More than this it is obvious that if any civilised Power holds the waters of the Upper Nile it may in the end be in a position to exercise a predominating influence on the future of Egypt. I cannot, therefore, help thinking that it will not be possible or desirable to maintain a purely passive attitude much longer'.

Although Cromer took it for granted that it would be preferable from all points of view if the reconquest of the Sudan were carried

out in the name of Egypt by Egyptian troops under British gui-
dance, he warned that this still 'involves the possibility of war with
France, a direction in which we have been drifting for some time
past in connection with Egypt and other matters'. The risk would be
increased if, as he assumed, Egyptian government funds were to be
used to pay for the reconquest. This would require the consent of
the International Commissioners for the Debt in Cairo, and it was of
course certain that the French, and probably the Russians would
object. 'Unless', Cromer warned, 'we are prepared to insist on our
point, even to the extent of fighting for it in case of need, we had
better leave it alone.' He added that 'unless the naval experts should
declare our capacity to hold our own, and more so, against the
French fleet' it would be better not to embark on the reconquest of
the Sudan.

Soon afterwards, in the summer of 1895, the Liberal government
fell, and the imperialist Joseph Chamberlain became colonial
secretary in Salisbury's third Conservative administration. Salisbury still believed that there should be no advance into the Upper
Nile until his Uganda railway had reached Lake Victoria. Early in
the new year however the situation changed. In France Captain
Marchand received permission to proceed with his expedition. In
eastern Africa the Italians, trying to expand from their base in
Eritrea, were coming under increasing pressure both from the
Mahdist forces on their outpost at Kassala, and from Menelik's
armies in the north of Abyssinia. The Italians appealed to the
British for help on the grounds that if they were defeated by native
African troops it would put all Europeans in Africa in danger. It was
too good an opportunity for the British to miss. It provided a
conveniently good excuse for an advance up the Nile in the direction
of Khartoum. To send some of the British and Indian troops then
stationed at Suakin on the Red Sea coast towards Kassala would of
course have been a better way of relieving pressure on the Italians
but that was not the direction in which Salisbury wished to go.

Although the plight of the Italians was still used as an excuse it
was not until ten days after the Italians had been defeated at Aduwa
on 1 March 1896 that the British cabinet formally authorized an
advance up the Nile. It was a cautious and limited advance but it was
a beginning. Armed with this authority Kitchener[4] wasted no time.

---

[4] General Sir Herbert Kitchener had been commander-in-chief or Sirdar of the
Egyptian army since 1890.

With the help of Thomas Cook's fleet of Nile pleasure-steamers which he requisitioned, he pushed ahead so economically in terms of men and of money that the cabinet soon sanctioned another small advance. Dongola was captured in September. Both Cromer and Salisbury thought it would be wiser 'to stop two or three years at Dongola before making any further advance', but Kitchener pleaded that he had got the Mahdist forces 'on the run', and that it would be quicker and in the long run cheaper to strike while the iron was hot. By November Salisbury and his cabinet were convinced by Kitchener's logic and authorized an advance to Berber. But there, Salisbury told Cromer firmly, Kitchener was to halt 'for some time', unless, he was careful to add, 'matters were hastened by the advance of some other power towards the Nile'.

By this time Marchand had nearly finished pacifying the coastal area, and was beginning to assemble his men and materials on the navigable part of the river Congo. Although spokesmen for the British government continued to talk of limited objectives and altruistic motives on the Nile, it was becoming clear to most people at home and to nearly everyone abroad that the real purpose of Kitchener's operations in the Sudan was the defeat of the Mahdist forces, the capture of Khartoum, and victory over the French in the race to the upper Nile.

CHAPTER VII

Marchand on the Congo and the Ubangi

Soon after his arrival at Brazzaville at the beginning of 1897 Marchand sent word to Lagarde at Addis Ababa: 'You may take it for certain that by the first of January 1898, and perhaps by the previous November, I shall be in occupation of Fashoda, and that you can make your arrangements from the east accordingly.' Marchand was prone to recurring moods of depression and euphoria but when this was written the prospects were certainly promising. The difficulties and delays of the caravan route from Loango were behind and he had in front of him 2,000 km or about 1,200 miles of navigable river from Brazzaville to Ouango. Of this, 800 miles on the broad main stream of the Congo and the Ubangi could be navigated in steamboats, and the remainder in whale boats and canoes. Marchand had already sent Largeau on ahead with an advance party and 2,000 porter-loads of supplies, and they had managed to do the journey from Brazzaville to Bangui in 27 days, an average of about 20 miles a day.

When he sent Largeau off on 1 November, Marchand never expected that he himself and his rear party would not be able to leave Brazzaville until the middle of March, and that it would be the end of April 1897 before the whole of the expedition had left Bangui. There were two main reasons for the delay. One was that they now had twice as many loads of stores in their possession as they had when they landed at Loango. Having opened the caravan route, Marchand found himself beset with pleas from officials, missionaries and traders in the interior to bring up the most urgently needed of their goods which had been held up for so many months on the coast. Apart from his reluctance to ignore pleas from his fellow-countrymen in such an awkward situation Marchand knew that he and his companions would become very dependent on the goodwill of these same officials and missionaries and traders once they reached the upper reaches of the Ubangi. The other reason for the delay was a shortage of river transport. The French Congo authorities had six steam-driven craft of variable age and condition but only one, a small screw-launch called *Faidherbe* was available for the expedition's use. The others were either out on loan, under repair or had been abandoned. The only other vessels in the territory were three old paddle-steamers or stern-wheelers of the Mississippi type belonging to the Dutch transport company, the Nieuwe Afrikaansche Handels Venootschap which was, not surprisingly, better known as NAHV.

Marchand eventually persuaded the local agent of NAHV to carry both the advance party under Largeau, and a second party under Sergeant Venail, which left early in January with a further 1,900 porter-loads of stores. It was part of Marchand's habits of leadership that he tried to avoid having all his eggs in one basket. He knew from years of experience in Africa how every operation however carefully planned was liable to unforeseeable accidents of nature and human frailty. He also knew that dividing his forces accustomed men to acting on their own, and served too to lessen the frictions of living together at close quarters for long periods on end. Just as he had in the beginning despatched the members and stores of the expedition from France in four separate parties, on different ships and by different routes, so now he divided his men and his materials into four sections for the journeys to Bangui and Ouango.

There was so little room on the small, out-of-date NAHV craft that all three vessels were needed in turn to transport each section of the expedition. This meant that the other sections had to wait for weeks at Brazzaville doing nothing until the three boats returned from Bangui. To speed things up Marchand tried to persuade the authorities in Paris to send out a larger ship. When this failed he once again turned to the Belgian Congo for help. In contrast to the meagre resources on the French side of the river, the rich Congo Free State had a large fleet of modern steam vessels at its disposal. The outcome was that the third and fourth sections of Marchand's expedition travelled in comfort and style on a much larger and faster ship called *La Ville de Bruges*, a screw-driven ship some 40 meters in length which could do twelve knots. This however was not the end of their troubles. Both the Congo and the Ubangi rivers were enclosed by hills and by walls of thick forest which formed a sort of corridor through which sudden gusts of wind sometimes swept with hurricane force. The *Ville de Bruges* was a flat-bottomed craft, and this, coupled with its high superstructure of two decks, made it vulnerable to such hazards. A vessel like *Ville de Bruges* had recently been caught by a gust of wind before it could take shelter and been overturned, and on their way upstream Marchand and Baratier nearly had a similar experience. When they left the main stream of the Congo and began the ascent of the Ubangi they found that it was full of sandbanks and reefs not marked on their charts. Another hazard was the low level of the water in the dry seasons. There was a particularly difficult stretch of river some 100 km south of Bangui. When Marchand reached this point in *Ville de Bruges* at the beginning of April he was assured by all the experts that there would be enough depth of water for them to pass. In the event it turned out, as so often happens in Africa, to be an unusual year, and in the end they had to unload all their stores and engage 65 canoes and over a thousand paddlers to finish their journey.

Even a boat as large as the *Ville de Bruges* did no more than 25 to 30 miles a day. It had to tie up every night in order that wood could be cut ashore to feed the engine-room boilers the following day. A special complement of wood-cutters was carried for this purpose. To fit themselves for their night's work the wood-cutters slept all day in a lighter attached to the side of the ship in attitudes of naked abandon and alcoholic stupor. Progress was also delayed, often to Marchand's impatient displeasure, by frequent stops at riverside settlements where local produce of all kinds could be got in exchange for coloured beads and implements made of iron. At one such place where foodstuffs were particularly plentiful he noticed that there was no meat for sale, not even the ubiquitous goat. The explanation, according to the ever-curious Baratier, was that the meat was kept for bartering with men who came in from the depths of the forest with occasional captives or slaves, for which the people of the village had a culinary taste. Baratier generally took great pains in his search for local colour but nineteenth century travellers' tales of cannibalism, like stories of sexual orgies and human sacrifice, need to be treated with caution. People in Europe and America who read books or listened to lectures about distant places seem to have expected primitive behaviour from primitive peoples, and it was not unusual for explorers and even missionaries to invent or imply such behaviour when first-hand evidence was lacking. Marchand and his companions were less prone than many to this failing but young Lieutenant Mangin had a number of young married sisters to impress and to shock, and his letters to them from the heart of Africa sometimes contained more detail perhaps than he had actually seen with his own eyes. Of the cannibals in this part of the Ubangi, for example, he wrote:

They go about their business with great dexterity. The quarry is first silently despatched with a throwing spear and the throat cut with a knife especially designed for the purpose; the stomach is then disembowelled. The back is broken with a single blow, and the victim is carried off by two men, one with the legs draped round his neck, and the other with the trunk on his back. It is all over in a matter of seconds.

Bobichon, the French officer in charge of this area of river and forest, liked and admired the people who lived there, and was at pains to explain that as a general rule they only ate people in times of great need. Bobichon was in turn respected and obeyed, partly perhaps because he did not try to interfere unduly with the customs and practices which they had evolved over the years to meet the special requirements of their life in the forests. So when Marchand wanted his thousand paddlers at short notice Bobichon got them without question or delay. Not all the French officials on the Ubangi were as sympathetic or as effective. They were often of poor quality and little education, and had become demoralized by ill-health in the steam-bath climate, by loneliness, and by what a commission of enquiry was later to call the inadequte pay, poor living conditions and the budgets *squelettiques*, the shoe-string budgets on which they were expected to run their districts.

In his service in French West Africa Marchand had seen something of the demoralization which set in when Europeans living in isolated and primitive places were deprived of the relaxations and refinements they were used to. Judging the moment to be right after dinner one night on *Ville de Bruges* he had a crate unpacked whose contents he alone knew. Inside was a mechanical piano. His companions listened in a state of enchantment as the piano regaled them with old favourites like *Ma gigolette elle est perdue* which they knew from the music halls of their youth in Paris and Marseilles, and from the barrel-organs which had played in the dusty, tree-lined squares of the country towns and villages where they had grown up. The tune, and others in the same vein, brought tears as well as smiles as each in turn evoked memories of sight and sound and smell and

touch which added up to each man's private image and memory of
France.

It was for the same reasons that Marchand took particular care of
the cases of wine and the tins of delicacies which they had brought
with them from France. If he thought they were getting too much
sun or were being unduly disturbed by the motion of the boat he
immediately had them moved or stowed away in another part of the
ship. When conditions allowed equal attention was paid to the
cooking. Although as a rule they used trained Senegalese soldier
cooks to prepare their meals most of the French members of the
mission seem to have taken a close interest in what they ate and how
it was cooked, and often applied their own expertise to the prepara-
tion of improvised dishes such as elephant steak, smoked hippopotamus and python stew.

The expedition had left France with sixteen European members.
By the time they reached Bangui there were only thirteen. The
three civilians had, each for his own reasons, left and gone home.
The military members found that in practice the civilians were not
up to the physical and mental stresses of the life they had to lead,
while the three civilians, for their part, found the disciplines and
arrogant behaviour of some of the soldiers difficult to tolerate. This
was especially the case with Castellani, *le panoramiste* as they called
him, who had been sent out by *L'Illustration* to accompany the
expedition and illustrate its exploits. Castellani wrote a book about
his experiences, and it is easy to see from his vivid, entertaining and
uninhibited descriptions of his companions why he was regarded by
them as 'at once the delight and the nightmare of the expedition'.
Baratier, he described, as a man of distinctive intelligence and
charm who 'had the signal quality of never being rude'; Dr Emily
was 'un homme serieux', whose presence always had a calming
effect and who was possessed of such marvellous eyes that 'if I were
a girl I would not hesitate for a moment'. Unorthodox statements of
this nature did not endear Castellani to Marchand who tended to be
conventional and old-fashioned in matters of this kind. Relations
between the two men were consequently often somewhat strained
but Castellani's pen portrait of Marchand had the merit of detachment and close observation. He described him as being below
average height with a dark complexion and lively black eyes; his
ears stuck out 'which', Castellani observed, 'is always a sign of great
energy'. He wore his hair close-cropped, 'a bit too much so for my

taste', and his face was neatly framed in a black beard except when he let it grow ragged and long. His head was set proudly on the shoulders, and his lithe, loose-limbed walk belied his underlying toughness. He always wore a grey felt hat which suited him much better than the traditional *képi* or peaked cap 'which make our overseas army officers look like clarinet players of the First Empire'. 'Marchand', Castellani continued, 'can be described as a cheerful, straightforward extrovert. His main character defect is that he hates to be contradicted but it would not be fair for me to hold this against him. In conclusion, if I am not to be accused of flattery, I must mention one more trait of character which in a leader of men must be accounted a fault – notwithstanding a strain of ferocity in his nature I believe him to be basically a kind, fair man who is easily moved to pity. And perhaps it would not be overstepping the bounds of discretion to add that, like King Henry IV of France and Navarre, he did not disdain the fair sex – to put it mildly'.

Marchand himself did not reach Bangui until 11 April 1897 but he had again split his party into four sections and had sent each on ahead on different dates and with different objectives. They travelled in large dug-out canoes to Ouango where the Mbomu and Uele rivers joined to form the Ubangi. Beyond that point the rivers were little known and largely unmapped, but local reports indicated that because of rapids and small waterfalls that was as far as the big canoes could go. Each tribe on these rivers tended to have its own distinctive type of canoe and its own particular style of propulsion. As a general rule, however, there were paddlers who sat or crouched in the stern, and men with long poles who stood in the bows and watched for sandbanks and rocks, and did their best to avoid or scare off the hippopotamus which infested the rivers. Starting at dawn and travelling until dusk, with a rest for an hour at mid-day, they could do twenty to twenty-five miles a day. Marchand still had some two thousand loads of other people's stores to deliver, and he had also had to take on about a hundred local men as interpreters, guides, servants and guards. So it was that, for the 450 mile journey from Bangui to Ouango, the expedition engaged a total of 175 canoes and over 4,000 local boatmen. No such demands had previously been made on the limited resources of the tribes on the upper Ubangi, and without the help of the local French officials they could certainly not have been met. Although the tribesmen were paid at current local rates[1] such large numbers of canoes and boatmen would not normally have been available. Marchand and his officers submitted their needs to Bobichon and his agents, and they in turn told the tribal chiefs and elders to produce so many canoes and so many men at such and such a time and a place. Bobichon's authority, and his understanding of the cannibal tribes in his district were enough to ensure that all the expedition's needs were met without serious resistance, and that the only disturbances which occurred were about women.[2]

It was during his own journey by canoe from Bangui to Ouango on 18 April that Marchand took a decision that was to change the whole course of his mission. In the scheme which he had originally submitted in 1895 he had planned to make his way north from Ouango towards Diem Zubeir and then north again to the Bahr el Arab. From there he had intended to take an overland route through southern Darfur and Kordofan which followed the line of the Bahr el Arab to its junction with the White Nile at Lake No and so on to Fashoda. He had three reasons for choosing this route. The first was that it would bring him quickly into country controlled by the Mahdists whose help he was confident he would get in any venture designed to discomfit the British. This route also had the advantage of avoiding the immense swamp of the Bahr el Ghazal. Thirdly it provided a mainly overland route and thus avoided the need to carry with them anything more than light portable aluminium lighters for floating their stores downstream when the opportunity arose.

This part of Marchand's plan had already been a matter of dispute in Paris before he set off, and had in the end been left for settlement between Marchand and Liotard on the spot in Africa. Liotard wanted Marchand to go eastwards from Ouango up the line of the Mbomu to Tambura and the territory inhabited by the Azande;

---

[1] Canoe men were paid two coffee-spoonfuls of glass beads a day; one spoonful was for the day's work and the other for sustenance. One spoonful of beads was the equivalent of 20 centimes in cash or half a chicken in kind. The normal proportion of white to coloured beads in these transactions was two thirds white to one of red or blue.

[2] The people of the upper Ubangi did not appear to mind their womenfolk consorting with the various members of Marchand's expedition but parents of unmarried girls and husbands expected to be paid the customary fees for abduction and adultery. However willing the ladies may have been, if these fees were not paid there was serious trouble.

thence he was to make his way down a small tributary of the Nile called the Sue and through the Bahr el Ghazal to the main stream of the White Nile.

Liotard's advice was not to be lightly ignored. He had served for many years in French Equatorial Africa and knew the area as well as anyone, and Marchand had been made specifically subordinate to him so long as he was travelling through his territory. There was also the important point that Liotard had himself been given instructions earlier to extend French administration eastwards into the valley of the Nile. For him as a civil governor this meant more than a quick, dramatic dash by a small military expedition to Fashoda. It meant a slow and painstaking process of establishing a proper administrative structure, of maintaining law and order, and of creating conditions in which French settlers and merchants and missionaries could function and prosper. This in turn meant seeking and gaining the co-operation and trust of the Azande who dominated both sides of the watershed between the Congo and the Nile in this region. In particular it meant persuading the chiefs and elders of the ruling Avongera clan that their best chance of keeping some at least of their considerable powers and privileges was to act as agents of the new French administration. Another reason for seeking the co-operation of the Azande was that they made very good soldiers. It was said indeed that in the competition for control of the upper Nile whoever had the Azande on their side would come out on top.

The ordinary Zande men and women were inclined to be friendly and well disposed to strangers but experience had taught them to be wary of anyone with a light-coloured skin. Experience had also taught them, however, that they had even more to fear from the people of the northern Sudan. During the time that the Mahdi and Khalifa Abdulla had been in control of this area the Azande had suffered on more than one occasion from raids from the north by Arabs using methods of memorable ferocity and cruelty to try and recruit conscripts for their armies and converts to their Islamic faith. The Azande were negroid peoples with their own ways and customs, and they had nothing in common, in appearance, language or culture, with the Arabs of the north. Liotard had gradually won the confidence and respect of the Zande rulers, and the last thing he wanted was for it to become known that a band of his fellow-countrymen was seeking an alliance with the hated Mahdists from the north. Such an association would not only upset the Azande but

might also prejudice his future relations with all the Nilotic tribes of
the Bahr el Ghazal and beyond – the Dinka, the Nuer, and the
Shilluk, who hated and feared the Mahdists as much as the Azande
and whose co-operation Liotard would also need for further east-
ward extensions of French control.

Liotard used a number of other arguments to try and persuade
Marchand to change his mind. One was that porters and paddlers
would be difficult to find in the country to the north. Another was
that the area had recently been so devastated by the Mahdist forces
that there would be little food and other supplies left for Marchand's
men. His most persistent argument was that if Marchand allied
himself with the Mahdists it would arouse so much hostility to
Frenchmen and France among the Nilotic tribes that Marchand and
his men would find it impossible to reach their objective.

Marchand had great tenacity in argument as well as in action. He
refused to admit the validity of Liotard's reasons or to accept that
Liotard knew better than he. In the end what made him change his
route were two inescapable facts. One was that, as stated above, in
the instructions given to him in Paris he was made subordinate to
Liotard and subject to his orders. This in itself might not have
deterred Marchand who, as a soldier, was not averse to disobeying
orders issued by civilians if he was sure he was right. What finally
decided him was the realization that if he insisted on sticking to his
plan to go north he would get little or no help from Liotard's
adminstration in securing porters and supplies and canoes. If he
went east, as Liotard wished, he would have the whole weight and
influence of the administration of Upper Ubangi at his disposal.
When he changed his plans on 18 April 1897 it was not because he
had been persuaded but because he realized that he had no other
choice.

Marchand remained convinced to the end that the change of
course was a mistake and that it seriously prejudiced his chances of
success.[3] There were those both at the time and afterwards who
believed that Liotard was prompted by jealousy, and that his real
purpose was to hinder Marchand rather than help him to do what he
himself had failed to do. Despite their disagreement Marchand's
relations with Liotard remained courteous and correct, and Man-

[3] In a letter to Terrier, Marchand said that the change was considered by everyone
'comme une insigne folie, une impossibilité totale, l'échec assure de la mission'.

gin, who was no respecter of persons described Liotard in moving terms as 'homme très simple, très bon et très droit'.

The most important result of the change was that Marchand now had to have a steamer of his own. Otherwise they would, as he put it, find themselves when they arrived at Meshra er Rek 'au fond d'un cul de sac infranchissable', in a dead-end without any means of escape. They had to have a steamboat not only to get down the Nile from Meshra to Fashoda but to ensure a reliable means of supply once they got there. Knowing that the British and the Belgians and even the Khalifa had steamers in plenty, Marchand as a more than ordinarily proud Frenchman, also wanted one for reasons of prestige. Although he did not finally decide to take the eastern route until April, he and his officers had known that it was a possibility. They had therefore been on the look out for a steamboat for some time, a boat, that is to say, that could be taken to pieces and transported by porters or by canoe when the rivers became impassable or they had to travel overland. Vessels that met such requirements were hard to come by in the middle of Africa. Baratier had discovered the remains of one called the *Jacques d'Uzès*, which had been abandoned on a remote stretch of river when it had capsized and its master had drowned. With his usual resource and determination Baratier had it recovered and cut up into portable loads. In the end, however, it had to be left behind because despite his efforts some pieces remained too large and too heavy to carry. A more suitable vessel was the *Léon XIII*, named after Pope Leo by the Catholic missionaries to whom it belonged. Although it was over 70 feet long, it had been specially built so that it could be broken up into 850 portable loads. It could do 10 knots and had a very shallow draught. Marchand accordingly started negotiations to purchase it with the colourful and autocratic local Bishop Augouard. In the end the combination of French government parsimony, ecclesiastical greed, and Papal politics[4] resulted in a stalemate which no one could claim as an honourable draw. Relations between Marchand and Augouard, who were both accustomed to getting their own way, became acrimonious with Marchand describing the bishop as 'un sot, ignorant, vaniteux et ambitieux', an ignorant, vain and ambitious

---

[4] Cynics averred that, although the papacy did not mind offending the Protestant British, it would be impolitic to let the Catholic Belgians think that it was aiding and abetting the French in the race to the Nile.

fool, and what in Marchand's eyes was worse, a Frenchman who put his church before his country.

That left the *Faidherbe*, the only steamboat in the French Congo still available and in working order. It was not ideal but, having failed to persuade the authorities in Paris to provide anything better, Marchand was left with no alternative. As the boiler plates had been riveted there were those who doubted whether it could be taken to pieces; if it were possible each half would still weigh over a ton. Others forecast that, even when stripped and emptied of its fittings and contents, the hull of the vessel would be too cumbersome and heavy to carry across country. To Marchand and his companions doubts and difficulties of this nature were challenges which they found it hard to resist, and when Marchand and the owners of the *Faidherbe* failed to agree on a price Marchand simply commandeered it and left it for others to decide in the courts whether this was requisition or theft. To overcome the technical difficulties of having a propellor-driven steam launch Marchand engaged the services of a French marine mechanic called Souyri.

It was at Kouango that Marchand had received the letter from Liotard which finally decided him to change his plans. Kouango, where Bobichon had his headquarters, was a tidy cluster of white-washed buildings, known as *Kouango blanc* where it was said, everything was white except the women. Within a few days of making his decision Marchand had issued a new set of orders. He sent Landeroin to Zemio to warn the authorities that the expedition was on its way, and would require 1,200 men in May and another 1,200 in September. Germain was sent to Ouango to take command of the party with the *Faidherbe* and to ensure that they got all the help they needed. Mangin and Largeau were despatched to various posts on the route ahead to engage porters and boatmen, and to make plans for the protection of the parties going through. Another officer was sent to the French frontier post at Tambura to warn the Zande chiefs of the expedition's arrival, and its likely needs of men and supplies. When they had done this they had orders to explore the headwaters of the river Sue and find a place where, after its long journey across the watershed on land, the *Faidherbe* could be reassembled and refloated in the basin of the Nile.

CHAPTER VIII

Across the Watershed

FROM Ouango to Tambura on the Nile side of the watershed was 668 km, about 400 miles. Although Marchand's new route followed the line of the Mbomu river he and his men made little use of the river itself because of the reports that rapids and waterfalls made it impassable. They had therefore to unload their canoes and find porters to carry their stores and their baggage over the rough native tracks which twisted and turned on the steep slopes of the river. The going was so bad that it took the advance parties of the expedition five months to cover the four-hundred miles to Tambura, an average of two and a half miles a day. Much of the time was spent in repairing and enlarging the track to make the going easier for the heavier loads which were still to come.

As usual Marchand was the last to leave. His base for this lengthy and difficult stage of the journey was at a place called Bangassou. Bangassou was in fact the name of the chief who lived there; when the chief died the place was apt to change its name, a fact which often caused problems when Europeans were making maps or trying to find their way.[1] Bangassou was the chief of a large group of peoples known collectively as the Nzakara, and was a powerful and formidable personage. Baratier took a photograph of him with 'quelques-unes des ses cinq cent femmes'. Bangassou put on a medley of European-style clothes for the occasion and this, together with his ample girth and his bevy of naked or near-naked young, middle-aged and elderly wives gave him what Baratier described as 'un air bon vivant'. Bangassou's accumulation of wives was, it seems, not so much for variety and plenty as for reasons of state and investment. He was head of a widely scattered association of clans and villages linked by kinship, and many of the women in his household were there as hostages for the good behaviour of the communities from which they were drawn. The element of invest-

---

[1] In this case, as in others, once the name had been put on a map it remained, and Bangassou is still Bangassou.

ment was provided by the dues customarily paid in cash or kind by
men found guilty of adultery. Bangassou's decreasing ability in his
over-ripe years to husband all his five hundred wives meant that he
could count on a steady income from this source. It also provided
him with meat. The Nzakara were occasional cannibals, and by
long-standing custom adulterers who were unable to pay their dues
were eaten. Except when times were hard, no one else was eaten,
with the exception of strangers to whom the same rules did not
apply. They never ate anyone who died of natural causes. Another
of their pagan beliefs was that there was life after death. For this
reason they sometimes buried a few possessions and one or two
wives with a departed chief to comfort him in the long days ahead.

Sultan Bangassou was a popular and respected figure in the eyes
of Marchand and his companions, partly perhaps because he provided them with a regular supply of porters. When the porters had
safely carried their loads to the next staging post at Rafai and had
returned to their base, Marchand paid them for their work at the
customary rate in white and coloured beads. Before he left, Marchand had the more difficult task of rewarding Bangassou himself. It
was important to pay neither too much nor too little. What Marchand paid, and its relation to services rendered, would quickly
become known in other places where Marchand and his expedition
would need help. Apart from his own interests Marchand was also
conscious of his obligation to Liotard and Bobichon, and to other
travellers who might come this way, not to spoil the market or queer
the pitch. In the end Marchand gave Bangassou six rifles and 250
rounds of ammunition; a revolver with 60 rounds; 2 bales of
material; 40 kilos of beads; 15 tarbushes; a bale of unbleached
cotton; a few pieces of silk; a music box; 8 air guns and 7,000
cartridges and one large carpet. Bangassou received the gifts with
the grace of a born receiver of wanted goods. After counting the
guns and making sure they were not out-of-date models, his only
hint of criticism was that of all the ills from which his poor country
suffered the greatest was gun-starvation.[2] Baratier amused himself
afterwards in working out the total cost in wages, subsistence and
presents of transporting 2,000 loads weighing 30 kilos each for a
distance of 142 km from Bangassou to Rafai. It worked out at 2,500

---

[2] The chief at Rafai was even more demanding; he got a high-velocity rifle with his
name inscribed in silver, the uniform of a full colonel of the old Imperial Guard,
some Arab robes and a Turkish sabre.

francs, that is to say sixteen centimes a load, the equivalent in English money of the time of 1½d.

Bangassou applied himself with equal care to the equally delicate matter of presents to his visitors when they left. Such presents would reflect both on his own importance and wealth, and on the standing of the recipients, and caused him considerable thought. Thus the age and condition of the girl presented to Marchand differed nicely from the corresponding attributes of the lady given to Baratier. Such gifts also presented problems for the recipients. To refuse any gift in local currency or kind would undoubtedly cause offence as implying that it was insufficient or unpleasing while acceptance, in the case of girls or other ladies, raised the sometimes very awkward question of what to do with them when the expedition reached its next destination. As a general rule they were kept for a few days, and then sent back unobtrusively to their homes.

The next stage of the journey was from Rafai to Zemio, a distance of some 200 km. Zemio was in Zande country, and the sultan, as he liked to be styled, was a large, corpulent man, bulging with self-confidence and good-living. He had a black beard and perpetually smiling, pitiless eyes that missed nothing. His country was fertile and rich, and he and his people had nearly everything they needed. They were strong, warlike people, and what they lacked they took from their weaker neighbours, diseased and decimated tribes like the Karrai who Baratier described as belonging to the 'lowest rung of the human ladder'. Carrying heavy loads for white men for two spoonfuls of beads a day did not appeal to the proud and prosperous Zande, and, when Marchand demanded porters for the difficult country ahead, the sultan simply sent his warriors out to round up the Karrai at night and flush them out of their hiding places like animals. One thing the Zande of this area lacked was meat. Because of tsetse-fly in the bush by the river and other watering places their cattle had died of trypanosomiasis. To make up for this lack of beef the Azande were reputed to have become occasional cannibals. This was all the more readily believed by travellers because the Zande were commonly known by the horribly onomatopoeic name of Niam-niam, although in actual fact the name meant no more in the language of their Dinka neighbours than big-eaters.

It was while Marchand was at Rafai making plans and arrangements for the next crucial stages of the journey across the watershed of the Congo and the Nile that he decided to send Baratier off on his own to explore the upper reaches of the Mbomu. Although local reports had indicated that it was impassable and even guarded by monsters he soon began to suspect that these reports were coloured by the reluctance of the local people to venture themselves and their canoes on these waters. For Marchand and the expedition as a whole it was a matter of great importance. If the river was really impassable for the *Faidherbe* it meant that the vessel would have to be dismantled, and carried or dragged in sections all the way from Rafai to Tambura and beyond to whatever point on the river Sue was found suitable for her to be refloated.

The *Faidherbe* had joined the expedition in May of 1897 at Kouango and had steamed up the river as far as the impassable rapids near Ouango. There on 4 June the resourceful Souyi had dismantled her, and reduced the whole vessel to pieces of portable or draggable size. While this was being done Germain and Dyé busied themselves making arrangements with Bobichon to engage porters and men to transport the vessel overland. In addition to the sections which could be carried there were others which were too large or too heavy for the porters. These were dragged up the bank of the river and put on to rollers made of tree trunks cut from the forest. They were then pulled or pushed along the river bank past the rapids. By working almost non-stop from dawn to dusk they completed the huge task of dismantling, transporting and reassembling the *Faidherbe* in eight days. They then pushed on as fast as they dared up the shallows and treacherous courses of the lower Mbomu.

Meanwhile Baratier had left on his reconnaissance, setting out, as he phrased it on 28 June 'in search of the monster of Zemio with three canoes, three Senegalese and three local soldiers, seven Yakoma,[3] a cook, seven days rations and a supply of rice, beads and cloth as presents'. He spent the next five weeks on the river in a dug-out canoe with a packing-case for a seat and with his charts and other papers spread out on a camp chair. He was in his canoe for twelve hours a day from sunrise to sunset with only a rough awning made of reeds to protect him from the sun. There were soundings to take, notes to make and maps to be carefully compiled. When he had set out on this mission Baratier admitted that he had pictured himself in imagination as a white man alone in primeval forest,

---

[3] The Yakoma, some of whom were to stay with the expedition to the end, came from the area of Ouango.

surrounded by cannibals and wild beasts. He was both disappointed and relieved when he discovered that the cannibals were smiling, friendly tribesmen who brought them presents of food at the villages and encampments where they tied up for the night. As for the wild beasts there were no charging elephant or roaring lion, and no poisonous snakes in hot pursuit. When they did encounter some wild animal and Baratier wanted to shoot it for the pot there was usually an African in his party who tried to dissuade him on the grounds that he and his clan had a special kinship with the animal concerned. The only wild beast which caused them any trouble was the hippopotomus, and Baratier noticed that there were few canoes on the river which did not have the marks of hippo teeth on their sides.

On 18 July after three weeks of slow and tortuous progress on the river Baratier reached the point where a tributary called Mboko joined the Mbomu. His careful soundings and observations suggested that the *Faidherbe* might be able to go that far under her own steam. At the junction of the two rivers Baratier was faced with a difficult choice. If he continued up the main stream of the Mbomu it seemed likely that he would find stretches of clear water. But the Mbomu's course was to the east rather than in the north easterly direction where Tambura lay. In the end he decided to risk taking the smaller and less well-known tributary which was reputed to go more in the direction he wanted. He was relieved to find in the end that it was more or less navigable for another hundred kilometres up to the point where it was joined by another stream known as the Mere. This, he believed, was as far as the *Faidherbe* would be able to go but it would nevertheless much reduce the distance over which the vessel would have to be dismantled and carried. It was therefore a discovery of the greatest importance for the whole expedition, and when he received Baratier's report at Tambura Marchand was relieved at the saving in effort and in time which Baratier's journey of exploration had now made possible. In his enthusiasm Marchand addressed his reply to Baratier's report to 'my dear fresh-water mariner'.

Baratier had encased his river maps and journals in a tin tube to protect them from the damp and from white ants, and despatched them as quickly as possible by runner to Bobichon who had joined Germain and Dyé on the *Faidherbe* for the journey up river. By the time they got Baratier's maps they had reached Zemio where they had expected they would have to dismantle the ship and arrange once again for it to be carried across country. They too, therefore, were relieved to learn from Baratier's maps that they could continue their journey on the river. It was slow going, as Baratier had warned it would be, and they had to advance cautiously, often hacking their way through falling tree-trunks and trailing vegetation, and sounding the bottom continuously for shallows and hidden rocks. They finally reached the Mere on 11 September. This, as Baratier had also foreseen, was as far as the *Faidherbe* could go under its own steam but by this time she had travelled 1,500 km up the river from Kouango and had pushed the navigable limits of the headwaters of the Congo further than anyone had thought possible.

*   *   *

The watershed between the Congo and the Nile in this region consists largely of wooded grassland where in the rainy season the grass grows to more than a man's height and the trees come into brief leaf and flower. At the end of the rains the grass is fired and what looked like a flat plain is revealed as undulating country with outcrops of rock interspersed with small streams. The streams meander and merge to form rivers fringed with bush which gets thicker and taller until in the end the rivers are completely enclosed in tunnels of dense living vegetation and the residues of dead and dying trees. In this type of country the actual watershed between the two largest rivers in Africa is not at all easy to see. In many places there is no visible ridge and the distance between the two slopes is so slight that one side of a field can drain into the Congo while the other goes into the Nile.

In an area so dominated by its rivers and streams the differences between the rains and the dry seasons are very marked. The rains fall roughly from May to October, and during that period many of the rivers become easy to navigate and much of the low-lying ground becomes impassable swamp. In the dry season the situation is reversed. One can walk on the dry baked ground but the level of some of the watercourses becomes too low for even the lightest of canoes. Here Marchand was faced with a number of problems. The *Faidherbe* had been able to take advantage of the rains to reach the limit of navigation on the Congo side of the watershed during the second week of September. Reconnaissance showed that the nearest point on the river system on the Nile side of the watershed where it would be possible to refloat the *Faidherbe* in the remaining weeks of the rainy season was a place called Khojali some 80 km north of Tambura. As Tambura was about the same distance from the river Mere this meant that the *Faidherbe* would have to be transported across country for a total of 160 km, approximately 100 miles. The first problem was, could the *Faidherbe* be dismantled and carried or dragged across 160 km of the watershed terrain? The second was, could enough men be found in Zande country to provide the necessary manpower for this formidable task, and once found could they be fed and kept fit? The third problem was, could it be done before the end of the rains?

These three problems were to dominate the lives of Marchand and his companions for the next three months. During this period they stretched their mental and physical resources to the limit and sometimes, it seemed, beyond the limits of ordinary human endurance. There were periods, sometimes unbearably long periods, when they had to wait on events or stay in one place doing nothing, but when there were things to be done they did not waste any time or miss any opportunity. The *Faidherbe* had arrived at the junction of the Mboku and Mere on 11 September. They first had to haul the ship out of the water, up the bank of the river and onto the dry ground, a formidable task which required hundreds of men and took a great deal of time. Souryi started to take the vessel to pieces the following day, and by 20 September the first pieces were on their way. Dismantling the *Faidherbe* and rendering it into movable sections was difficult work. Apart from the major problem of the boiler, there were other sections which still weighed more than the 30 kilos which were regarded as the heaviest load a man could carry. Many of the men who had been dragooned by the Azande chiefs into presenting themselves for work were unwilling conscripts drawn from the ranks of the weak, the diseased, and the undernourished. It was not the custom of the country to provide food for porters or other labourers, and in places where food was scarce the beads which were given in lieu were of little use. In these circumstances even the lighter loads of 15 or 20 kilos were sometimes too heavy, and progress was often painful and slow. It was not only for carrying loads that men were needed. The paths which served the day-to-day needs of the tribesmen were generally too narrow and too steep for the expedition's bulky and awkward loads, and additional men were therefore needed to go on ahead and widen the track, and to make fords across the numerous rivulets and streams. Altogether some 2,000 men were recruited in the area of Tambura for Marchand's expedition in the autumn of 1897, and both Liotard and Bobichon became concerned at the strain which these demands were making on the local resources and the goodwill of the various Zande chiefs. Despite these difficulties the shell of the *Faidherbe*, having been cut up into five sections each needing twelve porters, was successfully carried across country and reached its destination at Khojali in the middle of October. Although the indefatigable Souryi started straightaway on the process of reassembly, he was held up by the much longer time needed to manhandle the two halves of the boiler. He was also held up waiting for the spare parts, new steel plates and the marine paint which had been ordered from Brazzaville but had failed to arrive; and when they did arrive many of the rivets for the plates were found to be either too large or too small.

Marchand summed up these complex and laborious operations in his official report in the following statement:

A track 160 km long and 5 m wide was first hacked, carved and burnt through the high wooded grasslands on the watershed. The Faidherbe, cut into pieces, arrived on the river Sue on 14 October in the charge of Lieut. Largeau, and the mechanic Souryi started at once to re-assemble them. The other boats followed.

The brief postscript that 'the other boats followed' concealed what was in many ways the most remarkable feat of all. Souryi and Largeau had reduced the boiler to two sections before they departed with the shell and the ship's fittings, and it was left to Baratier with the help of Lieut. Gouly, the officer in charge of the French outpost at Tambura, to devise means of transporting the two halves of the boiler across the watershed. Each half weighed a thousand kilos, and the cast-iron of which they were made was so heavy that the whole weight of each section was concentrated in less than one cubic metre of space. Baratier's first idea was to put each section of the boiler into a cradle slung on a series of thick bamboos, ten at each side and two at each end. With a man to each bamboo, this meant twenty-four men to each section. Even so the weight carried by each man was over 40 kilos which was more than the average porter could carry for any distance. The situation was complicated by the fact that the porters available varied considerably in size and strength. Baratier also had difficulty in finding material for the cradles which was strong enough to take the weight. In the end he used a net made of the heavy twisted natural ropes and twines which local hunters used to snare elephant and other large animals. Although a trial showed that it was strong enough to hold the load, the porters had great difficulty in lifting it off the ground. When they finally managed to do so several of the bamboos broke. After several trials Baratier had to abandon the idea and start again.

The next method which he tried was to lift each half section into a dug-out canoe which was then pushed and pulled on log rollers cut from the forest and laid out on a prepared track. It was very slow going, and in the first three days they only managed to cover 14 km, that is to say about three miles a day. Nevertheless they persevered until the carriers tried to cross a gully too quickly and the canoe broke in two. Another method tried was a cart made of forest timber. In the absence of proper wheels old oil drums were used, but moving a heavily laden cart with such equipment presented a number of problems. Eventually some more conventional wheels were found but they had no axles, and attempts to improvise axles with sticks inserted between the spokes and bound with brass wire were not a success. In the end some proper axles were sent up from Bangui and with these the cart made better progress.

Many of the experiments with carts and canoes were carried out by the resourceful Gouly but it was the determined Baratier who in the end evolved the best system. On its way upstream the *Faidherbe* had been towing some metal rafts, one of which had once served as a cross-river ferry, and two whale-boats made of light-weight steel. They had come in useful for transporting stores. The rafts had been kept for the onward journey but it was not thought that the whale boats could be taken to bits and carried across the watershed. They had therefore eventually been unloaded and abandoned. Baratier now conceived the idea of using these whale-boats to carry the boiler. He made his way downstream by canoe until he found what he was afterwards to call the red boat. He hoped that there would still be enough depth of water in the river to paddle the boat upstream. But just when he wanted the rains to continue they stopped, and he had to spend a complete day cooking, as he described it, in the fiendish heat inside the hull while he undid all the bolts with a monkey wrench. As many of the bolt heads were worn or rusted he had to square them off with a hack-saw before he could undo them. When he had finished dividing the boat into portable sections he called on the local chief to provide him with porters with the inducement of a cartridge for each man supplied, and a gun for every hundred. When they reached the place where the *Faidherbe* had been dismantled Baratier reassembled the whale-boat and loaded one of the half sections of the boiler into the hull. He secured the boiler with ropes to stop it moving, and strengthened the hull of the whale-boat with stays and twists of brass wire to prevent it opening under the strain. When everything was ready he set off for the Nile. He left Gouly behind to recover the other whale-boat and transport the other section of the boiler in the same fashion.

Progress was slow but this time at least it was sure. It took Baratier sixteen days to do the 84 km from the river at Méré to Tambura, an average of three miles a day. He split the men into three parties; one to go on ahead and cut a broad track through the bush, another to chop down any dead trees or branches that were in the way, and a third to lay a path of log rollers and to drag the whale-boat which with its half-section of boiler weighed altogether more than 3,000 kilos. The going was easier when it was raining as the boat slid more easily on the rollers; when it was dry there was more friction and there were times when Baratier could even detect a nasty smell of burning.

At Tambura Baratier sent the men back to their homes. But when he asked the Zande chiefs of the area for fresh men to take him and his burden to his destination at Khojali on the river Sue he found that few were forthcoming. It took several requests, demands, and finally threats before the sultan at Tambura and neighbouring Zande chiefs were persuaded to meet his needs. Marchand had warned Baratier that on the upper reaches of the Sue a series of small waterfalls made it more like a staircase than a river but Baratier had by this time had enough of overland transport and porters and was determined to give the river a trial. By 5 November he had managed to get his whale-boat as far as the river and set out for Khojali with, as he put it, '10 paddlers, 4 Senegalese soldiers, 26 porters' loads of stores, 200 bottles of toddy and 75 bottles of wine'. The going was as difficult as Marchand had predicted. The stream soon became enclosed in a tunnel of vegetation; dead trees in every stage of decomposition barred their way and had to be dodged, moved, or cut with an axe. There were sandbanks and shallows and outcrops of rock in the river bed, and these soon gave way to rapids and falls which made Baratier declare that it was actually more like a ladder than a staircase. On the first day they did 3 km. They did the same on the second day. On the third all they could manage was 600 m. To make matters worse the rains again petered out and the level of the water in the river got lower every day. Baratier pressed on, as he usually did, but when after sixteen days he found he had covered less than 20 km and was faced with a waterfall with a ten-metre drop he gave up the river and took to the land again. He eventually reached Khojali with the red whale-boat and his half section of boiler on 5 December to find that Gouly, after travelling all the way by the overland route, had arrived there with the other whale-boat and his half of the boiler three days before.

By the end of 1897 all the members of the expedition had been established by Marchand in and around Tambura, and at various points on the river Sue. They had with them all their stores and equipment and what Marchand now grandly called his 'flotilla of ships'. It had taken them more than a year to traverse the basin of the Congo but while the longest and most laborious part of their journey had been accomplished the most difficult and dangerous part still lay ahead. But at least they had the satisfaction of knowing that, as Baratier said, 'from this hour all the watercourses which we follow will be going to the north and the east; we are now in the basin of the Mediterranean, the very waters which flow from the earth on which we stand, right here in the heart of Africa, go to replenish that great French inland sea'.

CHAPTER IX

The Rivals' Progress

At the end of 1897, as Marchand and his companions were taking up their positions at Tambura or on the river Sue, rumours were reaching Europe that the expedition had met with disaster in the Congo and that everyone had been killed.[1] Salisbury had once told Cromer that it was 'as difficult to judge what is going on in the Upper Nile Valley as to judge what is going on on the other side of the moon'. It was difficult enough for people in London and Paris to gauge what was happening and to distinguish rumour from fact; it was even more difficult for Marchand in a remote part of Africa where communications were slow and unreliable. Such official despatches and private letters as reached them from France took several months to arrive, and information from local sources in Africa often turned out to be no more than conjecture, deliberate misinformation, or alcoholic fantasy. It was especially galling for Marchand to lack reliable, up-to-date news; his aim was not only to get to Fashoda but to get there first. He very much wanted therefore to know how both his rivals and his would-be allies from Abyssinia were getting on.

Of his rivals the nearest were the two Belgian expeditions which had been sent out from the Congo Free State in the autumn of 1896. Marchand already knew that by the beginning of 1897 they were both within striking distance of the Nile. The smaller of the two expeditions under Chaltin had made good progress on the clear, high ground between the valleys of the Mbomu and Uele rivers, and in February he and his party of about 1,000 men crossed the watershed and engaged and defeated a force of Mahdist troops near the Nile at Rajjaf. Chaltin then set about establishing himself firmly on the river bank at Lado while he waited for the arrival of the other Belgian expedition led by Baron Dhanis. Although Dhanis's ex-

[1] A theory popular in Paris was that these rumours were inspired by the British or by the Belgians in order to ascertain, from the official statements which the French government were then obliged to make, how Marchand's expedition was faring and how far exactly it had got.

pedition consisted of 3,000 men and was altogether larger and better equipped the route which they had been told to take up the valley of the river Aruwimi did not make for a rapid advance. It took them through the great Ituri rain forest which, with its hostile pygmies, had so nearly destroyed Stanley on his mission to rescue Emin Pasha in 1888. The forest was so thick that little sunlight permeated through the trees, and it was unnaturally gloomy and quiet. In such an atmosphere every movement became a cause for alarm, and the sudden screams and grunts of unseen animals and birds made hearts leap and stomachs turn. Creepers and cobwebs brushed against faces and hands and left strange-looking rashes on the skin; every crawling insect and monstrous spider seemed to be the carrier of some loathsome disease. Nor did the pygmies like strangers in their forest. They watched as the men and the loads of the expedition approached, and then silently disappeared. They refused to provide the expedition with guides or with food, and as the long files of white men and their porters went by they closed in on the stragglers and picked them off one by one with poisoned arrows. The porters for the expedition came from other, distant parts of the Congo and were as much unwanted strangers as the Europeans. As they made their way uneasily through the alien forest they began to feel frightened and far from home. They started to complain that their loads were too heavy and their food too scarce. The Belgians, already disturbed by their own sufferings and fears, reacted with impatience and anger. Soon after they had crossed the watershed and were descending into the valley of the White Nile the porters in the vanguard refused to go any further. The disaffection soon spread to the rest of the column, and the great expedition which had set out with such high hopes quickly disintegrated into an unseemly scramble of frightened Belgians on the run and turbulent porters on the rampage. Dhanis himself was fortunate to escape with his life, and the whole enterprise was soon abandoned and disowned. Although the failure of the Dhanis expedition was a blow to King Leopold's designs, Chaltin was at the end of 1897 still at Lado waiting for instructions and reinforcements, and was no further from Fashoda than Tambura and the river outposts in the territory of the Azande where Marchand was waiting for the coming of the rains.

*   *   *

While Marchand looked on the Belgians as rivals the expedition which he feared most was what he continued to call *la mission Colvile*, long after Colvile himself had left Africa. When the French heard that Captain Macdonald was assembling a force in Kenya in 1897 and preparing to set off for Lake Rudolf and a secret destination further north they believed that it was some perfidious British device and that it was really Colvile's expedition under another guise. Macdonald had assured Lord Salisbury that he would reach Fashoda in less than a year but he had barely completed his preparations when in September of 1897 he found that he had a mutiny on his hands. His force consisted of nine British officers, an Indian officer and 300 rank and file of the 14th and 15th Sikh Regiments, 150 Swahili soldiers from the coast of East Africa, and 300 Sudanese under their own native officers and NCOs. To carry their considerable baggage, stores, tents, and equipment 300 local porters were engaged. The Sudanese, like the Senegalese used by the French, were cheerful, hardened, and efficient mercenary soldiers who were prepared to defend, protect, attack, terrorize and pillage almost anyone anywhere provided the pay and the rations were right. The men attached to Macdonald's expedition had once served with Emin Pasha in the southern Sudan, and had been left in Uganda when Emin Pasha had passed through on his way to the coast. They had the reputation of being good soldiers who responded readily to fair treatment, and loyally followed those who had taken the trouble to learn their language and understand their ways. It was these Sudanese who in September 1897 refused to go with Macdonald to the north, and finally deserted *en masse* with their arms and equipment.

The causes of the Uganda mutiny became the subject of heated argument. There were those, like Macdonald himself, who claimed that it was the culmination of long-standing grievances over pay, food, clothing, and work. Others said it was due to what one of them called 'injudicious management by young and inexperienced officers', particularly by officers fresh out from Britain or India who had come for the shooting and had small concern for their troops. There was a theory that the mutiny occurred because the Sudanese soldiers believed that they were going north to fight against the Mahdists who were their kith and kin in blood and religion. There was also another theory that the real cause was an order by Macdonald that the numerous women and children who always went everywhere with the Sudanese soldiers would be left behind except for one wife or one small boy per soldier.

Whatever the real causes of the mutiny the effect on Macdonald's expedition to Fashoda was disastrous. Not only did the Sudanese mutiny but they also killed some of their officers. They then decamped with their dependants and escaped to Uganda. Macdonald felt that he had to deal with the situation before he went north, and he therefore abandoned his expedition and went in pursuit of the mutineers. In Uganda the Sudanese joined forces with Kabarega and other dissident elements, and in the end it was six months before Macdonald felt able to return to Kenya and resume command of his expedition. So it was that at the end of 1897, as Marchand and his party were moving into position on the fringes of the low-lying, mosquito-ridden fringes of the Bahr el Ghazal, the bulk of Macdonald's own expedition were still encamped on the salubrious slopes of Mount Elgon in the highlands of Kenya waiting for their leader to return.

*   *   *

In the early part of 1897, when Marchand was on his way up the Congo en route to Fashoda from the west, the two French expeditions which were hoping to join him there from the east were making their way slowly across Abyssinia. Clochette got as far as Gore, about 400 km west of Addis Ababa but he had been badly kicked by a horse; largely because of the damage and the constant pain he had to give up the venture, and he died there soon afterwards. The other expedition under Bonvolet got no further than Addis Ababa. Frustrated as much by the seemingly unhelpful attitude of Lagarde as by the procrastinations of the Ethiopian authorities, Bonvolet went back to Paris in July to lavish blame on everyone except himself and to plead that, if he were equipped with six river gunboats, he could reach Fashoda and achieve all his objectives. He proposed that the gunboats should be shipped to Jibuti and then transported in sections on camels across Abyssinia to the river Sobat. Bonvolet failed to get his gunboats and did not return, but he had left his second-in-command Bonchamps in charge not only of his own expedition but also of what remained of Clochette's. When he reached Gore, Bonchamps discovered that it was not only ill health which had caused Clochette to abandon his mission.

Clochette had been held up at Gore for several months by what seemed endless and inexplicable delays in the provision of porters and guides, and in the grant of the official permission without which it was impossible for him to proceed. Bonchamps now found himself held up in exactly the same way. When he sought an interview with the emperor Menelik's representative, the amiable and wily Dejaz-match Tassama repeated the formula he had used to Clochette: 'You will have to wait here until I know the emperor's wishes.' When Bonchamps asked how long that would be the answer was 'About two months, perhaps less, perhaps more.' When pressed to try and expedite matters, Tassama shook his head and expressed surprise, as one civilized man to another, that anyone should want to go to that region of the Nile, which was hot and unhealthy and inhabited by black men who went naked and had feathered heads like chickens. Bonchamps had been assured in Paris that his venture would have the emperor's support, and he therefore sent a strong letter of complaint directly to Lebon, the French minister of the colonies. This elicited an equally strong telegram from Lebon to Lagarde instructing him to remind Menelik of his promises of support, for which he had already been well paid in arms and other forms of military aid, and to request him as a matter of urgency to give permission and facilities for Bonchamps to proceed. As the telegram plaintively concluded, 'we should by now have been safely established on the Nile'. In response Menelik assured Lagarde in writing of his continued readiness to facilitate the expedition; at the same time he sent verbal instructions to Tassama to devise new and less obtrusive ways of obstructing Bonchamps. Evidence now avail-able makes it clear that while the emperor Menelik was exchanging these amiable assurances with the French he was simultaneously negotiating in equally amiable and often conflicting terms with the British, the Russians, the Italians, and with the Khalifa Abdulla in Omdurman.

It was Colonel Wingate, sitting like a spider in Cairo at the centre of his intelligence networks in Africa and the Middle East, who provided the first reliable reports of what Menelik was up to. The result was that Wingate and Rennel Rodd of the Foreign Office were hurriedly despatched to Addis Ababa in April 1897. It was assumed that the French would have tried to persuade Menelik that the British also had designs on Abyssinian territory, and Rodd's instructions, which had been 'seen and approved by the Queen', were to convince Menelik that

the operations which the Egyptian government have undertaken against the Khalifa are solely for the purpose of regaining provinces which were formerly under Egyptian rule, and that there was no intention whatsoever of taking any steps which would be considered hostile to Abyssinia or which would involve any encroachment on Abyssinian territory.

Rodd's mission was a notable failure. Since his defeat of the Italians at Aduwa in 1896 the Emperor Menelik had grown in stature and self-confidence. He was courted now both by the British and the French, and even by his old enemy the Turks. The Russians were showing an increasingly ingratiating interest, and where the Italians had once bullied and bragged they now came hat in hand. Menelik was thus in a strong position, and he knew how to exploit it by playing one European power against another, even in matters of detail. Before he left for Addis Ababa, Rodd had written privately from Cairo to warn the Foreign Office that

the French had had a set of magnificent robes made here for the Emperor and the priests. The Sultan is said to be sending an Order in brilliants. The Russian gifts, now on their way, are said to be magnificent. We shall suffer by comparison if we only take the ordinary gifts which are sent to Barbarians . . . The Empress must be considered. She is said to be the only lady allowed to wear gold ornaments. A necklace of gold and some stones rather showy in character might be sent her.

Despite this timely advice the presents suggested by the Foreign Office were unimaginative and undistinguished. 'A portrait of the Queen in robes of State handsomely framed' was to be expected but the list soon descended to silver-gilt plate, 'not embossed much owing to difficulty of cleaning', candlesticks, carpets and brocade with 'a telescopic rifle of high finish' and 'a small quick-firing one pounder' to add weight. The best idea was an elephant, a suggestion which evoked the following reply from the India Office: 'I dare say we could manage an elephant from India if the King has someone to ride it but might it not be well to hear if he expresses a wish for it?'

There is no record that Menelik ever got his elephant, and when Rodd came to present his credentials and his gifts, the emperor's reply did not suggest that he had felt any strong sense of obligation or gratitude. When Rodd asked for an assurance that Menelik would not give any help to the Khalifa, Menelik replied that, while it 'was absolutely impossible that he should ever contemplate affording his traditional enemies any assistance', the most that 'he cared for the moment to put on paper' was an undertaking not to allow arms to be sent to the Mahdist armies through Ethiopia. Menelik had in fact been on friendly terms with his 'traditional enemies' for some time. He and the Khalifa had first been drawn together by a common interest in opposing the advances of the Italians to the south and west of their base in Eritrea. Before the battle of Aduwa, Menelik had sent a message to the Khalifa saying 'Now an enemy much worse that any we have had before comes against us. He comes to make slaves of you and me. I am dark skinned and you are dark skinned. Let us unite therefore and throw out this common enemy'. When Kitchener started his advance up the valley of the Nile, it was 'the red English' who were to be feared; and, when reports reached the Khalifa and Menelik that Marchand was coming in from the west and that the French had plans to create a single belt of French territory from Dakar to Jibuti, they both agreed that, despite their own religious differences, 'all whites were the enemies of God', and that they should therefore also be cautious in giving any encouragement or help to the French.

Thus, while Menelik continued to assure Lagarde that he would honour his promise to allow and help the French expeditions, he continued in private to hinder or at least to delay them. Marchand had told Lagarde that he expected to reach Fashoda at the end of 1897, so that it was with sharply increasing anxiety and anger that Bonchamps found himself still kept waiting at Gore all through the summer. While Maurice Potter, the expedition's artist, occupied himself drawing Galla girls at Gore, Charles Michel, the entomologist, painted equally stark pictures of what it was like waiting day after in the rain and the mist for something to happen; the constant flow of visitors when one wanted to be alone, the endless hours of solitude when one wanted company; the callers who all expected to be listened to and rewarded with presents and with food; the surroundings of dust, dirt and disease; the seemingly endless and pointless talk among themselves of what could and could not be done in the future, and of what should or should not have been done in the past; the daily inflow of reports and rumours that generally turned out to be untrue; the slow diminution of funds and supplies of food; the worry of finding enough food every day to keep the men and the pack animals fed and contented and fit for whenever permission came for them to go.

When at last Tassama told Bonchamps that he could proceed, many of the Abyssinian servants and muleteers refused to leave on the grounds, as if it were some new discovery, that the country to which they were going was desert where they would die of fever and thirst, and where the inhabitants were cannibals who would eat them alive. In desperation Bonchamps sent Michel back to Addis Ababa to plead with Lagarde to get the emperor to intervene. Finally in October the emperor's further orders were conveyed to the expedition. The new orders reiterated Menelik's wish to have Ethiopian flags planted on the east bank of the Nile and a supply of Ethiopian flags was provided for distribution in places along the route which the Abyssinians themselves were reluctant to travel. In addition Bonchamps was told that he must keep to the south side of the river Sobat. Apart from the fact that it was the most swampy and difficult side it meant that in order to get to Fashoda the expedition would have to cross the Sobat at its widest point. When the French protested Menelik blandly replied that his soldiers had once caught fever on the north side and he did not wish the expedition's guides and escort to suffer a similar fate.

The expedition finally left Gore early in December. Bonchamps had hoped that the delays might at least give time for the arrival of the portable boat which had been sent out from France to enable them to travel down the Sobat and thence down the Nile to Fashoda. It was known to have reached Jibuti but that it seemed was as far as it got. Unable to wait any longer they set off with every prospect, as Michel put it, of arriving on the Nile with orders to raise two flags and build two forts, 'sans bateau, sans hommes et sans argent'.

It was not a happy journey. Once they had left the temperate climate and familiar surroundings of the highlands and moved down into the steamy dampness of the Baro valley the Abyssinians developed fevers and fears which quickly reduced their numbers and fitness, and slowed down the expedition's progress until on 28 December it took them five hours to do 3 km. On 31 December 1897 they reached the junction of the Baro and the Sobat. Here they were within 150 km of Fashoda but it was as far as the demoralized and diminished expedition could go. On the first day of January 1898, instead of sending a telegram *Faschoda occupé!*, as they had hoped, Bonchamps and his companions turned back towards Gore. They had set off with 150 men and 140 pack animals. They returned with 80 sick men and only 27 of the animals. It was not the end of Bonchamp's efforts to reach Fashoda but it was a setback of disappointing and crucial proportions.

*   *   *

When at the end of 1896 the British government had agreed that Kitchener should continue his advance as far as Berber, it had also agreed to the construction of a railway from Wadi Halfa to Abu Hamed. The second decision was perhaps the more important. There were those who thought that Kitchener was better at logistics than fighting and that he was reluctant to push his troops forward until he had reliable means of keeping them reinforced and supplied. Although Kitchener had, in his time, used camels and feluccas, as commander-in-chief of the Egyptian Army reliable means of transport meant steam boats on the river and railways on land.

It was not until his engineers had completed two-thirds of the railway that Kitchener made any military moves. At the beginning of August 1897 he sent a force to Abu Hamed and by the end of the month it had gone on to occupy Berber. Lord Salisbury had ruled earlier that Kitchener should stay there 'for some little time', and this suited Kitchener too. He did not want to think of any further advance until the railway had been extended again from Abu Hamed to Berber. Nor were they alone in wanting a halt. Cromer, apprehensive as usual lest his financial reserves and carefully balanced budgets should be 'dissipated in military adventures' urged again that there should not be 'the smallest question of any further advance at present'.

Kitchener also had another reason for waiting. Some of the local encounters with the Mahdist troops which had taken place, together with intelligence reports provided by Wingate, suggested that the strength and fighting qualities of the Khalifa were greater than had been thought. This convinced him that he needed to support his Egyptian troops with soldiers from the British army. It was a view which at the time was neither shared nor welcomed in all quarters. British troops did not as a rule stand up well to the heat or the terrain of places like the Sudan. They cost more, and they required more water, food, accommodation, hygiene and medical services than was thought necessary for local forces. In one of his private letters to Salisbury, Cromer said, 'I doubt whether the unsuitability of the

British soldier as a fighting machine in the Soudan is sufficiently recognised at the War Office.' Even General Wolseley, who commanded the British troops in Egypt, did not think that British troops should be used until the railway had reached Abu Hamed and beyond, when 'they could perhaps be risked for a purely winter campaign.' They might have their drawbacks but the fact remained that British troops were better armed and better equipped than their counterparts in the Egyptian army.

The War Office supported Kitchener's plea but Salisbury and his civilian colleagues in the Cabinet did not. Parsimony and pusillanimity conveniently combined with foreign policy, as they had often done before, to hinder any addition to the British Empire. In a personal letter to Cromer, Salisbury admitted that 'for the sake of our relations with France, and with a more crusty potentate still – the British Treasury – I am anxious to avoid the introduction of British and Indian troops as long as I can.' In October 1897 when he and the Cabinet had considered Kitchener's request he said that he did not believe that the French had really 'moved any force, even a small one into the Nile valley'. If and when they did he was confident that the Mahdist forces would oppose and stop them, and that even if they did get to Fashoda they would find it impossible in practice to bring in enough supplies and reinforcements to maintain their position in any strength. So confident was Salisbury that the Khalifa would oppose the French that one of the arguments he used for not sending British troops to fight against the Mahdist forces in the Sudan was that 'by destroying the Dervish power we are killing the defender who holds the valley for us now.'

Caught between his own anxieties and the government's refusal to provide him with the means of dispelling them, and suspecting with good reason that Wolseley was intriguing to have him replaced by General Grenfell, Kitchener had what would now be called a nervous breakdown. In a very private and confidential letter in the archives at Hatfield House, Cromer described Kitchener as 'a sick man who has lost his nerve', and 'liable to fits of extreme depression.'[2] It was in one of these moods that Kitchener now

---

[2] In another letter in the archives at Hatfield from Cromer to Salisbury's sister, the countess of Galloway, he compares the two men: 'Kitchener is doing admirably. He has less polish but vastly more brains and character than Grenfell, however he has an eye to money – a sordid, unwarlike quality which somewhat commands my respect. I wish all soldiers did not hate one another quite so much. It causes trouble.'

tendered his resignation. Some thought that both his resignation and his breakdown might have been devices to get his own way. But Cromer believed that, with all his shortcomings of temper and temperament, Kitchener was the right man for the transport and supply problems involved in the campaign which lay ahead. He therefore used his considerable resources of oil and soft soap to persuade him to withdraw his resignation.

Although Cromer wanted Kitchener to stay, and realized that what he called 'an English expedition' would one day be 'an unavoidable necessity', he still did his best to put it off for as long as possible. As he told Salisbury in another of his private letters, he preferred to 'abide by Canning's dictum that if war is inevitable sooner or later, it is preferable that it should come later rather than sooner'. He went on to argue that 'as to the French, I would like to get there first but does it really matter?' He reiterated that the last thing we wanted was tracts of useless territory in the Sudan which it would be tiresome and costly to administer. What Britain really wanted was to ensure that the Nile basin did not belong to any other European power and that any trade there might be should be in British hands. The key to the situation, as he saw it, was Khartoum. Whether the French got to Fashoda first or not, it was doubtful if they or anyone else could built up a position of strength there if Britain held Khartoum. Cromer's conclusion therefore was that we should wait and see, and that 'we should not be hurried into action by fear of French activity'.

Towards the end of 1897, however, the situation changed. Both the civil and military establishments in Egypt became convinced, on the basis of reports from Wingate, that the Khalifa was concentrating his forces near Omdurman and had sent reinforcements to the north where one of his best commanders, Mahmud Ahmad, was encamped in the vicinity of Berber. It was feared that Mahmud was about to launch an attack which the Egyptian army on its own might not be able to hold. Cromer shared these fears and now came round to the view that British troops should be sent there 'whilst there is time' and that in this situation it might well be that the best means of defence was attack. On Christmas Day 1897 he wrote to Salisbury, 'I greatly fear that, whether we like it or not, an expedition to Khartoum next year will be unavoidable. It is no longer a question of anticipating the French on the Upper Nile . . . the real question is whether the Egyptian Army can hold the territory which has already

Jean-Baptiste Marchand

The *Faidherbe*

Le Petit Journal

Le Petit Journal
CHAQUE JOUR 5 CENTIMES
Le Supplément illustré
CHAQUE SEMAINE 5 CENTIMES

SUPPLÉMENT ILLUSTRÉ
Huit pages : CINQ centimes

ABONNEMENTS

SEINE ET SEINE-ET-OISE 2 fr 3 fr 50
DÉPARTEMENTS 2 fr 4 fr
ÉTRANGER 2 50 5 fr

Dixième année

DIMANCHE 28 MAI 1899

Numéro 445

MISSION MARCHAND
Une tranche du vapeur le *Faidherbe* dans la savane du plateau central, allant du Congo au Nil
DESSIN DE M. HENRI MEYER (D'APRÈS LA PHOTOGRAPHIE DU COMMANDANT MARCHAND)

Carrying a section of the *Faidherbe* from the Congo to the Nile

The *Faidherbe* dragged ashore

Arrival of the Anglo-Egyptian Flotilla at Fashoda, 1898

MARCHEZ! MARCHAND!

GENERAL JOHN BULL (to MAJOR MARCHAND). "COME, PROFESSOR, YOU'VE HAD A NICE LITTLE SCIENTIFIC TRIP; I'VE SMASHED THE DERVISHES—LUCKILY FOR *YOU*—AND NOW I RECOMMEND YOU TO PACK UP YOUR FLAGS, AND GO HOME!!!"

General John Bull and Major Marchand (*Punch*, 8 October 1898)

Le Petit Chaperon Rouge

Marchand and members of his mission between Harrar and Jibuti, 1899

Sergt. Venail   Lt. Fouque, Sergt. Dat   Cap. Mangin
              in Cap Baratier Col. Marchand Enseigne Dyé

been acquired.' On 31 December 1897 Kitchener telegraphed an urgent request for a brigade of British troops to be sent to the Sudan.

The Khalifa's records which were captured later after the fall of Omdurman show that he had in fact neither the means nor the intention of attacking Kitchener at Berber. It is difficult to avoid the conclusion therefore that this situation of crisis was engineered by Wingate and Kitchener in order to persuade Cromer to change his mind and to force the British government's hand. They believed as soldiers that the best time to complete the conquest of the Sudan was in the autumn and winter of 1898. For this to be possible they needed British troops, and they needed them to be sent without any further delay to the Sudan so that they could be acclimatized and deployed in order to be ready for operations at the end of the summer. Kitchener's telegram, supported as it now was not only by the War Office in London but by Cromer in Egypt, made it difficult for Salisbury's government to say no. There were other reasons too why the Cabinet felt obliged to agree to a demand they had so often rejected before. Secret reports reaching London both from Wingate in Cairo and from Paris suggested that Marchand had reached the basin of the Nile, and was acting in concert both with the Khalifa and the emperor of Abyssinia. It was clear by this time that there was no possibility of the Uganda railway being completed for some years, and that Macdonald's attempt to reach Fashoda had been seriously delayed by the mutiny of his Sudanese soldiers. Where only a few weeks earlier Salisbury and his Cabinet had believed that 'no sufficiently important English interest is involved to justify the loss of life and money', they now agreed not only to the immediate despatch of four battalions of British troops to the Sudan but also gave, on 25 January 1898, formal authority for Kitchener to advance to Khartoum.

CHAPTER X

Waiting for the Rains:
January–June 1898

AT no stage of their journey had all the members of Marchand's expedition been together in one place, but during the last quarter of 1897 and the first quarter of 1898 they at least shared a common base. This was at Fort Hossinger near Tambura where for six months Marchand directed the tasks and the movements of his men. Some were sent out to reconnoitre the route ahead and ensure by promises, presents, or threats that the chiefs and people of the areas concerned were co-operative. Others were told to build forts and staging posts for the next advance, or to go back and bring up supplies. Marchand himself, who did not care for inactivity either in himself or in others, once disappeared for weeks on a mission exploring the country to the east which seemed to have little connection with the expedition to Fashoda. On another occasion he was away for nearly a month just to make sure that one of his officers who had died in a remote spot had been decently buried. It was to Fort Hossinger that the various members of the expedition returned to report, and sometimes to rest for a few days before they were sent out again on another mission. Sometimes they came for medical treatment by Dr Emily. Most of them succumbed at one time or another to the effects of exhaustion and hard going, or to tropical diseases with French medical names like *fièvre hémoglobinurique* and *fièvre bilieuse hématurique* which made them seem even more alarming than the English equivalent of blackwater fever.

Although some members of the expedition were impatient to get on, and fretted at their long stay in the country of Sultan Tambura, there were compensations. The Azande would not willingly work as carriers or boatmen themselves but in other respects they were generally helpful and friendly. They kept the expedition well supplied with garden produce and there was fish, game and wild duck in plenty. The Zande womenfolk were particularly friendly. They were inclined to be persistent, and for some members of the expedition the difficulty was not in finding consorts but in avoiding them. For his part, Dr Emily, who was to become a distinguished medical general in the French army, was presented with a nine-year old boy by the sultan as a reward for medical treatment for himself and some of his wives. The boy stayed with Emily to the end, and eventually went back with him to France where he was assimilated in the French fashion, and rose to be a medical corporal in the Great War.[1]

The reason for their long stay in Tambura was that Marchand realized, as the rains petered out in October and November 1897 that, because of the time they had lost dealing with the situation on the coast and in manhandling their boats across the watershed, they would have to wait for the beginning of the summer rains in May or June 1898 before they could continue their journey. Some of his companions were reluctant to accept this conclusion, and thought that a small party should try and get through on foot or in light canoes rather than risk letting the British or the Belgians get to Fashoda first. Marchand said No to this idea with a firmness and finality which for a time strained his relations with some of his men, notably with Mangin. Mangin, and some of Marchand's armchair critics at home, were not above suggesting that Marchand was deliberately delaying his advance because he first wanted to explore, pacify, and incorporate all the Zande sultanates into a new French dominion with himself as its first governor. Marchand was not lacking in personal ambition, and he may have had this in some compartment of his mind; the reports which he sent home up to the end of 1897 had been signed and stamped *Chef du Mission Congo-Nil*, but in 1898 they start to bear a circular stamp in which *Mission Congo-Nil* is circumscribed by the name of a completely new territory called *Afrique Centrale Française*. From now on he claimed that he was no longer subject to Liotard's direction.

Marchand's reasons for waiting were nevertheless based on inescapable facts. The Nile side of the watershed sloped very gradually into a vast basin of impermeable clay. This basin, generally known by the Arabic name of its main river Bahr el Ghazal, is

---

[1] According to Professor E. E. Evans-Pritchard, Zande warriors would pay parents the equivalent of bride-price for a boy companion when they were away for long periods. The boys' duties were fetching water, gathering wood and making the fire, carrying the warrior's shield and other belongings, and keeping him company when required.

more like a shallow saucer than a basin, and its only outlet is in the north east where it escapes through a gap in the rim of the saucer and joins the White Nile to make its way north to Khartoum and Egypt. In the rainy season between June and November an intricate network of small watercourses carries the water from the slopes of the watershed into this shallow saucer where most of it remains, flooding over on to the flat plains and evaporating day by day slowly in the hot tropical sun. The whole area is so ill-equipped for dealing with the flood of water which comes into it that it has been calculated that out of sixteen thousand million cubic metres of water flowing into the Bahr el Ghazal every summer less than one thousand million reaches the main stream of the Nile. In this situation the Bahr el Ghazal soon becomes a swamp. To make matters worse, masses of floating vegetation called *sudd*[2] come down with the flood waters, choking the watercourses and adding to the inundation. The *sudd* also becomes a serious hindrance to navigation unless the watercourses are cleared. Partly because this was not done regularly during the disturbed conditions of the Mahdist rule, and partly for unexplained natural causes, the *sudd* was particularly thick and widespread at the time when Marchand was there. Although the rivers were choked with *sudd*, and the Bahr el Ghazal became a swamp in the period of the rains, it was the only time of the year when the rivers were deep enough for vessels like the *Faidherbe* and the whale-boats, and the flooded plains could be crossed by canoe. For the rest of the year the rivers were too shallow, and the plains became largely a sour, stagnant wilderness of mud and rank grass without crops, pasture, or habitation.

Apart from these difficulties Marchand was faced with other problems caused by the nature of the people who lived in this area, notably the Dinka and the Nuer. They were pastoral people who depended on their cattle for most of their needs, with milk and blood drawn from the living beasts as their main source of protein. In the rains they moved with their stock to certain areas of higher ground, and returned for the remainder of the year to the odd patches of pasture left when the water had receded. This harsh nomadic existence, and the constant need to protect their precious cattle from predatory lion and equally predatory neighbours, left them little margin between survival and starvation, and tended to

---

[2] *sudd*: from the Arabic *sadd*, an obstruction or barrage.

make them hostile and suspicious of strangers. Moreoever the complexions of the Frenchmen reminded them, much to Marchand's disgust, of the Turks and the Arabs who used to come from the north in search of ivory, slaves, and cattle.

The Dinka and the Nuer were tall, graceful people with ebony or copper-coloured skins, narrow heads, long legs, and beautiful backs, but Marchand and his companions were not the only visitors to find them unfriendly, unhelpful, evasive, untruthful and rude. Although the men displayed great courage and endurance they tended to have an effeminate appearance, whereas the women and girls were dismissed by the discriminating Emily as neither *jolies ni coquettes*, and by Baratier as sullen, and lacking in charm.

Neither the Dinka nor any of the Nilotic tribes would carry anyone's loads or paddle their canoes, and it was some time before they could even be persuaded to act as guides through the labyrinths of the Bahr el Ghazal. Nor, at first, could they be relied on to provide any supplies; they had few agricultural products, and they were reluctant to part with their cattle which were at once the pride of their possessions and the pivot of their lives.

Marchand knew that despite all these hazards a few determined men might succeed in getting through the Bahr el Ghazal in the dry season on foot and in light canoes, and so reach the clear water which would take them to the White Nile. They would however be unable to take the arms, equipment and supplies or the boats which they would need to establish and maintain a base at Fashoda. There was also the risk that they might be attacked by the Khalifa's troops both on their way and when they reached their destination. It was unlikely that the Dinka, who knew the expedition's full resources, would attack a small party but this would not apply of course to the more distant tribes. There was finally the danger that a small, lightly-laden party of Frenchmen might reach Fashoda and be the first to get there, only to find that they lacked the numbers and resources to resist a subsequent challenge by the Belgians or the British.

Although Marchand had to reject the idea of a flying column it did not mean that he did not sympathize with the feelings of those who favoured it. This perhaps was one reason why he now sent the restless Mangin forward to establish a series of staging posts for the next advance. The most forward of these posts was named Fort Desaix after the General Desaix who, during Napoleon's invasion of Egypt in 1798, penetrated furthest up the valley of the Nile. It was situated on the river Sue near the present town of Wau on the margin of the great swamps and plains of the Bahr el Ghazal. It was here that Marchand planned to assemble his men and supplies, and his flotilla of boats, for the last stage of their journey as soon as the summer rains made the rivers navigable. The choice of Mangin for this task also served to take the sting from his complaints and to remove someone whose outspoken dissent sometimes threatened to create dissension and discord during what had become a long and awkward period of waiting.

Although Baratier was always Marchand's loyal lieutenant he too fretted at the inactivity and was soon pressing Marchand to let him at least go on and reconnoitre. Marchand had been much impressed with the reconnaissance which Baratier had carried out earlier on the Mbomu but he was reluctant to send him out this time because of what he knew, from local reports and from the travellers' tales of Gessi and others, that dangers lay ahead. But in the end he let him go. His orders were for Baratier to make his way down the Sue by boat and see if there was a way across the Bahr el Ghazal in the dry season to the old Egyptian river port of Meshra er Rek, where there was reputed to be clear water all the way to the main stream of the Nile. He was also to make contact with the Dinka and assure them that they had nothing to fear from Marchand and his expedition, or from the powerful but benevolent nation of France which had sent them.

In January 1898 Baratier set out from Fort Desaix. He took with him Landeroin, 24 Senegalese soldiers and 10 of the Yakoma boatmen in the red whale-boat, the same portable steel craft which he had himself so laboriously dismantled and carried across the watershed three months before. They set out to cross an area about which little was known, and without any reliable records or charts. Romolo Gessi[3] had got marooned here for three months some twenty years earlier, and most of his men had died of starvation. But, as Meshra was less than a hundred miles away as the crow flies, Baratier calculated that it would not take him more than two or three weeks to get there and back, and he took food for his party on

---

[3] Romolo Gessi, born in Constantinople of an Italian father and an Armenian mother, was serving under General Gordon in 1881 in what was then the Egyptian Sudan. Gordon said of him; 'Ought to have been born in 1560 not 1832. Same disposition as Francis Drake. . . .'

that basis. In the event the journey took him nearly three months, and turned out to be one of the most dramatic and hazardous operations of the whole expedition.

Although Baratier's account of this journey was written many years later, when he was a general, it has the freshness and unfolding excitement of a day-to-day record, and gives a strikingly vivid picture of what it was like to travel in what was then one of the least known parts of Africa. Not least of the merits of Baratier's account is the tribute which he paid to his African soldiers and paddlers, without whose cheerful and uncomplaining courage and endurance he admitted he would not have survived.

There were times when the vast and seemingly endless expanse of reeds, rotting vegetation, stinking mud and shallow, stagnant water became so difficult that their progress was reduced to two or three kilometres a day. Sometimes even this was only possible after hours of pushing and pulling the boat through the reeds, and hacking a way with matchets and knives through the tangle of vegetation. In this featureless wilderness of mud and reeds there was rarely any dry land on which to camp or stretch their legs, no firewood with which to make a fire or cook a meal, no landmarks like trees or villages or distant hills to help them find their way. At night it was damp and chilly, and from sunset to sunrise they were pestered by the persistent singing and stinging of mosquitoes. Nor for a long time were they able to make contact with the Dinka tribesmen. They sensed that their progress was being watched, and that their strength and resolution was being carefully and mercilessly assessed, but they rarely caught sight of the watchers; when they did encounter them in their dug-out canoes or catch a glimpse of a figure standing silent and immobile on one leg, the contact was usually brief and unhelpful. It was not until they were completely lost, and running out of food that they were able, with gestures and offers of beads, to persuade the Dinka to act as guides or to bring in small amounts of dried fish and millet. At first they kept their distance. They were suspicious of strangers, especially strangers with pale skins. All people with pale skins, grey, white or olive looked alike to them; Arabs, Europeans, Jews, Turks, Armenians, and highland Abyssinians appeared to be equally unfinished, and smelt equally unpleasing, and were equally suspect. In this situation it was an event to be recorded with pride and a sense of achievement when for the first time Baratier's men were able to effect an exchange of beads for food hand to hand, instead of leaving it in some distant spot to be collected. Landeroin did his best to make himself understood and to ask the usual travellers' questions about where and how far and in which direction; but few of the Dinka knew any Arabic, and they seemed neither to know nor to care about any neighbourhood except their own. They knew all the channels and sandbanks and deeps and shallows of their own locality; they knew where there were fish to be had, where millet would grow, and where cattle could graze during the seasons of the year. But outside these confines of subject and place they had no knowledge or curiosity. They showed no interest at all in the Frenchmen's world, in its achievements and glories, or in its beliefs, traditions, or customs. The only products of a thousand years of French civilization which appealed to them were coloured beads, and occasional pieces of iron.

Baratier on the other hand soon realized that if he was to get through the Bahr el Ghazal and its bewildering maze of hazards, there were elements of Dinka custom and belief that he had to understand and respect. It was not just a question of getting through. They had to return the same way, and come back again later with the rest of the expedition. They also had finally to leave behind them a situation in which they could establish and maintain communications once they reached Fashoda. One of the first things they learnt was not to shoot storks. Where there was no dry land there were no animals, no gazelle or bush-pig to be shot and eaten, no elephant or hippopotamus to be hunted. In the depths of the swamp the only birds they saw were Marabout storks. Their flesh had a fishy taste but as their rations came to an end the Senegalese soldiers pleaded with Baratier to shoot them. But the Dinka made it clear by signs and explicit gestures that they looked upon these storks as their kith and kin, not in any circumstances to be killed and eaten, and Baratier dared not risk their displeasure. He and his men tried fishing but they lacked the fish traps and the throwing spears with detachable heads which the Dinka used to catch perch in the streams and the shallows; nor did they know how to simulate the sound of rain, as the Dinka did with drums, in order to bring up the lung-fish from their long dry-season sojourn in the mud. Another piece of Dinka equipment which they lacked were the poles fitted with cross-pieces at the end which the tribesmen used to propel their canoes over the surface of the reeds and the matted vegetation. As there was no wood the Frenchmen could not make them, and there was a time when Baratier got so desperate at their inability to move their canoes that he even thought of stealing some or of taking them by force. But he knew that however great their need, the goodwill of the Dinka was of greater importance.

It was a great relief when in the first week of February they got their first sight of papyrus and knew from this that they were within reach at last of clear running water. They began to see the outlines of trees on the skyline and the distant hazy shapes of hills. They began to encounter hippopotomus in the deeps and elephant in the shallows which they could shoot. They ate the meat raw to appease a hunger engendered by a diet of roots and water-lily bulbs. Later they smoked the meat and kept it to eat in the days ahead, and for the two Frenchmen there was the treat once again of *boulettes journalières d'éléphant fumé*, of rissoles concocted from a mince of smoked elephant trunk.

In the reeds Baratier missed the opening of the channel which went to Meshra er Rek but he pushed on to the north until he came to clear water. On 25 February, when he was within reach of Lake No and the main stream of the Nile, he turned for home. He calculated, with good reason, that Marchand would be concerned at his long absence and the lack of news. So great indeed was Marchand's concern that early in March he had sent Largeau off in the other whale-boat with an escort of soldiers to look for Baratier and his companions. In the event however it was Baratier who had to rescue Largeau. Lost, and unable to make any headway, Largeau had abandoned his whale-boat in the reeds and had been trying to make his way back on foot across country, floundering in the mud like fish out of water until, by an almost miraculous chance, they heard a rifle shot and so met up with those they had come to rescue. Baratier managed to fit Largeau and his exhausted men into his whale-boat, and they all finally got back to Fort Desaix on 26 March.

When Lieutenant Mangin had first arrived with Largeau and sixty men at the site of Fort Desaix all they had found was a cluster of dry-season huts, looking like heads of untidy, unbrushed hair. They belonged to one of the many small tribes which had for generations gained a measure of protection against the Azande at the cost of abject subjection to the Dinka. These tribes, the Djour, Ncolo, Ndogo, Belanda, Bongo, and Biray were ready to welcome the well-armed, white-faced strangers because they had less to lose, and they were soon making themselves useful and agreeable by bringing in plentiful supplies of millet, milk, firewood, and girls. Like the experienced soldier he was, Mangin chose a text-book site which combined the requirements of both hygiene and defence. As the weeks and months went by, and they were joined by Marchand and the others, Fort Desaix was laid out and developed into a secure, attractive and well-appointed station round the essential nucleus of a small, stone-built fort. It was more than a temporary staging place. It was meant in Marchand's mind to be a permanent post and an important link in a chain of communications which would provide the expedition at Fashoda with a sure means of getting reinforcements and fresh supplies, and of keeping in touch with Liotard and with France. Its ultimate purpose was to be one of several administrative and military stations in a new French territory in central Africa, and part of a continuous belt of French possessions from Dakar to Jibuti.[4]

With this in mind, living quarters of solid construction were built, and care was taken to provide the settlement with some of the essentials of civilized living. For a Frenchman this had to include a *potager*, a vegetable garden sown with lettuce, radish, cucumber, spinach, aubergines, garlic, and French beans. Planting French beans, *haricots verts*, was one of the first things the members of Marchand's band did when they came across a likely looking patch of river mud or silt. Landeroin was the main gardener but Mangin was also an enthusiast and he boasted in one of his many enchanting letters to his sisters that he had once planted 1,500 banana plants 'and thousands of other useful seedlings' in a place where they were unlikely to stay long enough to eat the crops. Another essential of French living was somewhere suitable to store and preserve the wine they had carried with them with such care all the way from Bordeaux and the Côtes du Rhone. They built special enclosures too for the cows and the beef cattle, the thousand head of sheep and goats and the three hundred chickens which they had acquired to supplement local supplies of game, partridge, wild duck and river

---

[4] The *outre mer* section of the national archives in Paris has the originals of the orders and proclamations, written in longhand on cheap squared-paper, in which Marchand, using the language and style of an emperor appointing his field-marshals to be rulers of conquered provinces, named the lieutenants and sergeants of his little band as military commanders of distant outposts of mud brick and reeds.

fish. One way and another the country provided Marchand and his companions with a balanced diet, and a welcome change from the hippopotamus stew and *filet d'éléphant* which had for long been their staple diet. Thus fortified with gourmet meals and good French wine, and with music and songs from Marchand's mechanical piano, they waited in the middle of Africa for the coming of the rains.

They waited at Fort Desaix all through the spring and the early summer of 1898. Day after day they watched the skies for signs. They watched the rivers too, the Sue and the Wau, for the first indications that the rain had started to fall on the slopes of the watershed. There is nothing in their records and journals to suggest that they prayed to their own god for rain, but they were tempted to solicit the services of the local rainmakers whose records of success in this field were perhaps just as good. For the Dinka and the Nuer the coming and the ending of the rains were vital to their survival, and rainmakers played an important part in their lives. They both expected two things from their rainmaking chiefs; rain and virility. Rain was like celestial semen, bringing life to barren ground, and the two functions were therefore closely linked. If the rainmakers did not come up to expectations, through ill-chance or increasing age, they were ceremonially buried alive.

The rivers began to show signs of rain in early May – a muddy darkening of the colour of the water, the gradual disappearance of familiar sandbanks and rocks, and the rotting tree trunks that had lain on the river bed like the carcasses of dead animals through the long months of waiting. Marchand carefully measured the depth of the water every day, comparing it with the draught of the *Faidherbe* which had been nursed almost inch by inch down the river from Khojali at the end of the autumn rains. By the middle of May it was deep enough for some of the smaller boats, and Marchand decided to send the still restless and impatient Mangin off again to try and get through to Meshra and set up a staging post there for the final advance. Mangin left on 17 May, with Sergeant Dat and fifty men.

Even by the end of the month the depth of water at Fort Desaix was no more than 50 centimetres against the 1.50 metres which the *Faidherbe* needed. Marchand was now faced with another very difficult decision. He badly wanted the size and the speed and the armament, even the mere appearance of his steam-driven ship. He wanted it not only to carry the men, the stores and the equipment required to establish and maintain a substantial outpost on the Nile but, if need be, to intimidate and deter any hostile forces there might be. He also wanted it to impress the Nuer and the Shilluk, the tribes which dominated the region between Lake No and Fashoda and with whom his masters and mentors in Paris were anxious that he should make treaties of friendship and protection.

To set against this were the disadvantages and dangers of further delay. Apart from the feelings of his companions who, like his sponsors in France, were continually urging him on, he had had a nasty scare in February when Dinka tribesmen brought in a report that 'a large body of Europeans' were in the region of Ayak, some 250 km to the east. Marchand's first thoughts were that it must be a force of Belgians advancing to Fashoda from Lado. It was not until he had hurriedly despatched several parties in strength to investigate that he discovered that the reports, like others brought in by the Dinka, had been deliberately meant to mislead or distract. He was still nagged by fears that a British expedition from Uganda might get to Fashoda before him. There was also the important matter of making contact with Bonchamps from Abyssinia who had been told to expect Marchand very soon. Finally there were disquieting reports of Kitchener moving slowly but inexorably up the valley of the Nile. Marchand knew that the summer rains which would enable his little flotilla to move down the river to Fashoda would also allow Kitchener to bring his fleet of gunboats and supply boats over the dry season barrier of the sixth cataract and so on to Khartoum.

In making his decision Marchand was helped by the fact that during their long wait on the river Sue he and his men had been able to build up his supply of river craft. By the end of May he had, in addition to the *Faidherbe*, a total of thirty-four canoes and five portable whale-boats and rafts made of metal, each fitted now with masts, keels and sails, and equipped with the billhooks and square-ended punting poles which Baratier had missed so badly on his reconnaissance. The *Faidherbe* herself had been re-painted and fitted with a new hull and was 'as good as new'.

'Ah! si la flotille peut marcher!' Marchand wrote in despair to Bobichon back at Bangassou. 'This damned river doesn't flow any more. Here we are stranded on the sand like flapping fish for want of 40 centimetres of water and not a cloud in the sky. What a situation! Here I am', he went on with more ebullience than accuracy, 'with a brand-new steamer capable of 14 knots, 8 boats made of iron or steel and 40 large dug-out canoes made at the point of the sword in sixty days by frantic efforts. I have thousands of cartridges, an enormous train of supplies, and I am rooted to the spot. Ah! Fachoda! Fachoda! Dieu, que c'est dur!' In another letter he explained that he and his companions were sustained in this situation by two driving forces; one was love of France, the other hatred of England, a hatred which, he admitted, was grudgingly tempered with a certain admiration and respect 'for an adversary which possessed all the qualities and grand defects which made a nation great'.

Marchand's statement that the canoes were made at the point of the sword did less than justice to those who actually made them. Baratier, who always referred to the Senegalese soldiers in terms of affection and admiration, made it clear when he came to write his account that the main reason why the canoes were made so quickly was the cheerful willingness and adaptability of these Senegalese in doing anything they were asked to do 'as escorts, carriers, paddlers, navvies, blacksmiths, carpenters and boat builders.' The canoes were built on the spot simply to provide a means of travelling up and down the Sue during the dry season when the water was too low for anything else, and they were left behind when the expedition moved on.

At the beginning of June there was enough water in the river for the rafts and the whale-boats but not for the *Faidherbe*, and Marchand decided to split his forces. One party would set off at once with the smaller vessels and make for Fashoda as quickly as possible with such supplies as they could carry. The rest of the expedition would stay behind until there was enough water to bring the *Faidherbe* down the Sue, and take them and the remainder of the stores via Meshra er Rek and Lake No to join the advance party on the Nile at Fashoda.

CHAPTER XI

The Approach to Fashoda

THE advance party left Fort Desaix on 4 June 1898. It was commanded by Marchand himself. With him went Baratier, Emily, and
Landeroin together with Sgt Vernail, fifty Senegalese soldiers and
twenty of the Yakoma boatmen. Although most of the rear party
were still further up the river with the *Faidherbe*, the fort was not
left empty. Liotard had sent a French officer and thirty-seven
soldiers to take it over and maintain a presence, and they, and a
large concourse of local notables and others who had ministered to
the expedition's needs, gave Marchand and his companions a good
send off with much flag-waving, tears, and embracings. As Baratier
recorded, it was *Vive la France! Le grand voyage est commencé!*

Of those who went with the advance party Marchand, Baratier,
Mangin and Emily made some record of the journey, either in
official reports or private letters at the time or in books written, with
the advantages and disadvantages of hindsight, many years afterwards. Their accounts are by no means the same. Dr Emily not
surprisingly recorded more medical detail than the others, and dealt
at considerable length with an operation he performed under
difficult conditions to relieve Baratier of a foreign body in his eye. It
had made Baratier blind for a time and he had handed over his
duties as navigator to Marchand who, Baratier noted with good
humoured, comradely satisfaction, twice lost the way and took the
party round in a circle to where they had started. Emily also
performed a delicate operation to remove an inflamed gland from
Marchand's neck which had been causing him great distress with
nightmares, insomnia and irritability. There were frequent refer-
ences in most of the accounts to the hardships and dangers, and
some may have stressed them to excess, but Mangin, who had done
the journey some weeks before, was perhaps understating the
difficulties when he wrote, in another of his irreverent brotherly
epistles, that 'Marchand made the trip without too much difficulty,
thanks to his men who stood in the mud all day and pushed'.

Everyone agreed that the first part of the journey was the easiest when for eight days they sailed or paddled down the river Sue and averaged 40 km a day. Although they had to tack and perform other nautical manoeuvres to avoid sandbanks and reefs there was usually enough depth of water, current or breeze for them to make good progress each day, while the firm, wooded banks of the river allowed them to tie up each night and camp, and find enough wood to cook their supper and light fires to keep out the chill. They stopped, like good Frenchmen, for two hours for luncheon in the middle of the day. Landeroin had been put in charge of the kitchen, *chargé de la popote*, as Emily put it, and once again he was able to draw on a wide range of local produce – millet, milk, and honey, fresh beef and mutton, wild duck and venison – while for their African soldiers and followers they were able to shoot elephant and hippo and then smoke the meat for the lean days ahead. They started each day at dawn, and went on until five or six o'clock in the evening. The long midday break was not the only interruption to their progress. Marchand was a courageous but also a compulsive hunter, and Baratier was sometimes perplexed, and sometimes one suspects more than perplexed, by his otherwise much respected chief's frequent stops to shoot more game and wild duck than they could possibly eat. Crocodile however they could and did shoot from the boats. The sandbanks were littered with them; some, like monsters from the past, were as much as 8 metres long. Marchand had a particular hatred of them and took an almost fiendish pleasure in watching young crocodile emerging from their eggs and then killing them one by one.

The expedition's troubles began on the ninth day when the stream with its current and firm banks started to give way to what Marchand called the 'veritable ocean of reeds' of the Bahr el Ghazal. The reeds grew as high as two and three metres above the level of the river, and the look-outs and pathfinders had to climb up the masts and see over the top. Even then there was little to see except a seemingly endless expanse of green, moving restlessly like waves in a quiet sea, and above them the harsh, hot sun in the pale blue bowl of an empty sky. In this expanse it was difficult to discover the channel, rarely more than ten metres wide, where the current of the Sue was still strong enough to make a clear passage through the reeds. The depth of water in these narrow channels varied. When it was deep enough for the boats to pass they often found that this was only because the channel had become blocked by debris; when the debris was hacked away the level of the water fell, and the boats were left stranded and had to be pushed. When the water was too shallow they sometimes had to build up an artificial dam of mud and grass to hold up the slowly moving stream in order to increase the depth. Baratier who had crossed the Bahr el Ghazal before noted that in some instances there was less water in the channels after a month of rain than there had been earlier in the dry season. This was because the floods generated by the rain brought down branches and other debris which formed barriers and held up the flow of the river lower down. In such circumstances not only was their progress infuriatingly slow and exhausting but it was difficult, even for the experienced Baratier, to pick the right way through the reeds and avoid ending up in a cul-de-sac. Guides with local knowledge would have considerably eased and speeded their passage but it was not until they had been in the swamp for seven days that they had the service of a local tribesman whom Mangin had sent out from Meshra er Rek to look for them and help them find their way through the maze of reeds.

In all it took Marchand and his party twelve days to cross the 40 km of swamp, that is less than two miles a day. There were times when, as Mangin had said, their only progress came from the efforts and strength of the Africans who stood in the slime and pushed the boats through the reeds and what Emily described as 'a horrible mixture of mud, stagnant water like liquid manure, reeds, water-lilies, dead wood, rotting fish and the foeted carcase of a dead antelope'. It was an area where nothing lived except a hotch-potch of rats, snakes, millipedes and ants. The nights were as bad as the days. Myriads of mosquitoes appeared even before dusk and hummed and bit all through the night. 'Clouds and clouds of mosquitoes . . . c'est un véritable torture!' There was no dry land where they could pitch their tents or put up their mosquito nets, and they all, Europeans and Africans alike, had to spend the night in the cramped and crowded conditions of the whale-boats and the rafts. Most of them gave up shaving and washing rather than use the stinking black water. With their ragged beards and their clothes in tatters, their faces drawn and lined and burnt black by the sun, and their eyes hollow from fatigue, they were hardly, Mangin delighted in telling his sisters, an elegant sight. For the fastidious Dr Emily there was the additional misery of what he delicately referred to as *le débarras intestinal*, the daily problem of having to empty his bowels in public without even a tree or a bush to help.

There was little at Meshra when they arrived to show that thirty years before, in the days of the Egyptian administration, it had been a river port with a clear water channel for steamers all the way to the main stream of the Nile. Through years of neglect and disturbance the approaches to the port had become choked with weed. Apart from this hazard they were now entering a region which the Khalifa's forces patrolled. Marchand had originally believed that the Khalifa would welcome his expedition, as engaged in a common cause against the British but, as the Frenchmen got closer and closer to the Nile and his own dominions, he saw them more and more as just another band of acquisitive white men. In view of this Marchand ordered his flotilla of little boats to advance in military formation. In the leading boat, the red whale-boat which they had recovered on their way through the swamp, were Baratier, Sgt Venail and an escort of soldiers. Next came the flat-ended aluminium raft, with Mangin and Sgt Dat and another escort of soldiers. In the middle, in a position of honour and command, was Marchand himself. Behind on the third raft was Emily, with Largeau bringing up the rear in the white whale-boat. Their orders were never to be more than 200 metres apart.

Aside from this need for vigilance the next part of the journey was easier. Although the current was still slight and there was generally little wind for the sails, there was soon a clear stream 50 to 60 metres broad through the *sudd*, and they could safely use the moonlight to keep going until well after dark. With their destination only three or four hundred kilometres away they were impatient to get on. They cut down their mid-day break to an hour, and were soon doing 30 and 40 km a day. Things were also easier at night. The river had firm banks where they could tie up and camp for the night, and there was wood to make fires and cook. There was papyrus ten feet high which turned to shades of red and gold in the evening, and giant ant-hills in whose hard, reddish-brown mass Landeroin scraped out ovens and baked bread. Away to the north there were wide, grassy plains teeming with game, and the rare welcome sight of grey-blue hills in the distance.

As the month of June drew to a close, and Marchand and his companions marked off the first few days of July in their diaries and calendars, they came to places whose names had been like visions in their minds for months and years, and made them feel a special excitement and pride as each was successfully attained and passed.

There was the confluence with the Bahr el Arab, the great river which came in from the west. There was Lake No and the junction with the Bahr el Jebel, the main stream of the river which came down from the great lakes and the Mountains of the Moon to form the White Nile. Each time they hoisted the French flag when they camped on the bank of the Nile they could boast that for the first time since the days of St Louis and Napoleon Bonaparte the tricolour was flying again on the river of Ptolemy and the Pharoahs.

At half-past four on the afternoon of 6 July they had their first sight of the round, pointed huts of the Shilluk. The Shilluk were another of the Nilotic tribes, kin in appearance and customs to the Nuer and the Dinka, and it was they who dominated the left bank of the Nile from Lake No to Fashoda. It was thus a moment of great excitement for Marchand and all his companions. 'Quelle anxiété!' Emily wrote, 'et comme nôtre coeur à tous fait toc, toc!' From these Shilluk tribesmen they would discover how far they had to go, if there were any forces of the Khalifa to contest their arrival, and whether any one else had passed this way. Now at last they would know if Fashoda was still there for the taking, and whether there had been any sign of Bonchamps or other French expeditions from Abyssinia. Most of all they wanted to know if the Belgians or the British had got there before them.

CHAPTER XII

Further Progress of the Other Expeditions

AT the end of 1897 the Belgian force under Chaltin had been waiting on the Nile at Lado for reinforcements and instructions. Although Dhanis had had sealed orders to make for Fashoda, Chaltin does not seem to have had similar instructions. Nor indeed would he have been able to carry them out if he had. He was in no position to advance, and was having difficulty enough in defending his outpost both against local tribesmen and against the forces of the Khalifa which had been defeated but by no means destroyed at the battle of Rajjaf. Although reinforcements were sent to him from the Congo early in 1898, Chaltin was still beleagured at Lado when Marchand and his expedition were embarking on the last stage of their journey in June. Marchand still thought of the Belgians as serious rivals, and it would have gone some way to reducing his anxieties if he had known that they were already out of the race.

*   *   *

Major Macdonald had once boasted that when Captain Marchand and his men eventually reached Fashoda they would find Macdonald already there to greet them with a champagne supper. In the early part of 1898, however, Macdonald was still in Uganda pursuing his Sudanese mutineers, while the main body of his large Nile expedition waited for him on the slopes of Mount Elgon. The Marquis of Salisbury was not at all pleased at this disruption of his plans, and he quickly arranged for three companies of Indian troops commanded by Major Martyr to be despatched to Uganda so that Macdonald could get back to his expedition and proceed on his proper purpose to the north without further delay. Even after Martyr reached Uganda and took over the pursuit of the mutineers there was little in Macdonald's many letters to Lord Salisbury or the Foreign Office to suggest that he was in any hurry to go north. His letters were mainly concerned with excuses for yet more delays, and with trying to make out a case for 'a special clasp' and a medal for all those, like himself, who had been involved in the mutiny and the pursuit of the mutineers. Macdonald tried to lay most of the blame for the delay in his own departure on Berkeley, the newly appointed Commissioner in Uganda, whom he accused of refusing to give up enough of his Indian garrison troops to provide Macdonald with an adequate escort. Berkeley riposted by disclosing that in June Macdonald had asked him privately to explain to the Foreign Office on his behalf that a combination of ill-health, mental stress, and shortage of men and supplies made it impossible for him to set off for Fashoda, and had asked his advice 'as to how the expedition . . . could be abandoned without himself and his officers incurring reproach'. Macdonald followed this up with a despatch of his own saying that, because of lack of co-operation from Berkeley, he now only had enough supplies 'to keep the field for 4 or 5 months'. This meant that if, as he put it, 'he pushed on to Fashoda' he would not have enough food and ammunition for the return journey. If Kitchener was not there to replenish him he would therefore face 'total disaster'. If, on the other hand, Kitchener were there, then Macdonald argued with inexorable logic, 'there is no point in my going there'. Having thus disposed of those parts of his instructions which he did not like, he now proceeded to rewrite them in a form which suited him better. 'So' he wrote, 'it appears to me that I should be best fulfilling your Lordship's wishes if I do as much as I can in the more eastern portions of the Nile basin which cannot be dealt with by gun-boats on the Nile'. What Macdonald had in mind was the conveniently closer and healthier uplands between the Nile and Lake Rudolf, and he explained that he was sending one of his officers to the north of the lake in order 'to make treaties up to the limit of Abyssinian occupation'. The carrot which he now dangled to make up for Lord Salisbury's disappointment, and to improve his own prospects, was that his venture would 'forestall the French and secure to our flag that great block of territory south and east of the limit of navigation of the Nile.'

This despatch, and others in the same vein, did not reach the Foreign Office until August of 1898 by which time their only interest was that they provided the reasons, as was acidly remarked in the margin by some official, 'why the Macdonald expedition gave up the idea of going down the Nile'. Nor did his excuses come as any surprise. Berkeley had been asked by Salisbury to keep a close eye on Macdonald, and had been keeping the Foreign Office informed of developments by telegraph. The result was that Salisbury had already telegraphed to Uganda[1] expressing his surprise and displeasure that Macdonald 'should have abandoned the work for which he was sent out', and making it crystal clear that 'we do not desire to establish posts on the Lake Rudolf country until the railway has reached a more westerly point'.

Although this was the end of Macdonald's expedition and of Salisbury's vision of an advance to Fashoda from the south, it was by no means the last that was heard of the matter. Both Salisbury and his close advisers in the Foreign Office had realized for some time that Macdonald would not get to Fashoda before the French, but having given Macdonald two sets of instruction in order to deceive the French and everyone else they now found themselves hoist on the uncomfortable petard of their own duplicity. It had been said many times in public, in parliament, and in official despatches that Macdonald's object was to explore the course of the river Juba. It was therefore necessary to persevere with this fiction even when, a year later, the Liberal opposition in the shape of Sir Charles Dilke and Henry Labouchere, snuffling in the political dirt like a pair of well-bred pigs in search of truffles, voiced their suspicions in the House of Commons and demanded an enquiry into what they described as 'one of the most absurd and silly expeditions ever dreamt up by the mind of man'.

*   *   *

The French government was no less displeased when it received the news from Abyssinia that Bonchamps had also failed to carry out his mission. He was accused of incompetence, cowardice, and misappropriation of public funds. Bonchamps riposted by blaming Lagarde, who was still the main French representative in Jibuti and Addis Ababa, of being deliberately unhelpful and obstructive, and he also accused Emperor Menelik of witholding with one hand what

---

[1] In 1898 this meant by submarine cable to Mombasa via Zanzibar, then overland by copper wire suspended on telegraph poles along the railway line as far as it went, and thereafter by runner in a forked stick. This landline was liable to frequent interruption: partly because the Kikuyu and the Masai fancied the wire as ornaments both for themselves and their womenfolk, and partly because elephant and rhinoceros were apt to rub against the poles to relieve irritation, with disastrous results for the poles.

he had promised with the other. Both accusations had some subst-
ance.

One reason why the French government was so displeased was
that it was now realized, from Marchand's experience in the region
of the Bahr el Ghazal, that once he reached Fashoda he could only
be kept supplied from the west by river during the six or seven
months of the rains, and that for the remainder of the year he would
have to be sustained through Abyssinia. It was thus more important
than ever that Bonchamps should try again to make contact with
Marchand, and that Menelik should be offered further inducements
to co-operate and extend his own dominions towards the Nile. One
of the inducements offered was the prospect of revenues for his
country, with a due percentage for himself, if the trade of existing
and future French possessions in central Africa were to be channel-
led through Abyssinia by means of an extension of the projected
Jibuti-Addis Ababa railway to the east bank of the Nile. It was
another grand concept, and it took a very detached official at the
Quai d'Orsay to point out that there 'were certain inconsistencies'
between the inducements now being held out to Menelik by the
ministry for foreign affairs on the one hand, and the colonial
ministry's vision of a continuous belt of French territory from Dakar
to Jibuti on the other.

The Emperor Menelik was of course as aware of the inconsistencies and duplicities of the European powers as they in the end were
to be of his. The British had warned him that the French had designs
not only on the west bank of the Nile but also on the east and
beyond. Menelik was equally concerned with stories he had heard,
largely from French sources, of the designs which both Kitchener in
the north, and Macdonald in the south had on lands in the Nile basin
and in the vicinity of Lake Rudolf which he regarded as within his
own sphere of influence. He now decided therefore that the time
had come for him to re-assert his claim to all these areas by sending
in armed forces to take possession of them.

As the Mahdists also claimed the areas east of the Nile, Menelik
first sent an emissary to the Khalifa in the spring of 1898 to explain
that the projected operations of the Abyssinian forces were merely
aimed at 'the Europeans', that is to say both the French and the
British who, to quote from a letter in Amharic later found in the
Khalifa's archives in Omdurman, 'intended to enter my country and
yours and try and separate and divide us.' He even sent the Khalifa

'a small flag of three colours' with the suggestion that 'if the English advance against him he is to fly it at the head of his army. When they see this they will do him no harm, and this will be the same if the French advance against him.' Although the Khalifa was advised by his elders that his own troops would not take kindly to him using a flag of the infidel French in this way, he thought it might still come in useful, and therefore kept it among his private possessions which was where it was eventually found.

The force which Menelik now despatched to the western approaches of his dominions was said to have numbered a quarter of a million. It was divided into three parts. One under his cousin Ras Makonnen, the father of the future emperor Haile Selassie, was sent to the area he coveted most, the area between the Blue Nile and the White known as Bani Shanqual which was said to contain gold. Another section under Ras Wolde Georgis went south and west towards Lake Rudolf, while the third under Ras Tassama was ordered to occupy the valley of the Sobat. Ras Tassama's army left Gore on 10 March 1898. With it went Potter, the artist attached to Bonchamps' expedition, and Faivre from the department of native affairs in Jibuti. Bonchamps himself did not go with them. He and Michel went instead to Addis Ababa to seek fresh instructions and more funds, and to try and locate the portable boat without which they knew they could never hope to reach Fashoda. The departure of Tassama's army from Gore was a colourful affair. Although no more than 4,000 were armed with rifles, there were many others with spears and shields. Each fighting man was attended by up to ten women,[2] according to his military rank, as well as one or two boys to carry his weapons, hold his horse, and act as a cushion when his master wanted to lie down and sleep. Each person carried enough food for a month after which they were expected to live off the country. To carry his belongings and to bear him in battle each soldier had a mule and a horse. In all, the concourse which set off from Gore numbered well over ten thousand men, women, children and livestock. Before they left they went to the church to receive a blessing, and to be assured, like medieval crusaders, that disembowelling and castrating the infidels and pagans were holy acts,

---

[2] These women played an important part in the army, and the two Frenchmen were full of admiration for their blend of tenderness and toughness. After walking and carrying for ten hours a day they would cheerfully collect the firewood, cook the food, make the beer and wash the feet of their menfolk.

and would be duly rewarded in heaven. Menelik's orders were for them to conquer the 'western regions and all ill-armed aboriginal tribes'.

Potter and Faivre were not the only Europeans to go with Ras Tassama's army. There was also a Russian colonel named Artamanov, and two Cossack soldiers. Artamanov was a member of a diplomatic and military mission which the Tsar had sent to Addis Ababa in 1897. It was not the first time the Russians had shown an interest in Abyssinia; but it was the first official mission. It was followed by a medical mission and a hospital, and led one traveller to observe that 'pills and bandages are making the first Russian footsteps in Africa'. These missions made a good impression in Abyssinia although Menelik himself, having been assured by Lagarde that the Russians were enemies of the British, could not understand how it was that Vlassov, the Russian minister, not only had an English wife but an English governess for his children. The Russians lived in a grand manner in Addis Ababa, and entertained with a lavish hospitality which was apt to continue, as a matter of national honour, until both guests and hosts were under the table. It was said that the military members of the Russian mission had been selected from the tallest and best-looking officers of the Imperial Guard so that they would not appear at a disadvantage with the tall and elegant young men, like Count Gleichen of the Grenadier Guards, who had accompanied the British mission under Rennel Rodd. Colonel Artamanov was one of these officers.

When Bonchamps and Michel had set out for Fashoda in 1897 they had travelled west from Gore down the valley of the Baro to its junction with the Sobat. This time Tassama's army went south to another tributary called the Ajouba and followed this down to its junction with the Baro near Nasir. Tassama did not send the whole of his army into this unpleasant area of heat, fever and swamp. Nor did he go himself. He sent one of his officers, Fituari Haile, with 800 men to accompany Potter and Faivre down the Sobat to the Nile where, the Frenchmen assured him, they would find Marchand already installed and the French flag flying. Artamanov and his Cossacks went with them.[3]

After a difficult journey they finally reached the junction of the

[3] Local tribesmen told Marchand later that the party included 'four European women', but there is sadly no evidence to show who they were or to which members of the expedition they were attached.

Sobat and the Nile on 22 June. It was a day on which Marchand and his advance party had taken from dawn to dusk to struggle 500 m through the Bahr el Ghazal. It was with a bitter sense of disappointment, almost of disbelief, that Potter and Faivre searched the waters of the Nile and its western bank for a sight of Marchand's boats or a French flag. They pleaded with Fituari Haile to wait for a few more days. Haile refused, in a series of short, sharp sentences which have the ring of truth. 'We have not enough food. My men are sick. The river is rising. We will die in the swamps. Let us go.'

The Abyssinians had already planted their flag on the east bank of the river but, lacking a boat, Faivre and Potter saw no way in which they could plant theirs on the far bank. The Nile at this point was about five hundred yards across. Potter was ill, and could hardly stand upright from fever. Fievre couldn't swim. At last, however, they found one of their African followers who, for a suitable reward, was prepared to swim across the Nile with a French flag. They first pulled the thatch from an abandoned hut and tied it inside a large wooden crate so that it floated, after a fashion, and then attached the flag to it on a stick. The volunteer made his way gingerly into the water, and started to swim, pushing the crate in front of him. This was too much for the gallantry and Caucasian pride of the Russian. With a cry of 'Il ne sera pas dit qu'un nègre aura été seul planter le drapeau français', he dived into the river and was immediately followed by his two Cossacks. They seized the float and the flag from the African, and swam to a small island on the other side of the river. There they put up the flag. They then all returned safely to the east bank.

The return journey was not a happy one. As Fituari Haile had predicted, the level of the Sobat rose rapidly and they only just managed to get through. Potter was killed by a spear thrust from an unknown assailant for a reason that was also not known. Faivre took Potter's collection of beetles and butterflies back to Gore where in the end he decided to stay. Bonchamps returned to Paris where he carefully compiled a dossier now in the French archives, labelled 'Causes d'impossibilité de jonction avec Marchand.'

*   *   *

By the beginning of 1898 General Kitchener was fully restored in self-confidence. Even more than usual he displayed what someone called 'the humourless face of one who is always in the right', and his staff found him increasingly difficult to live with. He had got his brigade of British troops, and he had got authority to advance to Khartoum. He did not intend to attack Khartoum until the Nile flood enabled his gunboats and supply barges to pass over the sixth cataract, and having satisfied himself that the introduction of British troops did not mean, as he had once feared, that he would lose command of the expedition to Grenfell, he now proceeded to insist that he needed a second British brigade in the final assault. By the beginning of April, when this second brigade was on its way,[4] he had concentrated in the vicinity of Berber a regiment of Egyptian cavalry, one British and two Egyptian infantry brigades, 24 field and horse artillery guns and 12 Maxim machine-guns. On Good Friday, 8 April, he attacked Mahmud Ahmed, who was entrenched with some 12,000 courageous but ill-armed men in a well-prepared position on the river Atbara. Kitchener's preparations for the battle had as usual been meticulously thorough, and with his overwhelming superiority of firepower his victory was quick, bloody, and complete. If Kitchener's treatment of the proud and handsome Madmud after the battle now appears merciless and distasteful, it was no worse, if that be an excuse, and probably better, than he himself would have received if he had been defeated and captured.[5]

From this battle on the Atbara two important lessons were learned. One was that the rank and file of the Egyptian Army, particularly those who came from the Sudan, were excellent soldiers. The other was that, while the Khalifa's troops lacked up-to-date weapons, they were still fearless and formidable opponents, and that the way to Khartoum was likely to be bitter, costly and hard. As Cromer remarked after the battle: 'We have evidently not cracked our Soudan nut yet. The Khalifa will stand and fight at Omdurman and I expect he will offer a rather formidable resistance.'

Well before Kitchener asked for a second brigade of British troops the Treasuries both in Whitehall and Cairo had been carefully working out the costs. As the first brigade sent to reinforce

---

[4] Brigades at that time normally consisted of four battalions. All the units of the first brigade had come from troops already in Egypt but in this case they had come straight out from England except for the Grenadier Guards, who had been included because 'the Queen wishes it', and were stationed at Gibraltar.

[5] Kitchener had once seen a man who had been tortured by the Mahdists, and thereafter always carried a bottle of poison to take if he was ever captured himself.

Kitchener had come from Egypt, and had to be replaced there by fresh troops from England, the cost of the campaign was already over £200,000. When the cost of sending out another British brigade was added the total bill, it was calculated, could be as much as half a million. Such a sum in 1898 had a very sharpening effect on the minds of both officials and politicians, and much thought had been devoted in London and in Cairo to the question of what return might be expected from such an expenditure. Up to then the official British attitude to the Sudan had been that it was Egyptian territory which had temporarily passed into the hands of the rebellious forces of the Mahdists, and that it was now being recovered by the Egyptian Army, with military and financial help from Britain. Although Egypt was sometimes treated as if it were a British protectorate, it was still subject to a number of international agreements. This meant that its financial benefits had to be shared with others. The extension of this limited control and profit sharing to the potentially rich cotton-growing areas of the Sudan seemed an inadequate return for the cost of its conquest. The private letters exchanged between Cromer and Salisbury, and the secret records of the Foreign Office show how this problem was approached and resolved in a pragmatic manner, with a regard for British interests in which considerations of consistency and principle seem to have played a very small part.

It was decided in the end that the best answer was to abandon the idea of treating the Sudan as Egyptian territory occupied by rebels, and to look upon it instead as 'an independent and sovereign Mahdist State'. Then, as Salisbury put it in an exploratory telegram to Cromer early in June 1898, 'We might treat Khartum as the capital of the Mahdi state; and the capture of Khartum would deliver by right of conquest the whole of the Mahdi state from Halfa to Wadelai into the power of the capturing army. The army consists of two allied contingents . . .'. The 'two allied contingents' were of course the British and the Egyptian elements in Kitchener's army of the Nile. To mark the joint nature of the operation the British and Egyptian flags would fly side by side in the conquered lands but, because her Majesty's Government had made such a large contribution, she would be entitled to a dominant position in the control and the material benefits of the conquered territories. As Salisbury put it: 'If we can establish this position we shall be free of a lot of diplomatic hamper.'

Although Cromer accepted this 'two-flags policy', as it was called, he was not the only one to see its imperfections. Salisbury's assumption that the capture of a capital gave the conquerer rights over the whole territory was not one to which all statesmen and international lawyers subscribed. There was also the snag that if the British were to base their claim to the Sudan on conquest, the French might make a similar claim once Marchand had got to Fashoda and had consolidated the position which he and Liotard had built up in Tambura and the Bahr el Ghazal. There was also the awkward possibility that Emperor Menelik might be found to have established himself by force on the east side of the Nile.

With these awkward thoughts in mind, and with Kitchener now busy building up a force of over 20,000 men some 40 miles north of Khartoum, Cromer sat down at his desk in Cairo on 15 June 1898, and started to draw up a memorandum on the policy to be followed once Khartoum had been captured.

CHAPTER XIII

The Occupation of Fashoda

WHEN on 6 July 1898 Marchand and his companions first made contact with the Shilluk, a large tribe of some two million people, the questions they asked were straightforward and simple. How far to Fashoda? How many days to get there? Are there any white men at Fashoda? Have any come this way from the south, or from the east? Are the Mahdists established in the fort at Fashoda? Do they still hold Omdurman and Khartoum? What news of the Egyptians and the English coming up the Nile from the north?

The answers they got from the Shilluk, first from the villagers and finally from the chief himself, were not so straightforward or so simple. Living as they did 500 km south of Khartoum on the highway of the Nile, in country which grew good crops of grain, the Shilluk had had dealings with strangers before. The strangers had guns and rifles which they used to secure what they wanted; ivory, slaves, conscripts for their armies, nubile girls, and less than nubile boys, together with supplies of livestock and grain. The Shilluk had thus become wary of strangers, wherever they came from, though experience had taught them that they generally had more to fear from Arabs and Turks and Abyssinians than from the softer and more gullible Franks, as most Europeans were called.

They had particularly good reasons for being wary in that summer of 1898. The Shilluk, like the other Nilotic tribes of the southern Sudan, had suffered much from the Mahdist Arabs of the north who despised them because they were black, because they wore little or no clothing, and because they refused to abandon their traditional tribal beliefs for the faith of Islam. To ensure the subjection and humiliation of the Shilluk, the Khalifa had in 1892 deposed and killed the hereditary *Reth*, as the king of the Shilluk was called, and replaced him by a nominee of his own called Kur Abd al Fadil. If Kur Abd al Fadil ever forgot that he owed the power and the privileges of his position to the Khalifa, the gunboats and soldiers which were sent down from Omdurman to Fashoda to collect conscripts and grain were frequent and forceful reminders. In these circumstances neither the *Reth* nor his people wished to do anything which gave, or could be represented by an informer as giving comfort or encouragement to a stranger. At the same time the Shilluk did not fail to notice that the Frenchmen and their formidable-looking black soldiers were both well-armed and determined, or that they had considerable largesse to offer, from beads and bracelets to firearms. They therefore tried to steer a middle course composed, in roughly equal measures, of appeasement and deception. From the start the answers given to the strangers' questions, and the response made to their advances, were based on this principle. This process of obfuscation was facilitated by differences of language and difficulties of translation.

Nevertheless some of the answers given to the Frenchmen's questions were true. The deceptions came later. Fashoda, they were told, was four or five days journey by river, or three days as the long-legged tireless Shilluk did it on foot. No Europeans had arrived from the south. The old Egyptian fort at Fashoda was still unoccupied and in ruins. The forces of the Khalifa were still firmly established at Omdurman and Khartoum and in all the country to the north. There had been no news of the English coming from the north. Thus far the news was good from the French point of view. After all these years and months of hardship and endeavour they would be the first at Fashoda after all. 'Our joy', wrote Dr Emily in a cliché that seemed to have no frontiers, 'knew no bounds'.

To be on the safe side they camped for the night of 8 July on an island in the river. They had had a difficult day, with rain and high winds and a particularly troublesome school of hippopotomus. The reeds and the long grass on the island were so dank and sodden that the soldiers had to sleep in the boats. To cheer themselves up, and to remind them that they were close to their goal, they planned a special dinner, but because of the weather and conditions on their island they had to be content with their usual meal of 'chicken soup, boiled chicken, chicken sauté or roast chicken'. However Marchand drew on their still plentiful supplies of champagne for them to raise their chipped tumblers and tin mugs to drink a toast 'À la plus grande France!' The following day was better with a pale blue sky which reminded them of the Côte d'Azur, and a fair breeze and the good current took them smoothly through a countryside of fertile fields and neat huts nestling in the shade of palms and flat-topped acacia trees. The tribesmen waved to them and called from the bank of the river, and with nostalgic pleasure they heard the familiar sound of cow-bells and the lowing of cattle. The next day they paid a call on the *Reth*. After the customary exchange of greetings and gifts – two fine bulls for them and a high velocity rifle for him – they moved on down the river, and at five o'clock on the afternoon of Sunday 10 July 1898 they landed at Fashoda. It was a moment of great emotion for them all; for the Senegalese, it seemed, as much as for the Frenchmen. Baratier could hardly believe it. 'Nous sommes à Fachoda!!!' Two days later, in the presence of the *Reth* and his council elders, and with the officers and men all in their best array, Mangin in his newly-appointed capacity as 'commander of the garrison of Fashoda' gave the order Present Arms! Captain Marchand moved forward with all the dignity and deliberation he could muster, a taut, erect, unmistakably military figure, and declared in a voice ringing with pride and emotion 'Au nom de la France, je prends possession de Fachoda.' With the flagstaff ready and the French flag furled at its foot the order was 'Au drapeau!' The flag unfurled, fluttered in the wind and slowly rose, but half way up the mast the halyard broke and the flag fell to the ground. When at last the rope was replaced, and the flag reached the top, Baratier was still able to record in his memoirs that 'le pavillon français monte dans les airs, dominant le grand Nil, fleuve française.'

The emotion and the euphoria did not last very long. Fashoda, and getting there first, had for so long been their aim that it was not until the morning after their Bastille Day celebrations on 14 July that they began to see it as it really was. Fashoda was no more than a small hump of dry ground in a flat, soggy plain of black cotton soil. It was fiendishly hot during the day, and made pestilential by mosquitoes at night. The only shade was a clump of leggy palms, the only buildings the ruins of one of the series of Nile forts which Sir Samuel Baker and General Gordon had built twenty and thirty years earlier when, as representatives of the Khedive of Egypt, they had imposed a brief interlude of order and comparative peace on the southern Sudan. The fort had been destroyed by the Mahdist soldiers, and little remained: a few crumbling walls of mud-brick, a single arch tufted with grass, a courtyard smeared with slime, and a moat full of stagnant water. The only inhabitants were pale yellow scorpions and a few thin, black snakes.

Another disappointment was the lack of news about Bonchamps and the expedition from Abyssinia which they hoped would be waiting for them at Fashoda or in the vicinity. Some of the Shilluk had spoken of a party of Abyssinians 'with eight Europeans' having come as far as the mouth of the Sobat to plant some flags and then hurry away. Other Shilluk had spoken of there still being a large expedition with horses and mules not far away in the valley of the Sobat. On the strength of this report Marchand entrusted his official reports and a bundle of personal letters to some couriers provided by the *Reth*, and gave them a letter which he addressed to *Monsieur le chef de la mission française venant de la côte Somalis*, imploring him to forward the letters and reports to France, and to come to their aid as quickly as possible.

While he waited for the couriers to return Marchand put everyone to work. There was enough to do, and as a leader he knew that the less time they had to think and to brood the better. The ebullient Mangin, with his enthusiasms and his unhappy knack of upsetting his fellows, was given the task of reconstructing the fort so that it not only commanded the passage of the river but also provided protection against attack from the land. It its heyday Fashoda had had a garrison of 800 men, and the fort had been a sizeable affair with nearly 2,000 metres of fortified walls. With 3 officers, 2 French NCOs and 50 of the Senegalese soldiers still in the Bahr el Ghazal with the *Faidherbe*, the French force at Fashoda in July was of very limited strength. What Mangin did therefore was to use the old bricks to build an inner fort 35 m square, and to bring in the outside wall to form a perimeter of no more than 800 m with squat, powerful-looking bastions commanding the northern and southern approaches, each with a wide field of fire. It was the fifteenth fort which he and his Senegalese soldiers had laid out and built in the course of their 4,500 km journey across Africa, but it was the first time that these versatile and seemingly ever-willing men had turned their hands to bricklaying and masonry.

To keep the boats light, and to increase their mobility for the journey through the Bahr el Ghazal, Marchand and his advance party had taken as little as possible with them. Most of their supplies and reserves of food, ammunition and equipment had been left behind with the rear party and the *Faidherbe*. They knew that it might be some weeks before the *Faidherbe* reached Fashoda, and that it was important therefore that they should use local supplies, and, if only for reasons of health, that they should grow their own vegetables and fruit. Almost the first thing they did when they arrived therefore was to plant *haricots verts* in the rich Nile mud, and Landeroin was soon busy resuscitating and enlarging the gardens which had been established along the bank of the river by the old Egyptian garrisons. The vegetable plots and the fruit trees were carefully irrigated, and the seed beds protected by awnings made of palm leaves from the scorching heat of the midday sun.

To encourage the local people to bring in their produce Marchand set aside an area inside the perimeter for a market. As it was situated in front of Dr Emily's hut it afforded him more opportunities than he truly cared for to observe the daily comings and goings of the local people and the produce which they brought. Chickens and eggs were plentiful, together with smoky-smelling milk and rancid butter, and dark-coloured wild honey stippled with the corpses of insects and ants which had been trapped in their search for sweetness. The Shilluk also grew good crops of millet and beans, and fished in the river for perch. They owned large numbers of sheep and cattle but these, and particularly the cattle, they would as a rule only part with for iron which they could turn into spears. The vendors were equally various, according to Emily – 'les vieux, les jeunes, les petites filles et les vielles guenons'. The girls, he noted in his journal, were tall, long-legged and harrow-hipped, their foreheads encircled with three bands of cicatrice, their heads shaved. The right breast was generally covered, the other left bare. Dr Emily thought that on the whole the men were better proportioned than the women, and that, with their elaborate hair styles and the long, graceful sweep of the single garment they wore suspended from one shoulder, they looked as if they were 'contemporaries of Pericles and Augustus'.

On 1 August the couriers returned with their letters undelivered. They said that they could find no trace of Europeans in the valley of the Sobat. Marchand realized that he and his advance party were now in a dangerously isolated and vulnerable position. Their total military strength was 6 French officers, 2 white NCOs, 98 Senegalese equipped with light rifles, and 10 Yakoma boatmen armed with old-fashioned muskets whose cartridges had got damp and did not always fire. Their only transport was their five metal boats propelled by paddles and sails. With the Nile in spate, their ability to move upstream against both the current and the prevailing wind was restricted. They had had no news of the rear party and the *Faidherbe*. They did not even know if they had left. The best they could hope for was that they would reach Fashoda by the end of the month.

Marchand's sense of isolation was increased by his growing awareness of the danger he was in, not only from the Mahdists but also from the Shilluk. The Khalifa's position in Omdurman and Khartoum and the surrounding country was still strong and undisturbed, and as soon as he heard that Marchand and his band had invaded his territory and installed themselves in the fort at Fashoda he quickly announced that, whatever their nationality, they were foreigners and infidels, and would be attacked and destroyed. Marchand had long ago given up any hope of amity or even neutrality on the part of the Khalifa but he thought he could count on the promises of friendship and help made by the *Reth* and his people when they had arrived. It was some weeks before he realized that Kur Abd al Fadil was a man of many aspects, and that his affections and his support went in the last resort to whoever he thought was most likely to win. Experience had made him practised in the art of survival. He had no liking for the Khalifa or for his mainly Arab adherents but having been put in power by the Khalifa he was careful to repay his debt in the hard currency of tribute and aid. When the Khalifa's agents demanded conscripts for their armies he supplied them. When they asked for cattle and grain they were despatched without delay or question. But he was careful to see that it was not his own Shilluk kinsmen who bore the brunt of these demands. He used his greater numbers and military strength to ensure that it was his weaker neighbours on the other side of the Nile who supplied the bulk of the conscripts and the cattle. In this way he gained and kept the admiration of those among his subjects who disliked the way he had been appointed and who might otherwise have supported the claims of other pretenders to his throne.

In the same way he went through the motions of befriending the French when they first arrived while carefuly observing and assessing their strength and the reinforcements they were likely to get from the west and the east. When he realized that there was nothing coming from the east, and that there was little chance of the *Faidherbe* arriving before the end of August, he came to the conclusion that it would serve his interests best if he reported Marchand's present numbers and armament to the Khalifa's agent in terms which invited him to make an immediate attack. When

Marchand tried to reduce his isolation by inviting the *Reth* to place himself and his people under French protection Kur Abd al Fadil declined, and gently reminded the Frenchmen that, while he would never attack white men armed with rifles, he nevertheless controlled the surrounding country and could deny them supplies if he wished, and pick off any raiding parties which they might send out to forage on their own.

The Mahdist attack came on 25 August. The *Reth* did what he could to divert Marchand's attention but, when he realized that the French had got wind of the attack from one of their own informers, he proceeded to mass his own troops on the open ground behind the fort, on the grounds, as he blandly told Marchand, that the Mahdist forces 'were as much a danger to him as to the French'. He was thus in a good position to attack the fort if he saw that the French were being overrun. In this way he could appear as the loyal subject and ally of the Khalifa should his troops win, without actually risking the lives and ammunition of his own warriors in any hard fighting. He would also be well placed to move in and get a fair share of the loot. If, on the other hand, the French held their position he could claim that this was largely due to his refusal to join in the Mahdist attack, and demand a reward or some useful quid pro quo for his neutrality.

Marchand had expected to be attacked simultaneously from the river and the land, and had disposed his forces accordingly. He had expected to be attacked at dawn, and look-outs were therefore at their posts to sound the alarm when at six o'clock in the morning two gunboats appeared from the north. Behind the gunboat were seven lighters in tow. The gunboats were armour-plated and carried an array of cannon. In the lighters were about a thousand men armed with rifles and other, less up-to-date weapons. They were accompanied, according to custom, by a gallery of women whose presence and cries were calculated to encourage valour and discourage retreat.

The engagement lasted until mid-afternoon. Marchand devoted sixteen pages of his official report to it, and Baratier used his pen like a palette knife to paint the event in vivid colours. 'Sur la nappe blanchâtre du Nil', he began, 'deux grands vapeurs emergent confusément de la brume matinale . . .'. The Nile is about 600 metres across at this point, with two clear-water channels separated by islands of reeds. To take advantage of the range of their cannon the gunboats chose the channel furthest from the fort and opened fire from about 1,800 metres. It should have been decisive but the fire was so badly directed and the shells of such poor quality that the contest soon declined into an exchange of small-arms fire. Marchand calculated that a third of the enemy's shells failed to explode when they landed while others went off as soon as they left the barrel and splattered the river with shot. Once the gunboats came within range of the French Lebel rifles the advantage swung to the French. There it remained until the steamers had passed the fort and were out of range.

Marchand's position of advantage did not last long. With the Mahdist gunboats holding their positions 1,500 metres south and upstream of the fort he again found himself in an awkward situation. The *Faidherbe* might arrive at any moment, and he feared what would happen if she came unsuspecting round a bend in the river and found herself face to face with the Mahdist gunboats with guns at the ready, and a thousand armed men in the lighters. There was also the danger that if, as he expected, another Mahdist force advanced from the north on foot, he might have to deal with an attack on two fronts. Marchand immediately set off with Largeau and his section of 35 men. They slipped through the fields of millet and eventually took up a position where they had good cover and were no more than 600 metres from the gunboats. At this range they were able to pierce the armour-plating of the gunboats with their rifles, and cause havoc and panic among the closely packed men and women in the lighters. Still fearing a land attack Marchand and Largeau hurried back to the fort leaving a Senegalese sergeant and 8 men to continue the fusillade. Two hours later the gunboats, with their boilers badly damaged by the gunfire, broke off the engagement and started to make their way downstream. They made one more attempt to land a party of soldiers but this was foiled by rifle fire, and the gunboats and the lighters were subjected to a withering fire from the main body of the French garrison as they traversed the face of the fort. The superiority and self-confidence of the French was now such that Mangin was able to take a party of men out of the fort and pursue the enemy from the bank of the river for another four kilometres.

It was a dramatic victory achieved at the cost of five wounded soldiers. While celebrating that night Baratier recalled how they drank a toast to the memory of Saint Louis, 'soldier, pilgrim and explorer, like us, who made war against the infidel enemy as we did on the banks of the same river on 25 August, his own saint's day'. They re-named Fashoda, Fort St Louis. It was, they calculated, 650 years since St Louis had captured Damietta at the mouth of the Nile.[1] Their joy was tempered by the knowledge that the battle had cost them 14,000 rounds of ammunition. That left them with 28,500. As Baratier commented, 'Two more victories like this and we will be properly in the soup'.

Five days later the Khalifa's troops came again. This time, with their two gunboats out of action and most of the rafts sunk or adrift, they came on foot from the north. But just before the attack was due to develop the *Faidherbe* arrived at the fort from the south. The Mahdists withdrew, and Marchand and his small force were relieved to fight another day.

The arrival of the *Faidherbe* at Fashoda on 29 August 1898 was for the members of Marchand's expedition perhaps the most joyful moment of the whole expedition, and the one which they were to recall with the greatest emotion. 'C'est le Faidherbe. C'est la France'. Baratier wrote many years afterwards: 'Quelle moment! Quelle émotion poignante!' He confessed that it brought most of them to tears when the *Faidherbe*, with colours flying, passed in front of the fort at full steam with all its hooters and sirens at full blast. The deck of the steamer was lined with the French officers and Senegalese soldiers in their best uniforms as they saluted the huge French flag which Marchand had raised over the fort, and exchanged greetings with their companions and compatriots, waving their scarves and their caps in excitement.

The arrival of the *Faidherbe* at that particular moment was like an act of salvation. Without it they might have run out of ammunition, and been left to defend the fort and finally their lives with their bayonets. The *Faidherbe* brought them much-needed reinforcements of officers and men, fresh supplies of ammunition and other necessities, together with news from France and the outside world in official communications, newspapers, and private letters. The *Faidherbe* was also a lifeline for the future, a means of getting

---

[1] St Louis, the canonized title of King Louis IX of France, was a brave and honourable man but the sixth crusade which he took to Egypt was a disaster, and he was only able to enter Damietta after it had been abandoned. The actual date of the event was 1249; another awkward historical fact was that part of King Louis' crusading army consisted of a body of English knights and yeomen led by an ancestor of the marquis of Salisbury.

further reinforcements, further supplies and further news, and if needs be further orders. One other thing was accomplished with the arrival of the *Faidherbe*. It brought all the members of the expedition together in the same place for the first time since they had left France in the summer of 1896.

The arrival of the *Faidherbe* and the rear party at Fashoda at the end of August almost on schedule had not been achieved without considerable difficulty and danger. Because of the persistent low depth of the water in the river they had not been able to leave Fort Desaix until 19 July, six weeks after Marchand and his party had gone ahead. The going was made additionally hard by the fact that they were towing several heavily laden canoes and rafts packed with the expedition's equipment and stores. On the first day they could only manage to cover 3 km. Fortunately it started to rain, and the depth of the water improved. They were soon doing 30 km and more a day and making good progress until, on 29 July, they reached the beginnings of the swamp and the *sudd* of the Bahr el Ghazal. It took them 23 days to do the next 50 km. For their African soldiers and boatmen it meant long periods of pushing and dragging the *Faidherbe* and the rafts through the slime and the shallows, cutting a way through the reeds and the debris for up to fourteen hours a day, and sleeping night after night in the rafts and canoes. There was barely room enough to lie down and no protection of their nets from the tormenting swarms of mosquitoes. They finally reached clear water on 19 July. It was, Sgt Prat recalled afterwards, like entering another country. Although the going was much easier and life was more pleasant for them all they were running short of wood for the boilers in the flat open plains and the *Faidherbe* had to rely more and more on a breeze and her makeshift sail.

Among the letters and reports from France which reached Marchand with the *Faidherbe* was the news, now six months old, that Menelik had sent his armies to the west and that one of them under Ras Tassama had orders to establish an Abyssinian outpost at Nasir on the river Sobat. On the strength of this report Marchand decided that, despite the failure of the first couriers to find any trace of the Abyssinians in that area, he must at once send the *Faidherbe* to make a fresh search by river as far up the Sobat as it could get. Once again he entrusted this crucial mission to Baratier. Neither he nor Baratier wasted any time. Two days after the *Faidherbe* arrived at Fashoda after its journey of 42 days, Marchand gave Baratier his orders, and the following day, 1 September, Baratier set off, with Dyé as always in command of the *Faidherbe*, together with 24 Senegalese soldiers and 10 of the Yakoma boatmen, and 2 metal boats in tow.

It was another heroic journey, made no less heroic than Baratier's better-known exploits on the Mbomu and in the Bahr el Ghazal by the fact that it did not succeed. The first part of the journey up the Nile, and then for 150 km up the clear stream of the Sobat, presented no difficulties and only took them four days. Nasir had been a small river post in the days of the Egyptian occupation but, where Baratier expected to see an established Abyssinian outpost, he found nothing but the crumbling and overgrown remnants of a place long abandoned and forgotten. Continuing upstream to the point where the Baro and another tributary merged to become the Sobat, Baratier was faced with the problem of which river to take. He was now in an area of swamp and *sudd* similar to the Bahr el Ghazal, and the courses of both rivers, choked and overgrown as they were in a welter of evil-smelling debris and rotting vegetation, looked equally uninviting. The choice was not made easier by the confusing and conflicting answers he got from the local inhabitants when he asked if anyone had seen or heard of Ras Tassama's soldiers or any Europeans. Some said Yes and some said No; some pointed one way and some another; others just shook their heads or said nothing. In the end Baratier took the Ajouba, down whose left bank some of Tassama's men with Potter and Faivre had briefly passed two months before. Baratier struggled on for three more days in a bewildering mesh of choked water channels and inlets that led nowhere, but he found nothing except an occasional Abyssinian flag which had been left by Tassama's soldiers. Baratier was not a man who gave up easily but judging that it was likely to be a futile quest, and that he and his force might be more useful at Fashoda itself, he turned at this point and went back.

Baratier and the *Faidherbe* reached Fashoda on 14 September. Although he was disappointed and disturbed by Baratier's news Marchand again wasted no time. Dyé and his crew must have hoped for some respite but two days later they were sent off once again. This time it was Largeau who went with them with orders to go back to Meshra and there to send word back to the French authorities in Ubangi for immediate reinforcements of men, ammunition and supplies, and for a number of machine guns.

Marchand's wish for more men and armaments was understandable. All the indications were that the Mahdist forces would try again to dislodge him and to avenge their humiliating reverses. Although the Dinka and Shilluk tribesmen brought in stories of fighting and of English successes, Marchland and his companions had come to distrust these local reports, and they continued to believe that it was from the Mahdists that the next confrontation would come.

Marchand knew that the Khalifa could still call on large numbers of men who, though poorly armed and imperfectly supplied, generally turned out to be brave, determined and fanatical fighters in the field. Marchand and his force, however, had the confidence of an earlier success to lean upon, and since their last engagement they had almost doubled in number and had received fresh quantities of ammunition and supplies. They believed that they also had the support of the Shilluk; since 3 September they had a treaty, signed, sealed and witnessed to prove it.

Kur Abd al Fadil and his people had been impressed with the way in which a handful of white and black Frenchmen had repulsed and then almost destroyed a Mahdist force with gunboats and ten times more men. At that stage however, with the forces of the Khalifa re-grouping and determined to avenge their defeat, the Shilluk and their pragmatic ruler thought it wiser to confine their admiration to fair words and fat cattle rather than enter into any formal alliance. It was better to sit on the fence than to risk making a mistake about which side would win. But when the second Mahdist attack was called off, and Marchand's position was improved by the arrival of the *Faidherbe*, Abd al Fadil seems to have judged that it was time to come down on the side of the French. His decision was hastened by the news which his spies in Omdurman brought him of the Khalifa's declining power in the face of Kitchener's advance. Marchand had eased the *Reth*'s anxieties about the future by assuring him blandly that the French and the British were old friends, and he had gone on to paint a rosy picture of the Shilluk being protected by French soldiers and rifles from their tribal enemies like the Dinka and the Baggara, while benevolent French traders paid good prices in silver dollars for their grain and their livestock, or offered them in exchange all the marvellous merchandise of the west. Under these comfortable and broad umbrellas of protection and prosperity Abd al Fadil himself would continue to be the spiritual and secular ruler of his people; and his son after him, and his son's son, and so on, for ever and ever.

It was a happy prospect, and there was the equally persuasive argument that at the moment the *Reth* was left with little alternative. He therefore informed Marchand that he was now disposed to conclude a formal treaty of protection and friendship, and on 3 September he appeared outside the fort of Fashoda with an assembly of elders and chiefs to sign it. The treaty with its exchange of solemn affirmations and undertakings had been done by Landeroin into grandiloquent French and equally grandiloquent Arabic, neither of which the *Reth* or his elders understood. The treaty consisted of nine articles, starting with a declaration that, when the Egyptian administration had withdrawn in 1884, the Shilluk nation had recovered its independence, and that it was therefore a free agent in resolving now to place itself under French protection. Other articles dealt with matters of trade, and there were the usual assurances that all native institutions, customs, and beliefs would be respected except those which were 'contraire à la humanité'. On the French side it was signed by Marchand, Chief of the Congo-Nile expedition, officer of Legion of Honour and acting High Commissioner for the French Government in the Upper Nile and the Bahr el Ghazal. For the Shilluk it was signed by Kur Abdil al Fadil as the Sultan and legitimate hereditary ruler of the Shilluk nation, in the presence of Tiol, son of Adiangue; Kake, son of Dio; Bol, son of Ayouel, Kake, son of Niakouetch; Awet, son of Adjak-Koufal; Yor, son of Agouer; Ayik, son of Ding; Ding, son of Ring; Aker, son of Yor; Ouol, son of Agouer; Koug, son of Ador; Akiets, son of Abour, and Niadok, son of Ding.

Four days later a similar treaty was signed with the Dinka chiefs and elders on the other side of the river; and on 15 September Marchand issued an Order of the Day declaring that his expedition had completed its dual aim of 'occupying the Bahr el Ghazal and establishing French domination at Fashoda'. When he drafted this proclamation and inscribed it in the modest paper-covered exercise book in which he recorded all his orders and proclamations Marchand could be excused if he felt a measure of pride and satisfaction both as a soldier and as a Frenchman. He had got to Fashoda, and he had got there first. In particular, he had got there before the British. He had repaired and rebuilt the fort, and established himself there in a strong position. He had made treaties and established a chain of

posts in the Bahr el Ghazal and the upper Nile which could provide
the basis for permanent occupation and administration by France.
He had hauled and sailed the *Faidherbe* to Fashoda, and thereby
secured a means of communication and supply, at least during the
rains. In his memoirs Baratier allowed himself his moment of
euphoria too. Given a few more months to deploy the men and
materials and machine guns which would soon come on the
Faidherbe with Largeau, he calculated that if and when the British
did arrive they would not only find a well-armed garrison three
hundred strong at Fashoda, but a string of French flags flying from
forts and outposts which had been established with the agreement of
the local tribes and their chiefs throughout the basin of the upper
Nile. They would also find hundreds of keen and willing Azande,
Dinka and Shilluk warriors being trained by French officers and
Senegalese NCOs to protect their new possessions. And in the last
resort, should Marchand and his company be unable to sustain this
position for very long on their own, had not M. Hanotaux himself as
Minister for Foreign Affairs assured them on the eve of their
departure from France: 'You are going to fire a pistol shot on the
banks of the Nile; we accept all the consequences'.

A few days later Shilluk messengers, 'covered in sweat' as
Marchand later reported to Paris, came in with news of a huge
Mahdist force of five gunboats and thousands of soldiers coming up
the river on its way to avenge their earlier defeats. The French stood
to their arms, and Mangin manned his defences for the remainder of
the day and all through the night. At six o'clock the next morning
two black Sudanese soldiers splendidly uniformed in the gleaming
red tarbushes and khaki drill of Kitchener's army of the Nile
presented themselves at the fort of Fashoda, saluted with what
Mangin described to his sister as 'un raideur toute britannique',
typically stiff British formality, and handed Captain Marchand a
letter.

CHAPTER XIV

Confrontation at Fashoda

WHEN Lord Cromer sat down at his desk in Cairo on 15 June 1898 to draft a 'memorandum on the policy to be followed after the capture of Khartoum' he had little to go on in the way of formal instructions from the British government. Policy, if policy there was, seems to have consisted largely of a series of private and personal letters in Salisbury's own hand. They reflected a general feeling in Britain that the valley of the Nile should continue to be entirely and exclusively in the British sphere of influence. But they also reflected the distaste of most governments of both parties during the Victorian age for colonial adventures, and a marked reluctance to go to the trouble and particularly the expense of taking on any more overseas responsibilities, however much missionaries and merchants urged them to do so. This applied especially to what Salisbury had called 'useless territory' like the southern Sudan. If something had to be done to protect the headwaters of the Nile or to keep other nations out, and it became necessary to occupy the area, then this, he insisted, after a look at the map of a region he had himself never seen, should be limited 'mainly to the banks of the White Nile and a portion of the Blue Nile'. Cromer shared Salisbury's views if only because he suspected, with good reason, that Egypt would be expected to meet most of the cost.[1] Cromer was inclined to treat Egypt as if it were a public company of which he was chairman. In this capacity he had spent much time and care in putting his finances on a sound footing and in building up prudent reserves. He did not wish to see this upset by any unnecessary expense; nor did he want to have the invidious task of trying to persuade the Khedive and his ministers to impose new taxes on their subjects for distant benefits which they themselves were unlikely to appreciate or to share.

In these circumstances it was not surprising that what Cromer

[1] Cromer later calculated that the total cost of the Sudan campaign was £2,345,000 of which 'rather less than £800,000 was paid by the British', and the rest by Egypt. The British contribution was entered in the accounts as a 'non-repayable grant'.

suggested was a compromise. He proposed that after the capture of Khartoum two flotillas of gunboats should be despatched, one small one to go up the Blue Nile, and a larger one, if possible under Kitchener's own command, to go up the White Nile. Although the British and the Egyptian flags should be flown side by side, it was advisable that the gunboats should 'carry officers from the British rather than the Egyptian service and wearing distinctive marks of British uniforms'. Kitchener himself did not think that British troops were suitable for garrison duties in places like the upper Nile valley because of the climate and the isolation. In making this particular recommendation Cromer was more influenced by Wingate's view that it was important that some British troops should accompany the flotillas, partly because the Nilotic tribes had such bitter memories of the behaviour of Egyptian soldiers and officials in the Sudan in the past, and partly because, as he put it, 'the Abyssinians despise the Egyptians'. It was Cromer himself who had said that, while the White Nile flotilla might possibly find the French established there, it was more likely to be the Abyssinians. Whichever was the case Kitchener was to make it clear that her Majesty's Government laid claim to the whole of the White Nile valley. But, Cromer asked in a pointed and awkward aside, was he to lay claim 'in the name of the British Government, or of the Khedive, or of both combined?' Definite instructions, he pleaded, should be issued on this point.

There is little in the Foreign Office archives[2] to show how these proposals of Cromer's were received in the lofty corridors and cramped cubicles of power in Whitehall and Westminster. They do however contain the various drafts, eight in all, which were prepared in the Foreign Office before the matter was submitted to the cabinet. Cromer was in England at the time, and both he and Salisbury seem to have taken a hand in the drafting. Cromer was also present at the cabinet meeting on 25 July at which the draft was discussed and approved. It finally emerged as an official despatch from Lord Salisbury as Secretary of State for Foreign Affairs to

[2] The FO seems to have been mainly concerned with arguments about money; whether, for example, Egypt should pay for all the horses needed to bring the 21st Lancers up to war strength or only for those 'expended during the campaign'. There was much argument too about Press correspondents. Kitchener, who once told a clutter of newsmen, 'Get out of my way, you drunken swabs', did not want very many, though he later conceded that a few might come in useful as independent witnesses.

Cromer as British Agent and Consul-General in Egypt. It was dated 2 August 1898. The Queen's approval to 'this important despatch' was given in her own by now very shaky and barely legible hand.

After making it clear, with the hesitant parsimony which was so often a feature of British imperialism in the nineteenth century, that after the capture of Khartoum 'no further military operations on a large scale involving any large expense will be undertaken for the occupation of the provinces to the south', the despatch gave authority for Kitchener to send out the two flotillas of gunboats recommended by Cromer. Although it was laid down that 'nothing should be said or done which would in any way imply a recognition on behalf of Her Majesty's Government of a title to possession on behalf of France or Abyssinia to any portion of the Nile Valley', the despatch stressed 'the necessity of avoiding by all possible means any collision with the forces of the Emperor Menelek'. The instructions for dealing with the French were less specific:

It is possible that a French force may be found in occupation of a portion of the Nile Valley. Should this contingency arise, the course of action to be pursued must depend so much on local circumstances that it is neither necessary nor desirable to furnish Sir Herbert Kitchener with detailed instructions. Her Majesty's Government entertain full confidence in Sir Herbert Kitchener's judgement and discretion. They feel assured that he will endeavour to convince the French force, with which he may come in contact, that the presence of the latter in the Nile Valley is an infringement of the rights both of Great Britain and of the Khedive.

Although it had been laid down in the despatch that the British and the Egyptian flags would be flown side by side in the Sudan, Cromer's question about sovereignty was left unanswered; 'these matters', it was blandly stated, 'can be considered at a later period'. Cromer was nevertheless told to make it clear to the Khedive that HMG expected that 'any advice which they may think fit to tender to the Egyptian Government in respect to Soudan affairs will be followed'. It left little doubt that the British government intended to conquer and claim the Sudan in the name of the Khedive, and then run it themselves. The despatch was addressed to Cromer, and although a copy was sent to Kitchener early in August, it went to him in the form of sealed orders which were not to be opened until after Khartoum had fallen. It was one of the unusual features of the Sudan campaign of 1896–8 that Kitchener received his orders from the Foreign Office, and that all attempts by the War Office and

Wolseley to take control of what they scathingly referred to as 'this FO war' were firmly resisted by the formidable combination of Salisbury in London and Cromer in Egypt. To reinforce the point Salisbury arranged for one of his sons, Lord Edward Cecil, who was a captain in the Grenadier Guards, to be attached to Kitchener's staff as an ADC.

While this despatch was being drafted and considered Kitchener kept himself and his staff fully occupied from sunrise to sunset with preparations for the final advance to Khartoum. Early in July his railway reached Fort Atbara. In August the Nile started to rise, and by the end of the month there was enough water for Kitchener to bring his array of gunboats and transport steamers over the shallows of the 6th Cataract, and to concentrate a force of 25,000 men and 100 guns on the banks of the river north of Omdurman. There he was faced by a Mahdist army of between forty and fifty thousand. On 2 September the Khalifa launched an attack at dawn on a broad and very vulnerable front of five miles, and in the course of the next few hours lost 10,000 men killed and some 15,000 wounded or captured. 'At half-past eleven', Lieut. Winston Churchill[3] recorded, 'Sir H. Kitchener shut up his glasses, remarking that he thought that the enemy had been given a good dusting.' After a break for luncheon Kitchener rode into Omdurman. Two days later the British and Egyptian flags were raised over the former governor-general's palace at Khartoum and a funeral service was conducted in memory of General Gordon. When she heard of this and the slaughter that had taken place at Omdurman, Queen Victoria wrote in her journal 'Surely he is avenged.'

On 3 September General Kitchener opened his sealed orders. A week later, having despatched a small flotilla up the Blue Nile, he set off up the White Nile with five gunboats, a company of Cameron Highlanders, two battalions of Sudanese infantry, a battery of artillery and four machine guns. He also had with him a glittering array of rising naval and artillery stars. Kitchener was not the only eminent Victorian who liked to surround himself with personable and promising young men, but in this case he seemed to have a particularly good eye for those with the advantages and ambitions to

[3] The Foreign Office records show that Kitchener objected strongly but without success to the proposal that Churchill should be allowed to combine the duties of cavalry officer and special correspondent for the *Morning Post* in order to get to the front.

achieve distinction. Apart from Colonel Wingate, who became a general, and Lord Edward Cecil, his staff included Lord Roberts of Khandahar's son, Lieutenant Roberts, who was later to win a posthumous Victoria Cross in South Africa. Of the officers of the Sudanese battalions, Major Smith-Dorrien became a general and governor of Gibraltar, Major Jackson became a civil governor in the Sudan, and two of the young captains, Maxse and Capper became major-generals. The flotilla of gunboats was a nursery of famous admirals – Keppel, Cowan, Beatty, and Hood. There were no representatives of the Press.

They set out in good spirits. Few of them knew their destination or their purpose but after the anxieties and carnage and stench of Omdurman and Khartoum they all expected an easy respite and some good rough shooting. Even the matter-of-fact Wingate confided to his diary that he 'could not have managed another ten days like those just past' and, although he was probably the only one who knew what Kitchener's orders were, he too looked forward to a rest. He knew by then that Fashoda was their objective; one of the Mahdist gunboats which had been engaged with the French on 25 August had made its way back to Khartoum without knowing that it had fallen, and had been promptly captured and it's crew examined. They reported the presence of Europeans at Fashoda but, although they drew what looked like a tricolour in the sand, they confessed that all Europeans looked alike to them, and that they had no idea of their nationality. On its way up the Nile a few days later Kitchener's flotilla encountered the other Mahdist gunboat, the *Safia*. Despite the damage done by the French, the captain was still full of fight but eventually he was overcome, and he and the ship's supply of firewood and livestock were taken on board to sustain and guide Kitchener's gunboats through the sandbanks and channels of the Nile. By 15 September they had covered most of the 500 miles from Khartoum, and were within reach of Fashoda. Kitchener decided that it was time to give warning of his approach and so reduce the chance of an accidental clash; he also wanted to make the point, in case Marchand did not know, that he had taken Khartoum, defeated the Khalifa's army and was now master of the Sudan. When Wingate sat down to draft the letter on 18 September he knew it was probable that the Europeans at Fashoda were Marchand and his party but, as the Captain of the *Safia* was equally unable to tell one kind of European from another, he could not be certain. He therefore addressed the letter to the 'Chief of the European expedition at Fashoda'. The letter itself was written in French.[4]

It was sent off by hand of two Sudanese NCOs a few days later when Kitchener's flotilla was some 15 miles north of Fashoda. It was delivered to Marchand, as explained in the previous chapter, at dawn on 19 September. According to Wingate, Kitchener then halted for a day 'in order to give the French time to reflect and consider their position before composing their reply'. He may also have preferred to put off his arrival until he had got some indication of how he was likely to be received. Marchand read Kitchener's letter out aloud to his companions at half-past six in the morning and had completed and despatched his answer by half-past seven. It was a spirited reply, and Marchand had not needed any time to reflect and consider his position. After congratulating Kitchener on his victory at Omdurman, he went on, as one soldier to another, to detail his own exploits in taking possession of the Bahr el Ghazal and in concluding a treaty with the rulers of the Shilluk which, he said, effectively placed the whole area of Fashoda under the control and protection of France. Having thus firmly and unequivocally established his own position, he formally welcomed Kitchener to the upper Nile and expressed his willingness to receive him at Fashoda 'in the name of France'. The letter was signed by Marchand in his capacity as 'Commissioner for the French Government over the Upper Nile and the Bahr el Ghazal'. It was despatched to Kitchener in a whale-boat manned by the Yakoma boatmen smartly attired in brand new red jerseys, and displaying what Wingate described as 'an immense French flag'.

Having received Marchand's letter Kitchener continued on his way up the river, and at ten o'clock that morning the first of Kitchener's gunboats came into view of the handful of Frenchmen in the small, toy-like fort of Fashoda. It was an impressive sight as the five large gunboats in line astern appeared one by one and steamed slowly up the Nile to take position in front of the fort with flags flying, gunports open, the guns manned and ready to fire, and the decks lined with a force of some fifteen hundred British and

---

[4] The letter referred to the occupants of Fashoda as 'Européens quelconques', a somewhat derogatory phrase meaning 'Europeans of a sort'. The French not surprisingly thought it was meant as an insult but to be fair it seems to have been so more than an attempt on Wingate's part to translate what the captains of the Mahdist gunboats had told him in Arabic about not knowing what kind of Europeans they were.

Egyptian Army troops. With his victory at Omdurman behind him and the preponderance of force now at his command, and with the arguments for Britain's title to the valley of the upper Nile clearly spelled out for him in his instructions, Kitchener should have been confident and at ease. But, as Wingate confided to his wife, Kitchener had been 'rather staggered' by Marchand's letter. His orders were not to do or say anything which would imply that any country other than Britain had any title to any part of the Nile valley, and here was Marchand, not only calling himself Commissioner for the Upper Nile and making treaties, but formally welcoming Kitchener in the name of France to part of a territory which Kitchener believed he himself had just conquered. Wingate's diary and letters make it clear that Kitchener had had 'some private letters', presumably from Cromer, and that his course of action when he met Marchand had also been discussed with Wingate on their way up the Nile from Khartoum. 'Of course', Wingate told his wife, 'the Sirdar and I had talked over all that he was going to do'. Wingate indeed claimed that it was he who persuaded Kitchener to fly only the Egyptian flag on the gunboats except for the one carrying the Cameron Highlanders. Kitchener had not liked this departure from the strict letter of his written orders but in the end he agreed. 'Damn it', he is said to have said, 'have it your own way!' Wingate also seems to have persuaded Kitchener to wear his Egyptian Army uniform, and he confided to his wife that he had had to urge an out-of-sorts Kitchener 'to be firm and stick absolutely to what we had arranged'.

Kitchener was apparently still nervous and ill-at-ease when, at half past ten, Marchand came on board the gunboat to pay an official call. In the end, however, Wingate was able to tell his wife that 'K., I am glad to say, pulled himself together and spoke well'. Marchand was accompanied by Germain, his second-in-command, and Kitchener had Wingate. As neither Marchand nor Germain spoke English the meeting was conducted in French. Kitchener spoke French but with an unmistakably Anglo-Saxon accent, and he chose his words with the same slow deliberation that he used when he spoke English. This not surprisingly made many of his French listeners smile, and lent itself to imitation which was not always kind.[5]

---

[5] Kitchener learnt his French as a boy when his eccentric and restless father lived in Montreux, and at Dinan in Brittany; and later when he served as a volunteer with a French army field ambulance during the Franco-Prussian war of 1870.

First-hand accounts of what was said on board the gunboat *Dal* vary according to the nationality of the writer and the time when they were written. General Smith-Dorrien, then a major, watched the proceedings through field glasses from another gunboat; 'After much bowing and scraping and saluting, what I supposed was a map was spread out on the table, then followed much gesticulation and apparently angry conversation. Distinct signs of hostility on both sides.' There seems little doubt that to begin with both Kitchener and Marchand were touchy and suspicious, and allowed themselves to be upset by small matters of procedure and protocol. The first exchanges were formal and frigid. Kitchener explained that he had orders to regain Fashoda in the name of the Sublime Porte and His Highness the Khedive. To this Marchand replied that he had had orders from the French government to occupy Fashoda and other parts of the upper Nile which had been abandoned by Egypt and were therefore without any lawful owner. When Kitchener declined further argument, and drew attention instead to his preponderance of force, Marchand's answer was that until he received orders to retire he and his companions were ready to die at their posts rather than haul down their flag. When Kitchener observed that such a situation could lead to war, Marchand's response was what Baratier described as *une profonde inclinaison de tête*, a solemn nod of affirmation. Having thus delivered themselves of the awkward burdens of their official instructions and their prepared statements, Kitchener and Marchand were able to relax and appraise one another as individuals and as soldiers. Marchand who, like most French army officers of his time, tended to admire but dislike the rich and successful English, found that a cautious regard for the tall, taciturn, red-faced, brusque, blue-eyed Kitchener was gradually overcoming his instinctive aversion, while Kitchener's conventional feelings of scorn and contempt for everything French became overlaid with a certain grudging respect for the enterprise and courage shown by Marchand and his companions. In these circumstances both men were able to move towards a practical and honourable resolution of the situation with which they were faced. They agreed first of all that the rights and wrongs of the British and the French positions in the upper Nile were outside their competence and should be referred to London and Paris. Meanwhile Kitchener would not require Marchand to haul down his flag or retire, while Marchand for his part would raise no objection to Kitchener hoisting the Egyptian flag at Fashoda and leaving a garrison there. Kitchener did not raise the question of putting up the British flag side by side with the Egyptian, and this judicious departure from his original instructions seems also to have been at Wingate's instigation. Wingate and Germain were then sent ashore to settle the details on the ground, and once the awkward questions of where exactly the flag and the garrison should be installed had been resolved to both parties' satisfaction, the atmosphere again improved. It was at this point that Smith-Dorrien saw through his glasses that a servant was climbing the ladder to the top deck 'with a tray of bottles and glasses, and these, full of golden liquid, were soon being clinked together by the two central figures who, until that moment, I had believed, were engaged in deadly combat.' The toasts of The Queen and The President of the French Republic were then drunk in lukewarm whisky and soda. Marchand was to say later that drinking 'cet affreux alcool enfumé', that ghastly smoky liquid, was one of the greatest sacrifices he was ever called upon to make for France. Nevertheless the atmosphere continued to thaw, and Marchand and Kitchener were soon to be observed leaning over the maps, describing their recent exploits of adventure and conquest to each other in detail and patting one another on the back in a flurry of mutual congratulation.

At three o'clock in the afternoon Kitchener returned the call, attended by other members of his staff, including Lord Edward Cecil who spoke excellent French. Although the Frenchmen were full of apologies for the modesty of their quarters and most of the tall British party had to bend their heads to get through the low doorways, Marchand had taken care to dress all his officers and men in gleaming new uniforms which had only that morning been taken out of the tin-lined cases in which they had been packed for this purpose in France three years before. His British visitors were duly impressed. They were equally impressed with the quantity and the quality of the wines which were set before them, notably the sweet champagne in which toasts were now drunk in rapid succession to a variety of occasions, causes and personalities. Wingate listened carefully, like the good intelligence officer he was, as the tongues of his hosts became loosened and less guarded in the increasingly convivial atmosphere. Kitchener was not a drinking man, and despite the obligations of the toasts in sweet champagne, his glaucous, cod-fish eyes seemed to have kept their customary, watchful glaze. He noted that some of the Frenchmen laughingly confessed that it had been a great relief when they discovered that the flotilla of gunboats advancing up the Nile towards them had been the friendly British instead of the ferocious Mahdist forces returning to the attack. He noted too that Marchand admitted that some of his men were sick or fatigued, and needed to be relieved, and that he had had to send the *Faidherbe* back to Meshra er Rek for reinforcements and fresh supplies. Wingate had brought the latest French papers which he had had sent specially up from Cairo. This should have been a rare joy to the Frenchmen but, as they reported the fall of yet another French government and the disturbing details and revelations of the Dreyfus affair, they were a mixed blessing. Marchand confessed afterwards that 'an hour after we opened the French papers the ten French officers were trembling and weeping . . . and for thirty-six hours none of us were able to say anything to the others . . .'

As Kitchener was leaving the French encampment he noticed some zinnias growing in the garden below the fort. *Oh! des fleurs! des fleurs à Fachoda! Oh ces Français!* the usually undemonstrative Kitchener was reputed to have exclaimed. Landeroin, who was in charge of the gardens and their produce, thereupon bowed and gathered not only a bunch of flowers but a basketful of peas, French beans, cabbages, and other products of his kitchen garden for presentation to the English general. This was said to have evoked cries of astonishment and admiration from the English officers who had imagined that in their isolated predicament the French must lack such luxuries as green vegetables. It came as a shock in this atmosphere of euphoria when, at the last minute, Kitchener told Wingate to deliver a sealed envelope, and informed Marchand that it was a formal protest at his presence on Egyptian and British protected soil. This done, he added that he was setting off immediately for the junction of the Sobat and the Nile to hoist his flag, and would then return straight to Khartoum. Before Marchand had time to read the letter of protest and compose a reply Kitchener had boarded his gunboat and departed. He left behind him a battalion of Sudanese infantry about 600 strong under Major Jackson, with a gunboat and four guns. As Baratier noted in his journal, the Egyptian flag was well guarded.

CHAPTER XV

Kitchener's Despatch

It was about 60 miles from Fashoda to the mouth of the river Sobat. Wingate noted in his diary that on 20 September they stopped for the night 20 miles south of Fashoda, and that he was busy preparing letters to be despatched from the Sobat to Emperor Menelik, to Harrington, the British agent in Addis Ababa, and to the 'OC Troops, Uganda'. The letter to Menelik made it clear, in language that was more military than diplomatic, that the British were now taking possession of both sides of the White Nile, and that any claim which Menelik may have made in the past to any part of the Nile valley had been nullified by the discovery of evidence in the records of the Khalifa captured at Omdurman that while ostensibly a friend and ally of the Queen he was conspiring with the Khalifa. Kitchener reached the mouth of the Sobat the following day, and finding no sign of any French or Abyssinian flags, he left an Egyptian garrison and a gunboat there, and was away by half-past four from what both he and Wingate quickly decided was a thoroughly unhealthy and unprepossessing place.

That night Wingate recorded in his diary that he had 'a long talk with Sirdar on general nature of despatch after which spent all day writing it; it is short and to the point – almost too short for my liking as it appears to me that all these incidents require very full and careful attention'. Much care went into the exact wording of this despatch to London, and, it seems, some argument too.[1] The early part dealt briefly with Kitchener's meetings with Marchand, and it was conceded that 'during these delicate proceedings nothing could have exceeded the politeness and courtesy of the French officers'. It was the concluding paragraphs which presented the most difficulty and were the most drastically crossed out and re-worded. The final version stated that Marchand

holds at Fashoda a most anomalous position – encamped with 120 men on a narrow strip of land, surrounded by marshes, cut off from access to the

[1] Six preliminary drafts of the whole or parts of the depatch are now in the government archives in Khartoum.

interior, possessing only three small boats without oars or sails and an inefficient steam-launch which has lately been despatched on a long journey south, short of ammunition and supplies, his followers exhausted by years of continuous hardship, yet still persisting in his impracticable undertaking in the face of the effective occupation and administration of the country I have been able to establish.

It is impossible not to entertain the highest admiration for the courage, devotion and indomitable spirit displayed by M. Marchand's expedition but our general impression was one of the utmost astonishment that a great nation like France should attempt to carry out a project of such magnitude and danger with so small and ill-equipped a force which, as their commander remarked to me, was neither in a position to resist a second Dervish attack nor to retire – indeed, had our destruction of the Khalifa's power at Omdurman been delayed a fortnight in all probability he and his companions would have been massacred.

The claims of M. Marchand to have occupied the Bahr-el-Ghazal and Fashoda Provinces with the force at his disposal would be ludicrous did not the sufferings and privations his expedition endured during their two years arduous journey render the futility of their efforts pathetic, and, in this land of contradictions, none, I venture to say, rank higher than the pretensions of M. Marchand, with his handful of men, to be High Commissioner of the Upper Nile and the Bahr-el-Ghazal – such claims are more worthy of *opéra-bouffé*[2] than the outcome of the maturely considered plans of a great Government.

The despatch was drafted, completed and signed on the gunboat *Dal* on 21 September, and when they returned to Omdurman on the 24th it was given to Cecil to take to Cairo for transmission to London. Although the despatch itself did not get to England until October a summary of it was telegraphed to the Foreign Office on 29 September. Meanwhile Kitchener had sent off two telegrams from Omdurman on 24 and 25 September; as they both reached London on the same day they were sent they provided the first news to reach Europe about the meeting at Fashoda and the situation of the French expedition. Kitchener's two telegrams conveyed the gist of his despatch but in some respects they painted an even more dramatic and desperate picture of Marchand's position: 'The position in which Captain Marchand finds himself at Fashoda is as impossible as it is absurd. . . . The futility of all his efforts is fully realised by Captain Marchand himself and he seems as anxious to return as we

2 Comic opera.

are to facilitate his return.' 'If', Kitchener concluded, 'the French government will at once give telegraphic instructions for the explorer M. Marchand and his expedition to leave Fashoda and come down the Nile I can now send special steamer with such orders to fetch them. I am sure no one would be more pleased than M. Marchand and his officers to secure release from their unpleasant position.'

When Kitchener's despatch was perused in the Foreign Office, parts of it, including the whole of the final paragraph, were thought to be so questionable or in such poor taste that they were side-lined with question marks or carefully bracketed for omission should it ever be published or communicated to the French government. There were in fact few parts of the despatch which were not misleading or untrue. Marchand was said in the despatch to be 'on a narrow strip of land, surrounded by marshes, cut off from access to the interior'. The site of the fort at Fashoda had been chosen with care by General Gordon when he was governor-general of the Egyptian Sudan precisely because it was protected by marshes on the landward side, yet was easily accessible by river both from the north and the south at all seasons of the year. Equally misleading was the statement that Marchand only had 'three small boats without oars or sails and an inefficient steam-launch'. Marchand had five small boats, all equipped with sails, paddles, and punt poles. The sails may have been makeshift but they caught the wind, and, although the paddles and poles were roughly made and oddly shaped, in the expert hands of the Yakoma boatmen they were very effective. Wingate may have scorned their home-made appearance but they gave the French a mobility and a quick and easy way of crossing the Nile which the British garrisons lacked. The *Faidherbe* was still on its way back from Meshra when Kitchener and Wingate were at Fashoda, and they therefore never saw it themselves, but Major Jackson, who got to know it only too well during the weeks he spent there, thought it faster and easier to handle than any of Kitchener's gunboats.

Nor was there any evidence to support Kitchener's assertion that the French were short of ammunition and supplies. With the arrival of the *Faidherbe* on 25 August they had replenished their stocks less than a month before the British arrived, and there were few essentials which they lacked for their defence or their day-to-day

living. The French may have been short of some of the things which
the British thought important, like tea, bully beef, toothpaste and
toilet paper but in regard to those things which the French believed
made for a civilized existence – wine, fresh vegetables, music, good
food, and female company both for themselves and for their soldiers
– they were better off and better organized than the garrisons which
Kitchener left on the river or, for that matter, Kitchener's own
headquarters when he was in the field. The contrast between the
situation of the French and the British contingents in the fort at
Fashoda was vividly described by the commander of the British
force himself:

The French force occupied the ruined town and fort of Fashoda which were
situated on a small knoll – the only rising ground in the neighbourhood. The
Anglo-Egyptian camp lay some 300 yards to the south of the French. The
low-lying land on which it was placed was covered with tall rank grass and
became a veritable quagmire after the torrential rains which fell every
afternoon and generally during the greater portion of each night. . . . And
the equipment of the troops was not of a nature to add vastly to their
comfort in such adverse conditions. . . .

The French were in better case to withstand the discomforts of a tropical
rainy season. Each soldier was provided with an excellent type of waterproof ground-sheet which could also be used as a sleeping-bag if desired; he
carried in addition a small but serviceable mosquito-net which added
considerably to his comfort. His light kit was carried in a waterproof bag.
Stores and supplies were packed in hermetically-sealed tin cases of a size
and weight for a porter's head. Rifles were provided with waterproof covers
and belts and straps of the equipment were made of stout canvas.

In the Anglo-Egyptian force one blanket per man constituted the sole
protection against the inclemency of the weather. Neither tents nor waterproof sheets had been provided, and mosquito-nets were unheard of.
Under the tropical downpour and the attacks of myriads of mosquitoes but
little rest was obtainable between sunset and sunrise. Kits were carried in
coarse canvas bags which were anything but waterproof. Equipment which
was made of leather became hard and uncomfortable to wear from constant
exposure to the wet and heat. Supplies were stored in sacks and no
waterproof sheets had been provided for their protection. Perishable stores
were in a state of transition – biscuits to pulp and flour to dough, while
vegetable rations of lentils, onions and beans showed signs of vigorous
growth and sprouted in the sacks.

In fine it must be admitted that, while the French were admirably
equipped for service in a tropical climate, the Anglo-Egyptian force was

lacking in practically everything which might ameliorate the conditions of
service in such a country. . . .[3]

When Kitchener in his luxurious three-decker gunboat passed
Fashoda on the way back to Khartoum from the Sobat, it was noted
that the soldiers of the garrison were 'busily engaged in drying their
clothes and blankets and clearing the ground of the rank grass'.
Kitchener did not stop but he signalled to Jackson by semaphore,
'Glad to see steps you are taking to make men comfortable'.
Jackson wisely kept his thoughts to himself.

Another questionable statement in Kitchener's despatch was that
Marchand was said to have told Kitchener that 'he was neither able
to resist a second Dervish attack nor to retire'. What he did say, and
what Baratier and others later told Wingate and Cecil, was that they
had heard from the Shilluk that a large force of Dervish gunboats
and soldiers was coming up the river to make a second attack, and
that they were very naturally relieved when they discovered that the
force was British. As to withdrawing, had he wished Marchand
could always have taken to his boats and escaped from Fashoda.
There is no evidence however that he ever thought of doing so, and
the indications are that he, together with his officers and his
Senegalese soldiers, remained confident to the end that they could
defend themselves against any Mahdist attack.

Perhaps the most misleading parts of Kitchener's despatch were
those in which he sought to cast doubts over Marchand's claim to
have occupied 'the Bahr-el-Ghazal and Fashoda provinces', and to
give credence instead to his own claim to have established 'an
effective occupation and administration of the country'. Kitchener
had, with his usual thoroughness and expedition, set up a military
administration of the country north of Khartoum but when he paid
his fleeting visit to Fashoda and the mouth of the Sobat he had had
neither the time nor the means to have done the same in the south;

---

[3] This extract is from an article which Major Jackson wrote many years later for
the semi-official publication, *Sudan Notes and Records*. He was somewhat less
circumspect in the private letters which he sent at the time from Fashoda to Wingate
and others in Khartoum. In one he wrote: 'Another d___able night, heaviest rain
yet, all drenched to the skin and all *tukls* (circular thatched huts) down, camp
ankle-deep in mud and water. Up best part of night . . . wading about and hauling
men out of debris of fallen *tukls*, no catch Fashoda in rainy season. . . . Rain or
millions of mosquitoes by night. . . . They bite through coat and trousers, so you can
imagine what men suffer. No women for men, and Shilluks and Denkas are most
particular. Something will have to be thought out. . . .'

and when soon afterwards he tried to send a gunboat into the Bahr el Ghazal it was stopped by the *sudd* short of Meshra er Rek and had to turn back. Marchand and Liotard on the other hand had between them by this time established a chain of outposts and garrisons throughout the Bahr el Ghazal and the country of the Azande. Marchand himself had been flying the French flag at Fashoda for over two months, and had concluded treaties with both the main tribes of the vicinity. Although Kitchener reported that the *Reth* of the Shilluk 'absolutely' denied making such a treaty and was 'delighted' to welcome the new Anglo-Egyptian administration, the evidence is that he did sign a treaty and that his denial was no more than a tactical move in what was for him a continual struggle for survival.

If Kitchener and Wingate had misrepresented the French position at Fashoda in one or two particulars it could have been due to misunderstanding or excess of zeal. But the number and range of the misrepresentations make it more likely that they were calculated and deliberate. There is also the evidence that Kitchener told Jackson not to accept any letters from Marchand or his companions, nor to allow them to use the Nile route either for their official reports or their personal letters. The result was that for the first crucial weeks the only accounts to reach the outside world were Kitchener's own. As Smith-Dorrien admitted, Kitchener 'wished the French and British governments to consider his own reports before any representations from Marchand could reach them'.

Kitchener's secret instructions were to use all possible means except actual shooting to get the French out of Fashoda. Provided there were 'no corpses', as Salisbury put it, he could do what he liked. This no doubt encouraged him to conclude that, if he himself failed to persuade Marchand to go, the next best thing would be to present the situation in such a light that the French government might be induced to instruct Marchand to leave. Records now in the archives at Khartoum suggest that Kitchener had already made up his mind before he got to Fashoda that it would serve his purpose best if it appeared that he had come to 'rescue' Marchand and his gallant little band from an impossible situation. This may have been another reason why he took no press correspondents with him to Fashoda, and why he prevented Marchand from using the Nile route for his own reports. With no reliable means of communicating with French agencies in Abyssinia or Jibuti, and with messages routed through the Bahr el Ghazal and the Congo still taking several months to reach France, Marchand had no means of letting his government know his own version of events or his own appreciation of the situation.

The Facts and the Fictions

THE day after Lord Salisbury saw Kitchener's first telegram from Omdurman on 25 September 1898 he sent a private note to the Queen saying that Marchand's position was 'very uncomfortable, that he was short of ammunition and supplies and anxious to get away'. The following day he sent copies of both of Kitchener's telegrams to Sir Edward Monson, the British ambassador in Paris, with instructions to read them aloud to Delcassé, the new French minister for foreign affairs but, he added, 'you had better not leave a copy'. As Delcassé's English was of politician rather than ambassador standard, Monson had the telegrams translated into French before he showed them to Delcassé, and then summarized the contents in an *aide memoire* which the minister could take away and show to his colleagues.

It was an awkward moment for Delcassé. He had only been in office for a few months since the fall of the previous government in June. There was perhaps a certain poetic justice in his now having to deal, as foreign minister, with the consequences of a project, the foundations of which he had himself laid when he was minister for the colonies. It was in any case embarrassing for a minister to have to depend on the ambassador of a rival foreign power for information about one of his own country's ventures, and in having to ask, as Delcassé anxiously had to ask Monson, if there had been any bloodshed; a few weeks earlier, on 8 September, Monson had reported that Delcassé had confessed that 'he did not know precisely where Marchand was as news took so long'. He had added, with one of his rare attempts at humour, that 'as the British force were so admirably served by all the applications of civilisation, he should soon have direct and speedy information of Captain Marchand's whereabouts'. It was a pleasantry he was soon to regret. The French government itself had had no news from Marchand since the end of June, and the report which it had received then was dated December 1897. It had taken six months of runners with cleft sticks, canoes, paddle-steamers and ocean-going ships for the report to get from Marchand's straw hut at Tambura to the Pavilion de Flore in Paris.

Marchand had said in December 1897 that he hoped to reach Fashoda in May 1898. His report had been addressed to the minister for the colonies, but between the time it was written and the time it arrived, the change of government had brought in a new and inexperienced minister named Georges Trouillot. The permanent staff of the ministry, encouraged by the *Comité de l'Afrique fran-çaise* and other interested elements, ensured however that he was not slow in taking action on two matters which Marchand had insisted in his report were of urgent importance. One was that after three years, 'dans les conditions excessivement dures et fatigantes', the members of the expedition should be relieved and replaced by fresh men, and that its stores and equipment needed to be replenished. The other was that he should be given clear and up-to-date instructions on what he should do when he reached Fashoda. Sending replacements of men and materials, such as a new boiler for the *Faidherbe*, was something which the department could and did manage on its own. For instructions, however, it was necessary to consult the ministry for foreign affairs, and on 4 July 1898 Trouillot wrote to Delcassé saying that he would like to hear 'your department's views on the tasks which the expedition should then undertake', adding that it was 'essential and of the greatest urgency to send Marchand precise instructions so that he will know what to do when he meets Kitchener's army'.

Despite this plea, and two reminders, it was two months before he got a reply. Delcassé and his wife were at their villa on the Côte d'Azur in August but it was not merely annual holidays at the seaside or in the country that was responsible for the delay. There had also been a difficult and protracted process of reappraisal. The answer, when at last it emerged on 7 September in a letter from Delcassé to Trouillot, was devious.[1] The reasoning was logical and clear; what made the letter devious was that it tried to make what was really a *volte-face* on Delcassé's part look as if it were no more than a matter of words.

---

[1] Another devious aspect of this letter was that Delcassé, or one of his officials at the Quai d'Orsay, tried to cover up the delay in sending a reply by giving the date of Trouillot's original letter as '4 Septembre'. The archives show that this was crossed out in blue pencil when Delcassé's letter reached the colonial ministry, and the correct month 'juillet' firmly inserted in the margin.

When, as minister for the colonies, Delcassé had launched Monteil's and Liotard's missions to the Nile, he had been prepared to accept, even to welcome a confrontation. At that time in 1893 and 1894 the only competitors in sight were the Belgians, and Colonel Colvile's supposed incursions from Uganda. Now, as minister for foreign affairs in 1898, he was faced with an entirely different situation. In the first place there was Kitchener's advance in the Sudan. In 1894 it had not even begun; by the time Trouillot's letter reached the Quai d'Orsay in July 1898 Kitchener was well on his way to Khartoum. By the time the reply had been sent on 7 September Kitchener had already taken Khartoum, and a confrontation between the small French force and a large Anglo-Egyptian army seemed inevitable. Another factor was the failure of Bonchamps and his companions to establish a base on the Sobat or to provide a means of sending reinforcements and supplies to Marchand through Jibuti and Abyssinia. Nor was it only in Africa that the situation had altered. The balance of power in Europe had also changed. Where once the Germans were encouraging and supporting French efforts to contest the British position in Egypt and in other parts of the world, in 1898 Kaiser William was one of the first and most fulsome with his congratulations on the British victory in the Sudan. It now suited him to placate and please the British government in the hope, among other purposes, of inducing it to support what von Bulow, the German foreign minister, described as 'our own very moderate demands for possessions in other parts of the overseas world'.

Delcassé knew, of course, that by the time he came to reply to Trouillot's letter, there was no possibility of fresh instructions reaching Marchand in time for him to act on them. It did however provide him with an opportunity of putting himself and the government in a better position should anything go wrong if and when Marchand and Kitchener came face to face. In his letter Delcassé therefore advised that Marchand should not now go as far north as Fashoda but should 'establish himself if possible on an island in the vicinity of the confluence of the Sobat and the Nile'. To escape any charge of inconsistency on his own part he tried to give the impression that this had been his intention all along. He went on to suggest that Marchand should concentrate on improving his communications with the upper Ubangi rather than push forward. If however he did happen to encounter Kitchener he should explain that he was merely protecting the approaches to the French possessions in the

Congo basin, and engaged, like the British, in a civilizing mission against the iniquities of the Mahdist regime. Any questions of national rights or claims that might arise should be referred to Paris for discussion with the British government.

Having thus, as he hoped, adjusted his position in tune with present realities Delcassé felt able to relax. When Monson saw him a few days later, he told London that 'having been hitherto used to encounter M. Hanotaux's petulance and hysterical susceptibilities on every occasion of contention, I was favourably impressed by the calmness displayed by M. Delcassé at this interview'. Delcassé had then assured Monson that there was really no such thing as a Marchand expedition; it was, he said, no more than a continuation of the instructions given to Liotard many years previously gradually to extend French influence towards the Bahr el Ghazal, and to take no steps which might give rise to a conflict.

Delcassé seemed in an equally relaxed and amenable mood when Monson had shown him Kitchener's telegrams on 28 September and expressed the hope that the French government would soon feel able to send orders to Marchand to withdraw. 'I can but hope', Monson told the Foreign Office, 'that his colleagues will be equally sensible.' Like Salisbury in England, Delcassé tended to conduct his country's foreign affairs as if they were his private domain, and with as little reference to his officials and his political colleagues as he could contrive. The situation at Fashoda was however clearly a matter which he had to take to the President of the Republic and to the Council of Ministers. Delcassé's usual behaviour at meetings of the Council of Ministers was parodied with exquisite exaggeration by Anatole France in his *Island of Penguins*:

The dwarf came into cabinet meetings with a brief case bigger than himself and crammed with papers. He remained silent and answered no questions, even those put to him by the venerable President of the Republic. Soon afterwards he fell asleep, tired by his incessant work, until all that was visible above the green baize table was one small tuft of hair.

On this occasion however he had little chance of remaining silent. What he remembered of Kitchener's telegrams, and the brief *aide memoire* which Monson had given him, did not by any means satisfy his colleagues, and he came under particularly strong pressure from Trouillot. Relations between Delcassé and Trouillot personally, and between their two departments had been frayed for some time.

Delcassé and his often supercilious officials at the Quai d'Orsay did not always bother to keep Trouillot informed about their negotiations with other governments on overseas matters, while Trouillot and his more robust ex-colonial officials at the Pavilion de Flore[2] seemed for their part to have ignored Delcassé's attempts to limit Marchand's activities, and continued to send him reinforcements of men and supplies.[3] In view of all the efforts which he and his department had made to meet Marchand's demands, Trouillot was not unnaturally incensed at the implication in Kitchener's telegrams that Marchand was short of ammunition and other items. After a heated discussion the Council of Ministers decided that it could not properly assess the situation solely on the basis of information furnished by its opponents or, as Delcassé put it more diplomatically to Monson the following day, the French government 'would be embarrassed to act without first seeing the report of its own agent'. As instructions to Marchand would take several months to reach him by the Congo route Delcassé asked Monson if a telegram could be sent *en clair* to Marchand at Fashoda via Cairo and the Nile route. The British government grudgingly acceded to this request but tried to make the worst of it by saying that they were merely conveying a message 'to a French explorer who finds himself in a difficult position on the Upper Nile', Kitchener warned that it might take some time for such a telegram to reach its destination. The official English version of the French telegram was short and to the point: 'Congratulations. We will not forget your services. You are promoted colonel. We have had Kitchener's account. Please send us your own, and your appreciation by hand of an officer to Cairo.' The full text in French was considerably longer and less laconic, and the crucial last sentence asking for '*les indications que vous êtes vous-mêmes en mesure de me fournir sur cet incident et sur la situation existant antérieurement à Fachoda*', went to 56 words.

Delcassé's telegram was despatched from Paris on 1 October, and reached Omdurman the same day. Kitchener sent it on a few days later in the gunboat *Kaiber* commanded by Captain Hood. Having

---

[2] The head of the African Affairs section was Gustave Binger, a tough and very able ex-Marine and former governor of the Ivory Coast.

[3] According to a British military intelligence report sent to the Foreign Office on 4 October 1898 three separate parties of men and supplies for Marchand and Liotard had been sent to the Bahr el Ghazal between February and May 1898, and a further party had left France on 9 September with 16 officers under Captain Delafon to pick up a 'strong force of Africans at Dakar'.

seen the text of Delcassé's telegram, he gracefully added his own congratulations to Marchand on his promotion. As it was the first time Kitchener had allowed any communication with Fashoda, both he and Wingate took the opportunity to despatch presents of tinned food and wine to the Frenchmen as a small return, as they put it, for the fresh fruit and vegetables which had been presented to them on their visit to Fashoda. The kindness was appreciated by the French, though some of them could not but observe afterwards that sending wine and tinned food, of which they had plenty, was like carrying coals to Newcastle, or taking water to the river, as the French say. The *Kaiber* reached Fashoda on 9 October, and Baratier left the next day with Marchand's report in his pocket and a number of personal letters hastily written by other members of the expedition. Although Baratier and Hood's ability to communicate with one another on the *Kaiber* was limited by the fact, as Baratier said, that 'he knew as much French as I knew English', at Omdurman Baratier was given a splendid tent with two rooms, a carpet and furniture such as he had not seen for years, and royally entertained by British officers whose good French made him ashamed of his own lack of English. He eventually reached Cairo on 28 October, and spent most of the first night sending off transcripts of Marchand's report to Paris by telegraph.

Delcassé was not the only member of the French council of ministers who hoped that Marchand's report would make everything clear, and resolve everyone's doubts. Attitudes and feelings on both sides of the Channel had hardened since Kitchener's accounts had become public knowledge, and both the aggressive faction represented by Trouillot and the colonial ministry, and the more cautious European faction represented by Delcassé and the Quai d'Orsay hoped, even prayed, that it would support their point of view and prove that each had been right. In the event both were disappointed, and Delcassé, who had hoped for so much, dubbed Marchand's report *déroutante* or confusing. The factual report and the expert appreciation which Delcassé had asked for turned out to consist largely of copies of the telegrams which Marchand had composed between 10 July and 27 September, the originals of which he had tried without success to send via Abyssinia. His account of the meeting with Kitchener was unhelpfully bare and brief, and his most recent appreciation of the situation had been written as long ago as September. It was a perplexing mixture of good news and bad, of satisfaction and depression. 'Nôtre situation politique', he wrote, 'est excellent . . . but it will deteriorate as time goes on in view of our opponent's superior strength.' They had plenty of ammunition[4] and supplies but the 'situation sanitare', the health of his officers and men gave cause for anxiety, and it was essential that they should be relieved as soon as possible. 'We are cut off on all sides. It is impossible to put up any longer with the conditions of isolation and imprisonment which the English have imposed on us here, and, if in 12 days I get no orders by the Nile route, I will risk going off in a boat to Khartoum to demand communication with Paris. . . .' 'This' Marchand concluded 'is all I can put on paper. I think I would be more use to you in Paris. I await your decision.'

Marchand must have known that his report was incomplete and inconclusive, and he had indeed expressed his regret for 'the lack of first-hand information when you need it most'. The only excuse which he offered himself was 'his inability to communicate with France by other routes'. Others suggested that the *Kaiber*'s stay at Fashoda was too short for Marchand to compose a full statement but, apart from the fact that Marchand had had plenty of time for writing since Kitchener's visit, Jackson was later to make it clear that he had offered to hold the *Kaiber* at Fashoda if Marchand wished for more time to complete his report. It is difficult to avoid the conclusion that Marchand left gaps in his report deliberately in the hope that he would be summoned to Paris himself for further questioning. This would enable him to stir up support for his case, and to try and stiffen what he rightly believed, from his reading of the latest French and English papers, to be the wavering resolve of the French government.

In fact however when Delcassé heard that Baratier was bringing the report to Cairo he sent instructions for him to come on to Paris before he had even seen what was in the report. These instructions were waiting for Baratier when he arrived, and the demand for his presence in Paris was so insistent and urgent that, after sitting up all night transmitting the text of Marchand's report to Paris by telegraph, poor Baratier had to leave early the following morning without being able to enjoy any of the enthusiastic welcome and civilized diversions which his countrymen had laid on for him. It was

---

[4] Marchand reported that they still had 90,000 rounds.

less than he deserved and considerably less than he had hoped for. Even the sea journey to France, which could have provided him with a few days of relaxation, was marred by the discovery that General Kitchener was on board the boat to Marseilles. Although they both sat at the captain's table, and exchanged polite civilities, Kitchener's presence caused what Baratier termed 'un certain froid à bord'.

Baratier reached the *gare de Lyon* in Paris after ten o'clock on the night of 26 October. It had taken him and his companions over two years to reach Fashoda, mostly on foot or in small boats and canoes propelled by paddles. The journey by the Nile route, by train and in vessels propelled by steam, took him exactly 16 days. Despite the lateness of the hour, Baratier found an immense crowd waiting to greet him and give him a hero's welcome. Even the platform, he noted, was 'black with people', and outside the station a crowd of five thousand or more was so thick that he and his carriage had difficulty in getting away.[5] It was an enthusiastic crowd, a cheering, shouting, gesticulating, alternately laughing and weeping crowd which engulfed Baratier in a choppy sea of handshakes, embraces and two-cheeked kisses. It greeted him with cries of 'Nous resterons à Fachoda! Nous y resterons!' The cries evoked in Baratier emotions of joyous pride and anxious relief in roughly equal quantities. He was both happy and relieved at this seeming evidence that his countrymen took pride in Marchand's achievement, and shared his determination not to retreat. He had need of such reassurance. That very morning on the train he had seen reports in the papers that the French ambassador in London had asked the British government to provide Marchand with food and ammunition, and to rescue him and his party from their hopeless plight. Baratier knew that this could only have been done on instructions from Paris, and it was with a sinking feeling in his heart, therefore, that he saw that the welcome which had been arranged for him at the station had been attended by private personages like Étienne and Colonel Monteil and other representatives of the *Comité de l'Afrique française* but not by any notable member of the government. Baratier was due to see Delcassé the following morning. He knew that the foreign

---

[5] Or, as Baratier himself put it, 'mon omnibus ne peut se dégager de la foule' – the omnibus being the kind of horse-drawn conveyance which, in that happy era, used to take people at a leisurely clip-clop from the station to their hotel, and which in this case had been hired to take Baratier to his father's house in *avenue de Villars*.

minister had called him to Paris before seeing Marchand's report, and he was beginning to wonder, despite the tumultuous welcome he had received first at Cairo, then at Marseilles and finally in Paris, whether Delcassé and the French government had not already made up their minds about what they would or would not do at Fashoda.

The Moment of Decision

BARATIER'S appointment with the French foreign minister was for eight o'clock in the morning. Ministers and officials at the Quai d'Orsay may have had a reputation for being away from their desks at midday from twelve to three, and of leaving early to visit their *cinq à septs* before going home to their wives in the evening, but with M. Delcassé in charge they seem to have started work considerably earlier than was the custom in Whitehall. When Baratier arrived Delcassé advanced to greet him with his arms and eyes raised theatrically to heaven, as if resigned to forces beyond his control. It was not long before Baratier began to suspect the sincerity of his congratulations and the quality of his intentions. At another meeting the following day Delcassé plied him with questions about the state of their supplies at Fashoda, and about their health and morale, until Baratier finally came to realize, with a mixture of surprise and shock, that far from wanting to know how long they could hold out, the minister was looking for excuses to recall them. Having angrily and acidly assured Delcassé that they lacked neither food, ammunition, weapons nor will, Baratier turned on his heel and left the room. Later that day he took his perplexity and his anger to M. Étienne and the *group colonial* in the Chamber of Deputies.

Baratier would have been less surprised if he had been in Paris, or had seen all the French and English papers during that autumn of 1898. It has been explained how, when Delcassé came to reply to Trouillot's letter on 7 September, the realities of the international situation had already induced a touch of caution into his earlier enthusiasm for Nile expeditions. By the time he had seen Kitchener's telegrams, and taken the meeting at Fashoda to the council of ministers at the end of the month, his caution had become more pronounced. Paris was not the only capital in Europe where those who had their ears to the ground thought they could detect the first unlovely sounds of politicians changing course.

By the end of September both Delcassé in Paris and de Courcel in London had come to realize that Salisbury and the British government were now unlikely to accept the force and logic of the French arguments. The French case was still that in international law the basin of the upper Nile was *res nullius*, and belonged to no one by right, and could therefore be claimed by whoever got there first; if this were questioned, it could still be maintained that the French occupation of Fashoda and the Bahr el Ghazal gave France at least the same title as the British claimed at Wadelai, and the Belgians at Lado. The difficulty was that neither Salisbury nor Monson were any longer prepared to argue along these or any other lines. They took their stand in the valley of the Nile on the less arguable proposition that might is right. As Delcassé told his wife in a private letter on 28 September, 'All we have is arguments, and they have soldiers on the spot . . .'. Another reason why Delcassé was beginning to think he might have to give way at Fashoda was a further deterioration in the domestic situation in France. The alleged rights and wrongs of the Dreyfus affair continued to reveal deep emotional and intellectual divisions which were being exploited by the forces of both the right and the left with diminishing regard for the merits of the case itself. The popular demonstrations, strikes, and clashes with the police which erupted in October helped to deter the government from taking a stand which could lead to a conflict with England which a divided France was in no position to wage, and for which no one wanted to pay.

In these circumstances the most that Delcassé could hope for was to extract some concessions from the British in exchange for ordering Marchand and his men to withdraw from Fashoda. When Marchand's expedition was first conceived in 1895 the expectation was that it could be used to oblige the British to refer the whole question of Egypt and the Nile to an international conference at which France would be entitled to a large say and a share of the spoils. When these hopes had to be abandoned for lack of support from those like the Russians whom France had thought were her friends, there still remained the possibility that Marchand's achievements would enable France to retain a part of her gains in the Nile valley. When this too became a pipe dream because of the speed and scope of Kitchener's advance from the north, Delcassé still believed that if he played his hand with finesse and skill, he might yet be able to persuade the British to allow him to keep some of the Bahr el

Ghazal or at least a port on the Nile river system in exchange for withdrawing Marchand from Fashoda.

This was not mere wishful thinking on Delcassé's part. He had good reasons for believing in the autumn of 1898 that Salisbury might be willing to make some such concession in return for a quick and painless solution to what in some respects was also an awkward situation for the British. Delcassé knew that Salisbury desired good relations with France as a counter to the growing power of Germany; that he preferred diplomacy to force in the settlement of international disputes, and that he and his Conservative colleagues wanted to avoid doing anything risky or costly which might send down the price of Consols or put up the rate of income tax. De Courcel got on well with Salisbury, and Delcassé had learnt from him privately that Salisbury's real interest in the Nile valley was confined to the main course of the White Nile between Lake Victoria and Khartoum, and that he had no wish to assume the burden of administering and paying for what he had already dismissed as 'tracts of useless territory' and 'wretched stuff' like the Bahr el Ghazal. He also knew from his various official and private sources in Egypt that Cromer shared this view.

Although Delcassé and Salisbury had met briefly on Salisbury's way through Paris to his villa on the French riviera, negotiations were conducted at first between Delcassé and Monson in Paris, and later and more fruitfully between Salisbury himself and de Courcel in London. Such negotiations were necessarily delicate and secretive at the best of times, and they were complicated in this case because they had to be conducted against a background of increasingly strident opposition and suspicion in the press and the parliaments of both countries.

In France the opposition to Delcassé's conciliatory approach was brought to a head when he took the issues raised by Marchand's meeting with Kitchener at Fashoda to the council of ministers on 26 September. Angered by the imputation that they had neglected to keep Marchand properly supplied with men and materials, and already suspecting that the devious Delcassé was planning to avoid rather than relish a confrontation, Trouillot and his supporters engineered a series of resolute articles in right wing papers like *Le Gaulois* to make it as difficult as possible for the government to withdraw or to compromise over Fashoda. One article in particular on 27 September quoted Trouillot in terms which promoted Delcassé to tell Monson that 'it was a pity his colleague could not hold his tongue'. The headlines were framed both to catch the eye and to stir the emotions: 'Marchand cannot be disavowed or recalled!'. 'The hour of tergiversation is past . . . the heroism of Marchand and his soldiers must not be thrown away.' 'The honour of the flag is at stake!' To support this heady stuff the hundred or so politicians who formed the *group colonial* raised their voices and shook their fists in the Chamber of Deputies. With the government already under strain as a result of domestic issues a group of this size was not to be taken lightly. It also made it politically necessary for Delcassé to indulge in a number of flamboyant gestures and statements in public, both to protect his political flanks and his public rear in France and to impress the British and others abroad of his determination and intransigence. Even the cynical Monson was impressed. In late September and early October he was telling London in a series of melodramatic telegrams that Delcassé was not bluffing when he said that France would rather go to war than give way. As evidence he quoted *Le Matin*, generally regarded as Delcassé's mouthpiece, with its headline on 5 October 1898 that 'the only answer worthy of France is No!'.

On the other side of the Channel Salisbury faced similar pressures. Some of the strongest pressure came from Liberals in opposition like Rosebery, Asquith, and Grey, and from former Liberals like Chamberlain who had crossed the floor of the House in the 'eighties in protest against Gladstone's leanings towards Irish Home Rule. The imperialism of these Liberals and Liberal Unionists was based perhaps more on political realities than on enlightened principles. Their enthusiastic support for occasional colonial adventures and clashes with foreigners may not have appealed to their intellectual admirers in Bloomsbury and Cambridge but it did attract the cheers and the votes of large numbers of those who worked with their hands. Little wars in Africa, and confrontations with the French and the Russians were often more popular with the masses than with the middle classes who had to pay for them in increased taxes. Rosebery was thus on firm political ground when he said in a speech at Epsom on 13 October that no British government which showed signs of giving way at Fashoda would last a week. The Fabians and the *Daily Chronicle* might preach that British policy in Egypt was hypocritical, and that the upper Nile was not worth a war but the Yeovil Working Men's Liberal Association was closer to the grass roots of British society when on 20 October it attacked the government for weakness over China and praised it for its firm stand on Fashoda. In England the exuberance and bellicosity of the press, and its lack of moderation, truthfulness and good taste was even more marked and more widespread than in France. Even *Punch* disgraced itself with a cartoon in which an organ-grinder's monkey was depicted wearing a French army uniform.

Although many of the journals in France also devoted themselves, as Monson explained in one of his long-winded despatches, to expressing 'opinions of the type to which, in the current vernacular, the epithet "Jingo" has been consecrated', he reported that the general feeling in France was lukewarm and pacific. While emotions and verbal bellicocity were easily aroused by talk of the national honour and the flag, there was an underlying, hard-headed bourgeois assessment that no real French material interests were at stake in the Nile valley. Hanotaux, out of office and anxious to return, judged it politically opportune to express the opinion that 'nobody knew where Fashoda was or cared three straws about the Marchand expedition', and scathingly described the Bahr el Ghazal as 'a country inhabited by monkeys and black men worse than monkeys'. Hanotaux was not the only ambitious politician who noticed that some of the strongest opposition to a war with England over Fashoda was expressed in the provincial papers of the rich, sea-port towns of Marseilles and Bordeaux, and the solid centres of trade like Lyons and Toulouse. It was no coincidence that the same point of view was put forward in England in north country journals like the *Manchester Guardian* which did not think that the Bahr el Ghazal was worth a war and saw no reason why the French should not be allowed to keep it.

Against this public background of push and pull the search for an acceptable compromise in London and Paris continued in private for several weeks. The nearest the two parties came to an agreement was on 12 October when de Courcel and Salisbury had had a long and amicable discussion in London. On the strength of a decision reached by the French council of ministers on 3 October Delcassé had let it be known that he was now ready to withdraw Marchand from Fashoda if, as Monson put it, 'we can build a golden bridge for this retrograde movement'.[1] What he meant by a golden bridge was

[1] It was probably Delcassé himself who inspired an article in *Le Matin* on 10 October which argued that 'the abandonment of Fashoda is perfectly compatible

some concession in the Bahr el Ghazal which would enable him to claim that it had only been made possible by Marchand's heroic exploits, and that it was he, Delcassé, whose diplomatic skill and tenacity had achieved it. When de Courcel put this forward in their talk Salisbury responded by suggesting verbally that Marchand should retire from Fashoda and from all the places in the Bahr el Ghazal which he had occupied on the tacit understanding that the question of allowing the French to have some outlet on the Nile would be considered later when present passions had died down. De Courcel not surprisingly tried to translate this vague undertaking into something more specific. Both he and Salisbury became cautious to the point of vacuity when it came to putting undertakings and commitments into words, and in reporting what de Courcel had said to him Salisbury commented that 'the extreme indefiniteness of his language, and the rhetorical character he gave to it . . . made it difficult to know what his proposition was'. The meeting ended with Salisbury saying that while he would consider the ambassador's proposals he thought it might be better 'to wait until they were submitted in a more precise and tangible form rather than enter upon a discussion which under the circumstances would have been fruitful of misapprehension'.

In the letter which he wrote to Salisbury that evening the French ambassador was far from indefinite. He made it clear that the outlet which France claimed and which was hers by right was the whole of the Bahr el Ghazal and the Bahr el Arab. This was more than Salisbury himself had in mind, and considerably more, he knew, than his own colleagues and the Liberal leaders would be prepared to accept. He hastened to reply, in a letter of frigid Englishness, that 'but for the information contained in your letter I would have quite misunderstood the effect of our conversation'. With de Courcel fearing that he had not asked for enough, and Salisbury concerned that he had offered too much, the last chance of a negotiated settlement was lost. It was not the only occasion when misunderstandings occurred over what exactly was said or not said on the

with the national honour. We must realise that it is imprudent to saddle ourselves with useless and extravagant policies, and with annexations in the Mountains of the Moon which might, for all the good they are, be on the moon itself'. 'France', it continued 'had to resist the hungry edge of appetite lately shown by the *parti colonial* for the acquisition of fresh black territories and for the responsibility of governing more cannibal tribes.'

subject of Fashoda. On 10 October, for example, the British government took the step, unusual in diplomatic practice, of issuing a Blue Book containing the text of the communications exchanged while negotiations between the two governments were still in progress. Two weeks later the French government riposted with a Yellow Book of its own. Neither publication was calculated to facilitate calm and dispassionate consideration of the problems involved, and comparison of the records of discussions made in French and English by each side led Monson to remark on 'the impossibility that a long conversation between the two disputants . . . can be reproduced identically by the two parties concerned'.

Although Delcassé was still confiding to his diary on 23 October that his terms remained: 'Recognise an outlet for us on the Nile, and I shall order Marchand's withdrawal', he was already on the edge of persuasion by de Courcel, and by President Faure himself,[2] that there was now no hope of the British negotiating so long as Marchand was still at Fashoda. Even Salisbury, who was reported by de Courcel to be 'less intransigent at heart than his colleagues, his adversaries and the general run of English politicians', was no longer inclined or able to make any concessions, or indeed, do anything to sweeten the pill for Delcassé. Perhaps the last straw was when Salisbury failed to respond to Delcassé's impassioned plea, as one man of affairs to another, that unless he was given something he would have to resign and would be replaced by someone more difficult and 'more combative'.[3] De Courcel's advice was to withdraw from Fashoda unconditionally without further ado, and to hope that one day in the future there might be an opportunity for 'une petite négociation sur le Bahr-el-Ghazal'. Extra force was given to this pragmatic advice by the disclosure in the *Pall Mall*

[2] Félix Faure, President of the Republic 1895–99, had been closely connected with colonial expansion in the 'eighties and was one of the founders of the *Comité de l'Afrique française*. However he thought Marchand's venture was a foolish mistake, and came out in favour of withdrawal from Fashoda. A rich, self-made man of humble origin, the grand style of living he adopted as president earned him the nickname of 'Le Roi Soleil'; criticized once for not taking sides on a controversial issue he replied 'What do you expect? I am the equivalent of the Queen of England'.

[3] The fragile combination which made up the Brisson government fell apart on 25 October. After a few days' tactical hesitation Delcassé placed himself, his parliamentary following and his newspaper at the new government's disposition, and thus achieved an uneasy but continuous succession at the Quai d'Orsay. Such frequent changes of government at moments of crisis in France caused Salisbury to observe 'in such a confused situation an ultimatum was hardly necessary'.

Gazette on 28 October of the decisions taken by the British cabinet the previous day. These decisions were said to be:

1. Marchand must be withdrawn unconditionally; no promise or undertaking to be given as to access to the Nile or such like.
2. When he has withdrawn, this and other matters will be considered on their merits.
3. Every facility for withdrawal will be given.
4. If Marchand is not withdrawn there will be no interference with his remaining at Fashoda, nor will any date for his withdrawal be fixed. No reinforcements will be allowed to reach him. He will be treated courteously as a foreign visitor, and regarded in no other light.
5. It will therefore be left to France to adopt any active measures that would precipitate a conflict.
6. As precautionary measure the Mediterranean Fleet would be strengthened.

Confirmation from the French naval attaché in London of British fleet movements, and a report from one of Delcassé's secret agents in England, said to be a 'well-placed Englishman', that the Cabinet had been 'obdurate and unanimous', may have helped to convince Delcassé and his new colleagues that there was now no alternative to unconditional surrender.

Having made up its mind to give way the French government applied itself to the familiar tasks of finding excuses and scapegoats. 'The problem is', Delcassé wrote in his diary, 'how to combine the demands of national honour with the necessity of avoiding a naval war which we are absolutely incapable of carrying through, even with Russian help.' It seems unlikely on the evidence now available that the French government ever seriously considered the possibility of using force to resolve the situation at Fashoda, and there is no doubt that in 1898 the French navy would have been no match for the British. With its bases at Gibraltar, Malta and Alexandria, its numerical superiority and its wide range of conventional warships the British navy was a formidable force. The French navy on the other hand was in a vulnerable state of transition, and contained such a mixture of old models and experimental designs that it was called a *flotte d'échantillons*, a fleet of samples. Delcassé judged that in a conflict with the British it would be at the bottom of the sea in a fortnight.

Although the weakness of the French navy was a crucial factor it was not something which could be admitted by any politician or used as a reason for withdrawing from Fashoda. Delcassé might be able to pretend to Monson privately that Marchand had gone to Fashoda 'on his own initiative and in an excess of zeal' but this too was an excuse which he knew could neither be advanced nor substantiated in public. In the end Delcassé and his colleagues came to the conclusion that their best line of defence lay in claiming to withdraw Marchand and his force in their own interests, because they were short of food and ammunition, and suffering from sickness and exhaustion. This, of course, tallied with the picture and the excuse temptingly offered by Kitchener which the written report that Baratier brought back from Marchand himself did little to dispel. It contained enough disquieting news for Delcassé to write in his diary after he had read it: 'So my line is clear – if England does not accept my proposal I publish Marchand's journal and recall the heroic band'. He must have hoped, when he summoned Baratier to Paris, that Baratier himself would provide enough first-hand evidence of shortages, and of ill-health and low morale to support Delcassé's case. De Courcel had even suggested calling Marchand himself to Paris for the same reason on the grounds that he would be 'the most convincing advocate for an order to withdraw'.

In the event Baratier was a disappointment. He proved to be not only unhelpful in providing such evidence but an ardent and angry exponent of the contrary view that Marchand and his men had both the means and the will to remain at Fashoda. When Delcassé learnt that Baratier had been to see Étienne and *group colonial* in the Chamber of Deputies, and had told them that there was nothing in the situation at Fashoda to warrant the French government giving way, he angrily ordered him to return immediately to Cairo. When Baratier asked what instructions he was to take back to Marchand he was told that they would be waiting for him when he returned. By half-past eight that evening he was on the train to Marseilles, and on the following day, 30 October, three days after he had arrived full of hope and excited pride, he was steaming back to Alexandria in a mood of bitter disillusion and black despair.

A few days later, on 3 November, having telegraphed his instructions to Cairo, Delcassé instructed de Courcel in London to inform the British government that 'in view of the precarious situation and state of health of Marchand and his companions the government had decided to leave Fashoda'.

CHAPTER XVIII

The Withdrawal

THE French government's decision to abandon Fashoda was tele-graphed to the chargé d'affaires at Cairo on the morning of 3 November. The timing could not have been more aptly or cruelly contrived as it was the day on which Marchand himself arrived at Cairo. In his preliminary report from Fashoda he had asked for permission to bring the rest of his report to Paris himself. He had added that, if he did not get an answer in twelve days, he would, as he put it, 'risk going off in a boat to Khartoum to demand com-munication with Paris'. Marchand was as good as his word. On 24 October, that is after a lapse of 14 days, he begged a passage to Khartoum for himself and Sgt Dat on one of the British supply vessels, and with the help of the various British civil and military authorities along the way, he reached Cairo by special train in the very quick time of ten days.

Delcassé had not been at all pleased when he heard that Mar-chand had left his post at Fashoda for Cairo. He was afraid that people would think that he had authorized Marchand to leave while he himself was still engaged in negotiations with his own colleagues in Paris and with the British in London. He described Marchand's action as 'an incredible and unpardonable escapade'. Nor, at a time when he was about to say that the expedition was being withdrawn from Fashoda for its own safety and welfare, was Delcassé pleased to be told by the French representative in Egypt that Marchand had arrived 'in very good health', and claimed to have left the post at Fashoda 'in the best possible state from all points of view'. Nor was this the end of Delcassé's embarrassments. When Marchand reached Cairo and learnt of the French government's decision to withdraw from Fashoda, he sat down and composed a telegram to the minister for foreign affairs. It was despatched in cypher at four o'clock in the morning, and was couched in terms which suggest that he had been very well dined and wined by his compatriots in Cairo. 'At a time', he signalled, 'when the ministry of foreign affairs must be so distressed about our retreat from the Nile it is not appropriate for me to speak of my own heartache but I must say that the decision to evacuate, without even waiting for the rest of my reports, is to abandon unchallengeable rights acquired by us, and an excellent position. . . .' He went on to express his *stupéfaction prodigieuse* at Kitchener's deliberate misrepresentation of the true situation at Fashoda – 'our political position was strong; in the matter of supplies we had enough ammunition to deal with five Dervish attacks, and enough food to sustain the Europeans for a year and our African soldiers for a good two months . . .'. As to suggestions that they were bottled up by the British garrison at Fashoda, '. . . all I need is ten minutes to wipe out Jackson's troops and his guns'. 'If', he went on, 'there is any question of anyone needing an escort to move in this area, it is they and not I who need one. Here in central Africa I am *chez moi*, in my element.' He concluded with a poignant plea: 'How can I command the respect and obedience of my African soldiers if they see with their own eyes that France is at the end of the road?'

Delcassé's reply did nothing to soothe Marchand's feelings. He tried to argue that no rights had been surrendered. 'All we have done is to accept that, as you yourself have always said, Fashoda does not provide a satisfactory all-weather outlet on the Nile, and to accept the reality, based on your own experience, that it would take too long for the reinforcements and replacements which you say you need to reach you.' 'Not justified', the signal continued, in a rare lapse into telegraphic brevity, 'in exposing the expedition to the risks and hardships you yourself have described, and the government has therefore decided that the outpost should no longer be regarded as essential.' The last part of the message, the nub of the argument, was pointedly addressed to the chargé d'affaires rather than Marchand himself: 'Marchand has not the authority to engage the whole of France in defence of his position'.

By this time Baratier had arrived from France with his own account of his visit and of the contrast between the enthusiastic warmth of his reception by the public in Marseilles and Paris, and the unwelcoming coldness of his meetings with Delcassé. This encouraged Marchand to send off another telegram in terms which revealed the feelings of seething anger and contemptuous scorn which they both now had for the politicians in Paris. When Lefèvre-Pontalis, the French consul-general in Egypt hesitated to transmit a telegram in these terms, Marchand threatened to send it *en clair* through the Egyptian Post Office. The text of the telegram was as follows:

Must accept this terrible decision as imposed on us by the international situation but I absolutely refuse to accept your public explanation that reason for withdrawal is the bad situation of the expedition. If you insist you must recall me and send someone else to do it. I will only do it if you give the real reason i.e., the general political situation. I would rather resign than do as you say.

There was no reply from Delcassé but two days later a telegram from the ministry for the colonies went some way towards meeting Marchand's point with the statement that 'in the interests of France as a whole the government has decided not to keep its post at Fashoda'. Coming from the ministry which had issued the orders for the expedition in the first place, and which had since been its strongest supporter, this was like a *coup de grâce*, the merciful cutting of the throat of a victim being burnt at the stake. From now on, most of the telegrams and despatches both on the French side and the British were concerned with the arrangements for evacuating the French force at Fashoda and the disposal of its stores and equipment. Both the British government in London and the British authorities in Egypt and the Sudan offered practical help, and even a gruff Anglo-Saxon brand of sensitivity, to try and make this awkward operation as painless and dignified as could be; the British can be as ungraceful as anyone in defeat but in victory they often display generosity and tact. This did not stop Kitchener and Cromer, and Salisbury himself for that matter, making it clear, sometimes brutally clear, that things would be made thoroughly difficult if the French tried to stay on at Fashoda or to delay their departure. Marchand and Baratier, for instance, were not allowed to leave Cairo for Fashoda until they had committed themselves to early evacuation. By going to Cairo, and thus becoming completely dependent on the British for their return to Fashoda, they had both unwittingly underlined the weakness of the whole French position on the Nile.

The first thing that had to be decided was the route. Various possibilities were considered, of which return by the way they had come was the least attractive.[1] For a mixture of altruistic and

[1] Marchand told Delcassé in a letter from Cairo that he would have a revolt by his African soldiers on his hands if he was forced to go back through the Bahr el Ghazal and the Congo.

Machiavellian reasons the British offered the temptingly easy facilities, speed and comfort of the Nile route. This was obligingly accepted by the French government in Paris, and as proudly and stubbornly rejected by Marchand. Alternative routes by way of Khartoum, Suakin and the Red Sea, which would not expose Marchand and his men to the view of the Egyptians and the scorn of the European communities in Cairo, were also rejected. Having disappointed and humiliated Marchand in every other way, the least the French government could do now was to let him have his own way on this point, and Marchand and his companions were adamant in insisting that they should be allowed to finish their journey in the way it had started, that is to say, that they should continue to use the same means – the *Faidherbe*, the whale-boats and canoes, and their own physical resources and strength to go up the Sobat as far as they could into the heartland of Abyssinia, and then complete their crossing of the continent by whatever local means were available through Abyssinia to Jibuti.

This in the end was the way they went but it was not achieved without disagreement and argument. There were immediate objections from Kitchener and Wingate who suspected that Marchand wanted to go via Abyssinia, not so much to save face as to try and impress French influence on the peoples of the Sobat valley. For this reason orders were sent to Jackson at Fashoda to send a gunboat up the Sobat to stop Marchand staking any claims by hoisting French flags or making treaties on his way to the highlands. Nor did Harrington, who was still the British agent in Abyssinia, like the idea. His main concern seemed to be the reactions of the new French consul in Addis Ababa – 'a very young man who was in such a state of violent excitement and irritation over Fashoda' that Harrington thought it would be better if any questions relating to Marchand were dealt with in Paris and London. Lagarde himself did not object to the plan but he advised Marchand to leave his heavy baggage behind as 'it is not the custom for Abyssinians to act as porters like the natives of west Africa'. He made a formal request to the emperor for Marchand and his men to cross Abyssinia on 9 November, and it was granted with surprising ease and speed some ten days later.

There were also a number of practical problems to be settled on the Nile. Marchand and Baratier left Cairo on 13 November but they spent some days in Khartoum, and it was not until 4 December that they got back to Fashoda. During these three weeks the details of their evacuation were worked out between Marchand and Wingate on the spot, and between the French and British governments in Paris and London. These exchanges were frequently interlaced with strands and knots of suspicion and misunderstanding on both sides. Marchand had proposed a series of complicated manoeuvres which were designed more perhaps to demonstrate his independence, and his reluctance to be beholden to the English, than to hasten his departure. His plan was to take the *Faidherbe* to a temporary base on the river Sobat with the main body of the expedition and all the stores and equipment which would be needed for the onward journey through Abyssinia to the coast. The *Faidherbe* would then return to Fashoda, and take on the surplus stores which the expedition had accumulated there, and transport them up river to Meshra er Rek. She would then return to the base on the Sobat and take Marchand and his men as far up the river as was possible. If by that time there was insufficient water in the Sobat for the *Faidherbe*, Marchand and his men would continue on foot, and the *Faidherbe* would go back to Meshra, there to be dismantled and carried overland to the French Congo. On this basis Marchand calculated that he would haul down his flag at Fashoda on 1 January 1899, complete his navigation of the Sobat by the 25th, and reach Gore in the highlands of Abyssinia a month later.

For Kitchener and Wingate this was far too long, and too full of imponderables. They wanted to complete their occupation of the upper Nile basin as quickly as possible, and to be free of the awkward and potentially inflammable presence of the French at Fashoda. They therefore offered to put one of their own gunboats at Marchand's disposal to take his surplus stores from Fashoda to Meshra straightaway. This would have enabled Marchand both to leave Fashoda without further delay, and to proceed up the Sobat while there was still enough water for the steamer to navigate its upper reaches. They offered at the same time to transport by the Nile route any members of Marchand's party who were unable or unwilling to continue the journey across Africa on foot. Knowing that Marchand would be reluctant to accept any offer of help, however useful or convenient, if it made him seem to be dependent on the British, Kitchener had these offers put through official channels to the French government in Paris. Delcassé and his political colleagues accepted the British offers with alacrity. Apart from the savings in time and in money, they wanted to see a quick end to the dangers of conflict which still existed at Fashoda itself. To make life as unpleasant as possible at Fashoda for the French and so discourage them from delaying their departure, Kitchener had instructed Jackson to confine them to their fort. Marchand and his men fretted at these restrictions and did their best to evade them. Fearing that in this situation incidents could occur by accident or even by design Delcassé shared the British view that the sooner Marchand left Fashoda the better.

Marchand's regard for Delcassé and for politicians in general was not increased when he learnt that the French government had formally described the British offers of help as 'these graceful gestures', ignoring Marchand's cynical but perhaps not quite unjustified protest that the real reason for Kitchener's offer to send one of his own gunboats to Meshra was to have an excuse to despatch 'half a battalion of Egyptian troops' to take possession of the French outposts which Marchand had established there and elsewhere in the Bahr el Ghazal. In the end neither the *Faidherbe* nor a British gunboat went to Meshra er Rek as the approaches to the port had by this time become so choked with *sudd* that no steamboat could get there. However two of the French sergeants who were unwell, and six of the Senegalese soldiers, took advantage of the other British offer and went back to France by the Nile route; with them, according to Dr Emily, went some of the expedition's surplus stores – 'several boxes of ammunition both for their rifles and their cannon as well as considerable quantities of coffee, sugar, flour and bales of cloth and drums full of coloured beads'. This was by no means the end of Marchand's reserves. Twenty tons of perishable goods were also handed over to Colonel Jackson and his garrison troops, together with what Jackson himself described as their 'surplus supplies of champagne and wine'. Even allowing for the fact that on its successful visit to Meshra in October the *Faidherbe* had brought back further supplies, this evidence of the surplus at Marchand's disposal at Fashoda must have given both Kitchener and Wingate, and the French and British governments themselves considerable food for thought; as Baratier put it, the gift of these stores to Jackson and his unhappy and ill-equipped garrison was 'their only vengeance' for the way in which Kitchener had misrepresented their situation at Fashoda. Hardest of all perhaps for the Frenchmen to hand over were the gardens of vegetables and flowers which they had made and tended with such care, and their two precious milch cows.

Marchand finally left Fashoda on 13 December 1898, almost five months to the day since he had arrived. With him went seven French officers, two French sergeants, 100 Senegalese soldiers and 50 Yakoma boatmen.[2]

The departure was an emotional and difficult occasion for both sides. Although there had been moments of tension and ill-feeling, especially when Marchand was away and Germain was left in charge, relations between the French and British officers had as a rule been polite and sometimes cordial, while relations between the Senegalese soldiers and their Egyptian Army counterparts had often been embarrassingly friendly. When Colonel Jackson received his orders to prevent the French leaving the fort or getting supplies from the Shilluk he seems to have applied them without enthusiasm or conviction. One reason for this was that he knew, and the French knew, that he had not got the means to enforce them. The *Faidherbe* could always evade or outstrip his own gunboats while the manoeuvrable little whale-boats enabled the French to move on the river largely unchecked whenever they wanted to forage or send out parties to reconnoitre. Letters and journals and other personal records make it clear that during this period of official awkwardness there were frequent unofficial exchanges of civilities and courtesies, with the French sending presents of fresh vegetables and meat from game they had shot on illegal outings, and the British and Egyptian officers providing English and French newspapers and books, offering facilities and even credit for any purchases the French cared to make at the two shops run by Greeks which had been established in the British compound, and any help that was needed in stamping and conveying private mail. Dr Emily and the French-educated Egyptian doctor attached to the British garrison were on particularly good terms, and regularly exchanged gossip, bottles of wine and each own's particular cure for local ills like guinea-worm, beri-beri and hookworm. Another matter they discussed in great medical detail over claret and Greek brandy was

---

[2] Mangin had been sent off a month before with one other officer and fifty soldiers in another attempt to find an overland route into the Abyssinian highlands. When the decision to evacuate Fashoda was taken word was sent to him by runner that he should continue his journey to the east and meet the main body of the expedition at Gore.

the treatment of the terrible wounds inflicted by Nile crocodiles. One can sense from these personal records that, while their countries' governments and newspapers seemed to be locked in the grip of conflict and mutual abuse, even at times to be on the brink of war, at Fashoda itself the soldiers of both sides were drawn together by their common need to survive the heat and the rain and the mosquitoes, and the days and the weeks of almost insufferable boredom, anxiety, and stress.

Both Emily and Baratier wrote appreciately in their memoirs of the luncheon which the British officers gave to the French on the day before they left, and of the deep emotion they all felt when, in a generous gesture, Colonel Jackson presented them with the flag of captured Mahdist gunboat *Safia* on the grounds that it was rightfully more their trophy than his. Sadly, neither of the Frenchmen thought it politic to make any mention of the dinner which, according to Jackson, they themselves had given to the British the evening before. However they all recorded the actual moment of departure and the tense, last-minute delay while Marchand, proud and sensitive to the last, sent Baratier to request that the French flag should not be replaced by the Union Jack until they were out of sight. Jackson granted the request. Although he and the other British officers thought that the French government had been wrong to send Marchand to Fashoda, and that the British government was right to insist he must leave, they had nothing but admiration for the courage, resource, and determination displayed by Marchand and his band. Many years later Baratier was to recall this moment of departure with a moving blend of sadness and pride. Jackson had had a guard of honour drawn up on the bank of the river in front of the British camp. The French convoy of vessels moved slowly past with the *Faidherbe*, beflagged and its deck lined with troops, in the van, and behind it, in line astern, the five little boats with the Yakoma paddlers dressed in smart red jerseys for the occasion, and matching the rhythm of their paddles with song. The British and Egyptian officers drew their swords in salute; the guard presented arms, the band played the Marseillaise.

Not least of the Frenchmen's embarrassments was having to explain their withdrawal to their Senegalese soldiers. The Senegalese were mercenary soldiers but they were intensely loyal to officers they liked, and shared some of their pride in being French. But, as Emily was able to observe without sentiment, they quickly put disappointment and past events behind them, and dwelt with zest on the novel excitements and delights which, it was said, lay easily before them in *le pays des Blancs*, as the cool highlands and their paler coloured Abyssinian inhabitants were known by those with darker skins who lived in the hot plains and swamps below.

CHAPTER XIX

The End of the Journey

AFTER its brave start the *Faidherbe* and its following of small craft made more hesitant progress. The Yakoma boatmen no longer sang as they paddled; the only available firewood for the ship's boilers was damp or green and gave out little heat. Dr Emily used a number of medical metaphors to describe how the engine panted and puffed and wheezed itself hoarse as it strove to make way against the strong, steady stream of the White Nile. Progress was no better when they reached the river Sobat. The Sobat was no more than a hundred metres across at this point and not nearly as wide as the Nile but, with its upper reaches in the nearby highlands of Abyssinia, the current was faster. The days that followed seemed tiresome and endless, and the nights were no better because of the persistent mosquitoes and the difficulty, on a river bordered with reeds, of finding somewhere to camp. It was not easy for the Frenchmen in their mood of anger and frustration to have to admit that the best relief to the tedium was their encounters with the British, first at the fort which Kitchener had established at the mouth of the Sobat and again at Nasir some 200 km up the river where another outpost had been set. These posts were part of the network which Kitchener and Wingate were busy spreading, despite their instructions, over the whole area of the Sudan but these two posts had been established with particular celerity, partly to make sure that Menelik did not try to push his frontiers towards the Nile, and partly to keep an eye on Marchand's activities. For these reasons the Sobat was also being regularly patrolled by gunboats sent out from Khartoum. Marchand and his companions now found themselves being received and entertained at these outposts and on board the gunboats with a friendliness and tact which surprised and embarrassed them.

Marchand's party reached Nasir on 18 December, and it was not long before they had their first sight of the distant Abyssinian hills. It was a pleasant change. The flat featureless plains and reedy swamps started to give way to firm, tree-studded banks where they could camp at night and light fires, and put up their camp beds and mosquito nets. There were gazelle to be shot for the pot, and wild duck, and better firewood for the ship's boiler. There were occasional ragged straw huts set in patches of untidy cultivation. The naked, clean-limbed nomads standing immobile on one leg gave way to peasants, dirty, dishevelled and clothed. It was in this borderland region where the nature of the country and the inhabitants changed that the boundary between the pagan Nilotic Sudan and Christian upland Abyssinia was soon to be set.

Although the countryside was easier and the climate less steamy and less hot the going on the river itself got worse. The sandbanks gave way to rocks, and the course of the river became a succession of shallow, fast-flowing rapids and deep, boulder-filled pools. Instead of hippopotamus, and crocodiles sprawled with jaws agape while egrets picked pieces of fish from their teeth, there were herons and pelicans standing about awkwardly like actors waiting for a cue. There were stretches of river now where the *Faidherbe* could no longer tow the rafts and the whale-boats, and they had to be laboriously propelled with paddles and poles; when they became stranded on the rocks the men had to get out and push. For the *Faidherbe* herself progress became increasingly difficult. There was a constant danger of the vessel getting caught on the reefs and of being holed on a hidden ledge of rock. Finally on 5 January she struck a reef and started to sink. They beached her on a mudbank and tried to repair the damage. While the work was in progress Marchand went on ahead to reconnoitre. He found that the course of the river was beset by a series of waterfalls. It was clear that this was as far as *Faidherbe* could go.

They spent two days digging out a hollow in the bank. When it was finished they manhandled the ship up the side of the river into the hollow.[1] They left it there with its tricolour still at the mast. It was a proud and sad moment for them all. It had carried them and their stores on the Congo, the Ubangi, the Mbomu, the Mere, the Sue and across the Bahr el Ghazal to the Nile and from Fashoda it had carried them again up the Nile and the Sobat. Into the same hollow went the five small craft, the rafts, the old ferry, the red whale-boat and the white. It was the end of the journey for them too.

---

[1] This hollow on the upper reaches of the Sobat was meant to be a last resting place but the British, awkward to the end, found her there and removed the hull.

Without their boats the expedition needed other forms of transport for their belongings and supplies, but it was some time before they found anything to take their place. They were in a country on the upper reaches of the Sobat where neither Landeroin's Arabic nor the Nilotic languages of their Nuer interpreters were understood. Although they could make the elements of their needs known by signs they could not negotiate nor, in a country where everything was new to them, could they cajole or threaten as they had sometimes done before to get porters or food. After days of wearying and fruitless endeavour, of facile promises and mute denial, Marchand set off in desperation with forty men to try and find some answer to their problems or some authority on which they could depend. A few hours after he had left a body of willing porters presented themselves for work. Smiling and singing, as if there had never been any difficulties, they carried a first consignment of the expedition's loads for one day's long march. They left promising to return the following day to carry the rest of the loads. A week later the expedition, now split into two and immobilized by their own belongings, were still waiting, a day's march apart, for the porters to return.

As if to underline the fact that the expedition had entered an exotic land peopled by amiable but baffling eccentrics, Marchand and his reconnaissance party suddenly reappeared, mounted on horseback and at the gallop, accompanied by Abyssinian notables and a motley host of attendants, some on mules or horses, others running and keeping up with the riders by hanging on to the animals' tails. As the expedition made its way up into the Abyssinian uplands its progress took on what Dr Emily termed a number of fairyland qualities. The stores were loaded onto horses while the Frenchmen were mounted on splendidly caparisonned mules. In many parts of Abyssinia it was the horse which carried the loads, and the mules which carried people; that is to say the rich, the powerful, the priests and guests. The lowly and the women walked or ran beside the mounts. Marchand and his men now found themselves accompanied by a large concourse of local people of both sexes who displayed a close and persistent and often embarrassing interest in every detail of their activities. The countryside was beautiful but the route itself was difficult. The rugged mixture of craggy mountains and deep clefts reminded Emily of his native Corsica, and he likened the wooded valleys and tumbling streams to Auvergne and

Dauphiné. After many months of slender and sometimes monoto-
nous rations they now found themselves being plied day after day
with offers and gifts of butter and honey, bread made of wheat or
maize, a variety of peas and beans, onions, artichokes and sweet
potatoes. There was meat in plenty, beef and succulent mutton from
fat-tailed sheep. Their camps were again thronged each evening
with women and girls who came in with their produce and with
generous offers and gifts both of themselves and of *tej*, an intoxicat-
ing Abyssinian brew made from honey.

They reached the small country town of Gore on 28 January 1899.
Here they found Mangin and his party waiting for them, having
arrived only a few days before after a difficult and exasperating
journey through the lesser known country to the north. It was not so
much the awkward terrain or the hazards of travelling in unmapped
country which had held them up as the quixotic behaviour of the
Abyssinian general Dimisi who had detained them on the particularly infuriating grounds that they were English spies. It took some
time for Mangin to persuade him that he was a friend and an ally.
Coloured beads and copper wire may have sufficed in the lowlands
but they were not by any means enough for persuasion in Abyssinia.
The governors and generals who mattered wanted harder currency,
like high-velocity rifles, double-barrelled shotguns, and silver dollars bearing the effigy of the eighteenth-century Empress Maria
Theresa of Austria which, by one of the accidentals of history, were
still the most widely accepted currency in Abyssinia.[2] Having at last
persuaded Dimisi that he was not an English spy Mangin found that
he was no more free as a friend than he had been as an enemy.
Dimisi confided to Mangin that he had received orders to go among
the negroes and the Arabs whom he despised in a country which he
did not know, and wanted Mangin and his soldiers to take him by
the hand and be his guide and protector. It was only after what
Mangin told his sisters were 'unspeakable scenes' that he had finally
managed to get away and continue his journey.

Once it had been accepted that the expedition should withdraw
through Abyssinia Marchand had asked for a supply of warm

---

[2] Their use in Abyssinia dated from the time when much of the trade in the Middle
East was based on Venice, and from the brief period between 1797 and 1866 when
Venice formed part of Austria. They were thoroughly inconvenient as coinage, being
too large and too heavy, and with a value of about 4 shillings worth much more than
was needed for most local transactions.

clothing and blankets, together with 10,000 francs' worth of Maria
Theresa dollars, to be sent out from France through Jibuti and to be
ready and waiting for him at Gore. He knew that the blankets and
warm clothing would be needed in the night-cold highlands especially for his African soldiers and followers, and it infuriated him
when he found that the blankets had not arrived. He did not know
who was to blame but both he and Baratier were in bitter mood, and
ready to put the blame with equal inconsequence on Paris, on
Lagarde and other French representatives in Abyssinia, and on the
Abyssinian authorities themselves. They had counted so much and
for so long on help from the east, both from the French expeditions
and from the emperor Menelik, that their irritation had become
pervasive. They found another cause for irritation while they were
at Gore. Owing to what Mangin called the Abyssinians' 'capacity
for inertia' and to the rapacity of the professional muleteers, it was
two weeks before they were able to leave. Although the more
phlegmatic Emily did his best to put a gloss on their stay at Gore by
paying tribute to the generous if quixotic hospitality of their Abyssinian hosts and their elaborate network of social rituals and good
manners, he too found it difficult not to be vexed by the behaviour
of the muleteers who seemed to have and to abuse what amounted
to a strangle-hold on the entire transport system of the country.

It took Marchand and his men a month to do the 400 km journey
to Addis Ababa, an average of 8 miles a day. It was not at all like
their earlier journeys of adventure, excitement, exploration and
danger, sustained by patriotic fervour and the challenge of a race.
From having been a small, compact band of tough, taut, dedicated
soldiers they seemed to have degenerated into a bunch of easy-
living tourists, scornfully described by Mangin himself as 'un gros
convoi of 11 Europeans [a number of other Europeans having come
out from Addis Ababa to meet them], 139 Senegalese, 33 Yakoma,
a dozen or so servants, a hundred or so Abyssinians, 233 horses and
mules'. As they made their way in leisurely stages through the
rolling hills and high plateaux they looked like some minor Biblical
migration on its way to a promised land. The missing blankets finally
reached them as they were approaching Addis. As the town is
between seven and eight thousand feet above sea level the blankets
were very welcome but they did little to lessen Marchand's bitter-
ness.

They reached the outskirts of Addis Ababa on 10 March. Here

too it was another four weeks before they were able to move on. Their accounts of what they did in Menelik's new capital and of how they were treated both by their hosts and by their compatriots are by no means the same. For reasons which perplexed and vexed them Lagarde treated them in public with some reserve as if they were an embarrassment and an unwelcome reminder perhaps of his country's and his own failures. Lagarde would therefore have liked to see them leave as quickly as possible, and the main reason why they were held up for so long was the Abyssinian emperor's own uncertainty about whether it would be politic to grant them an audience or not. He had promised so much and performed so little that he may perhaps have been torn between the advantages of making amends, and the disadvantages of inviting recrimination. He wanted to continue the good relations with France which had brought him and his country so many benefits in the past but he did not want to upset the British who were now so clearly the dominant power in his part of Africa. In this awkward situation Menelik diplomatically absented himself from his capital, pleading sometimes that he was unwell and at others that he was occupied dealing with rebellious subjects. French historians generally incline to the view that the emperor resolved his dilemma by continuing to absent himself to the end but Harrington reported to London that there had been a formal audience, and Dr Emily later gave a detailed and evocative account of the expedition's reception, with the emperor receiving them reclining on cushions of state at ten o'clock precisely on the morning of Monday 3 April 1899. It seems that in the end the emperor's curiosity was stronger than his caution. He particularly wanted to view Marchand's Senegalese soldiers performing military drill and to see with his own eyes the black Yakoma boatmen from the Congo who, he had been assured by his advisers, 'had tails, ate women and children for breakfast, curdled the milk of nursing mothers, caused the pregnant to miscarry and feasted on human flesh all night'.

At last on 13 April Marchand and his companions managed to get away. They were still well provided with horses and mules but their progress was impeded by what Dr Emily later described in his book as 'a troublesome affliction' which affected both the European and the African members of the expedition, and for a time put as many as forty to fifty men out of action every day. In other respects it was an uneventful journey through unexciting country. They reached the ancient, picturesque and insanitary town of Harar on 28 April. They were entertained on its outskirts by a body of French Catholic missionaries who had established a hospital for lepers there; after a few days' rest in this pleasant, well-watered country, whose staple crops were cannabis and coffee, they embarked on the last stage of their journey. It took them through one of the hottest, driest and least attractive areas in the world. They had equipped themselves with camels and goat-skins filled with water to see them through the fringes of the Danakil desert and the arid approaches to Jibuti but, by what was nearly a calamitous mischance, it poured with rain when they were there, and in the end it was sudden, surging torrents of water, and slippery, barely passable mud which were their hazards instead of the heat and the thirst they had been led to expect.

They saw the French flag for the first time on a small white fort 37 km from the sea. In the fort was a detachment of soldiers posted to protect the men who were constructing the first section of the railway which French engineers were building to provide a link between the port of Jibuti and Addis Ababa. It was on this stretch of railway that Marchand and his men ended their journey. Although the train was decked with flowers, and they were welcomed with embraces and speeches and champagne, it was not quite the ending they had envisaged or hoped for when they first set out in 1896 to plant the French flag at Fashoda. As Marchand completed his heroic journey on this makeshift train he might have had the thought in his mind that, if his venture had received the help and support he was promised, this brief stretch of line might have been the beginning of a great railway to be constructed with French expertise all the way from Jibuti to Dakar; on such a railway French citizens and French goods would have been able to travel across Africa under the French flag without having to seek permission or to be beholden to any other power. He could also have wondered what might have happened if he had not been held up for six months at Loango securing a safe passage for his expedition and held up again with transport difficulties on the Congo and the Ubangi. Without these delays he could have been established at Fashoda by the summer of 1897. At that time Kitchener was the only other rival still in the race, and Kitchener was still six or seven hundred miles from Fashoda with a large, undefeated Mahdist army in his way. If the French had occupied Fashoda then they would have had time to reinforce it properly with men and supplies. They would have had time to make treaties of friendship and protection with all their neighbouring tribes and to have trained their young men into soldiers of France. In such circumstances they would have been hard to dislodge either by diplomacy or by force, and Marchand's objective could have been accomplished. Even with these delays the situation might have been saved if, when Marchand reached Fashoda in July of 1898, he had found an Abyssinian army encamped on the other side of the river with a French expedition waiting with reinforcements and supplies, and a line of communications firmly established across Abyssinia with the French port of Jibuti. Marchand and his companions did their best to respond to the cheers and the cries of acclaim as they entered the small town but it was small wonder that behind their polite smiles and bows of appreciation their real feelings were of anger, and bitter disappointment and a deep, brooding despair.

CHAPTER XX

The Aftermath

WITH the decision to withdraw from Fashoda, the visions of a commanding position on the Nile and of a continuous belt of French territory across Africa may have vanished, but there were still reasons for hoping that something might yet be harvested or at least gleaned from the seeds which Marchand and his companions had sown. When Lord Salisbury had spoken to the French ambassador in London on 27 October he had made it as clear as the diplomatic language and usage of the time allowed that, while there could be no discussion of territorial claims as long as Marchand remained at Fashoda, this would no longer be the case once the French government had told him to leave. As Salisbury himself put it in a telegram to Monson in Paris a few days later:

. . . whatever was at present abnormal in the diplomatic relations between the two countries would cease. It would then be open to the French government to raise a discussion upon the frontier in those regions, and their representations would be considered by Her Majesty's Government in the same spirit which they would bring to the consideration of frontier questions which might arise between England and any other nation in any part of the world.

Salisbury had often spoken in belittling terms of the Bahr el Ghazal, and Cromer had also expressed his reluctance to incur the trouble and expense of administering such an expanse of unproductive country. They argued that all Britain and Egypt wanted there was to trade, and that could be assured in other less burdensome ways. Salisbury was therefore, as he put it, 'not disinclined to compromise and would be prepared to give France the Bahr el Ghazal if they would stop obstructing us in Egypt'. In these circumstances it was not surprising that when Paul Cambon arrived in London to take up his post as the new ambassador on 12 December 1898 both he and Delcassé believed that there was a reasonable chance that they could extract some concessions from the British. They knew by then of course that neither Salisbury's Conservative government nor the Liberal opposition would let them keep Fasho-

da or anywhere else on the main stream of the Nile, but they hoped
that they might be able to keep a port like Meshra er Rek or Fort
Desaix which would give France access to the Nile river system.
They particularly hoped to be able to keep Tambura and the
country of the Azande where treaties had been made and posts
established both by Liotard and by Marchand.

It was with these hopes in mind that Cambon was soon to be
observed in London 'poring diligently over maps with the Marquis
of Salisbury'. The Foreign Office found the new ambassador friendly and helpful, and when Cambon dined with the Queen at Windsor
he was careful not to let anyone guess from his expression or his
appetite that he would write to his mother afterwards and say that
'in my household such a dinner would not have been tolerated'. In
order not to upset what seemed a promising situation, or prejudice
their chances of getting some concessions, the French government
decided not to raise any objections when, on 19 January 1899, the
British government proclaimed an Anglo-Egyptian Condominium
over the Sudan. The French may have also been influenced by the
way in which Britain continued to flex her naval muscle with much
ostentatious activity in the dockyards and on the high seas. In
ordinary circumstances France would have been the first to object to
the condominium as a devious device whereby all the power in the
Sudan would be in British hands, unfettered by the international
obligations and tribunals which the French found so useful, and
Cromer found so tiresome in metropolitan Egypt. In practice the
only part played by the Egyptian government in the condominium
was to make up any deficit there might be in the cost of administering the Sudan, an obligation which was to cost the Egyptian
taxpayer close on a million and a half pounds up to 1913 when, by
good government and parsimonious financial control, the Anglo-
Egyptian Sudan finally managed to balance its budget.

This forbearance however, did the French little good. When it
came to the point Salisbury had changed his mind. On 11 January
Cambon broached the matter on the assumption that Salisbury
'should now not be indisposed to discuss the differences which
separated the two countries at the present time', but Salisbury
replied that he was 'quite willing but must make it clear that there
was one point on which opinion in England was very strongly and
specifically fixed, and that was not to share with France political
rights over any portion of the valley of the Nile'. Salisbury's change

of mind was partly a matter of party politics, and partly the result of pressure from Cairo. On the domestic front there had always been a strong feeling among his Conservative colleagues both in the cabinet and on the back benches that Egypt and England must have absolute control of the White Nile. While Salisbury as a rule took less notice of the opinions of his colleagues and the Press than most prime ministers he had to be careful for his own political position not to alienate too many of his supporters, or to allow himself to be outflanked in imperialist zeal by Rosebery or other empire-building members of the Liberal opposition. What seems to have influenced him most however was the advice he was now getting from Cromer and Kitchener. In October 1898, when he had been inclined to compromise, he had instructed Kitchener to draw up possible boundaries between French and British possessions west of the Sudan. Salisbury had hoped that there would be some concessions to offer to the moderate Delcassé which could be displayed as feathers in his cap, or as favours, perhaps, for which other favours could one day be asked in return. Kitchener seems to have understood Salisbury's wishes, and he claimed that the boundaries which he eventually proposed involved what he described as 'granting large concessions to the French', on the grounds that he had left to France some areas in the north which had formerly been claimed by the Egyptians. In fact his proposed boundary followed the line of the watershed between the Nile and the Congo basins, which meant that the whole of the Bahr el Ghazal and Tambura would be included in the Anglo-Egyptian Sudan. In the north he even suggested an extension of the Sudanese province of Darfur to the west towards Lake Chad which would have cut off the French possessions in the Congo basin from those in north and west Africa.

The reasons which Kitchener gave for wanting the whole of the White Nile basin to be in British hands were, firstly, that the watershed between the Congo and the Nile was a natural boundary and that such frontiers were the easiest, and the cheapest, to control. The second reason was that, as he put it, 'if the French obtain control over the warlike Dinka tribe they will organize a force which will give us trouble'.[1] The third reason was the importance of not

[1] This was probably a misunderstanding on Kitchener's part due to the fact that neither he nor Wingate had ever been to the Bahr el Ghazal. It is true that a British military intelligence report had described it as 'the finest recruiting ground in the world' but the tribes it had in mind were the Zande and the Nuer, not the Dinka. Marchand and Liotard also had a high opinion of the Zande as potential soldiers.

letting the French have a port on any part of the Nile. As Sir John Ardagh, the Director of Military Intelligence argued in one of his secret reports, 'the region of the Bahr el Ghazal may not be of much value but it is of the greatest importance not to let France establish a clear-water port which would enable her to claim rights of navigation on the Nile'. Kitchener's final reason echoed the vision of Victor Prompt that if the French were allowed to keep any post on the Nile they could, if they were one day so minded, manipulate or divert the waters of the river in ways which could seriously affect the flow of the Nile on which Egypt and the rest of the Sudan depended.

The arguments for keeping the lands claimed to the north of the Bahr el Arab were different. Apart from a wish to have a link with existing British outposts in northern Nigeria in an area in which the French and the British had been at loggerheads for some years, Kitchener was influenced by claims put forward with persuasive charm by the sultans of Darfur that they had historical and other ancient rights to the lands of their neighbours to the west. Kitchener supported these often dubious claims so much that Salisbury had to warn him that 'if your demands are excessive we may find it hard to defend our frontiers both on the spot and in parliament!'

In the end, a settlement was reached in a remarkably short space of time. The boundaries finally agreed left the whole of the Bahr el Ghazal and the basin of the White Nile in British hands; in the north the British abandoned their demand for a corridor to Nigeria and accepted a compromise settlement of the rival claims of the French-backed sultans of Ouadai and those of their own protegés in Darfur. A French plea for purely commercial rights on the Nile waters was withdrawn in the face of a British demand for reciprocal rights on the Ubangi. These processes of argument and agreement were made easier by the fact that it was not then considered necessary or even desirable to pay much attention to the wishes of the people who lived in the areas in dispute. One result of this was that in the end the Azande found that they and their traditional lands were divided between the British, the French, and the Belgians.

The agreement was finally signed on 21 March 1899. Marchand does not seem to have been told about the negotiations or the agreement, either during the time he spent at Addis Ababa in March or when he arrived at Jibuti in May. The French government's reluctance to face Marchand and his companions with the details is understandable. The agreement not only put an end to the expedition's objectives and hopes but it surrendered all that had been so laboriously and sometimes painfully won by occupation and by treaty both at Fashoda itself and in the whole of the Bahr el Ghazal and Tambura. It was little compensation to a forthright soldier like Marchand that, at Delcassé's request, the agreement took the less obtrusive form of an annexe termed an Additional Declaration in a general settlement of Anglo-French differences in western Africa.

Marchand himself, however, and other French chauvinists who felt as he did, continued to criticize Delcassé and his colleagues as weak and unpatriotic politicians who had put their own personal reputation and interests before their country's. But it could also be argued that they were logical, hard-headed realists, and that the agreement they reached with the British government was as good as the parlous condition of France then allowed. They recognized that Britain had a stronger navy and a better industrial base than France, and that if they had dug in their heels out of sentiment or allowed the situation to drift or erupt into hostilities it would have been yet another war that France would have lost. They also recognized that France's position was seriously weakened by its own domestic situation, particularly by the divisive effects of the Dreyfus affair. It did not make matters easier when at a crucial time on 16 February Félix Faure, the President of the Republic, died suddenly at the age of 58 from a heart attack attributed by gossip to over-exertion in someone else's bed.

When they had been negotiating the details of the agreement Cambon and Delcassé had tried hard to retain a Nile port or at least a part of Tambura. Their resolution had been weakened however by the realization, from a close reading of Marchand's own reports, that because of the seasonal variations in the depth of water in the river Sue and the problems created by the *sudd*, the area of the Bahr el Ghazal could not after all provide the year-round, clear-water port that was needed. Nor were Marchand's reports of the economic potential of the region encouraging to private investors and overseas merchants. For both these reasons the big commercial concerns which had a large say in the policies of the *parti colonial* had already started to lose interest in the basin of the Nile and had turned their attention elsewhere.

Another factor which Delcassé and Cambon had had to take into account was the balance of power in Europe. The attitudes of the other major European powers during the Fashoda crisis had made it clear that France must look afresh at its traditional alliances. Although Austria, Germany, Italy, Russia and Turkey had all at one time or another encouraged France to confront the British in Egypt and the valley of the Nile not one of them had been prepared to offer any effective help. Russia in particular had been revealed as an unreliable ally, while the Germans made it clear that they would not go beyond words and a muffled rattling of sabres unless the French renounced the lost provinces of Alsace and Lorraine. As this was something no French government could possibly do, it left their traditional rivals the English as the only real alternative. The movement towards an Anglo-French alliance was necessarily a gradual process, and it needed several years and several setbacks before it came to fruition in the *Entente Cordiale*. But both Delcassé and Cambon saw earlier than most that this should be the objective. They saw too that one of the prices France would have to pay for such an alliance would be to relinquish its ambitions and claims in Egypt and the valley of the Nile. Yet even this sacrifice of what had for so long been a cardinal feature of French foreign policy had its compensations. As France tacitly and in the end openly gave up Egypt and the Nile to the British, so, for its part, did the British come to abandon its commercial and strategic interests in north eastern Africa and accept that France should have a free hand in Morocco. It turned out in the end to be a good bargain for France, and one which had a strong appeal to all the elements which made up the *parti colonial* in metropolitan and overseas France – the business houses, the strategists, the soldiers and the imperialists and those who sought an outlet for France's own increasing population. Morocco was described by a spokesman for the *Comité de l'Afrique française* as 'one of the finest countries in the world with 30 million hectares of arable land – half the area of France and room enough for 15 to 20 million Frenchmen. . . . It is in Morocco that you will find phosphate deposits and iron ore, wheatfields and olive trees. It is there that you will find markets for the cotton goods of Rouen and the Vosges, wool to supply our weavers in Roubaix and Tourcoing, railways to build and harbours to develop . . .' There too, the generals of the French army knew, they would find a population of tough and warlike tribes, who could be trained into soldiers to serve the interests of France in all parts of the world. Finally Morocco was geographically close to metropolitan France, and provided a convenient bridge therefore between those who believed that France should be strong in Europe and those who wanted expansion overseas.

There was one other factor which Delcassé and his colleagues had to take into account. Colonel Marchand and his companions had become the heroes of discontented conservative opinion in France, and the focus of the activities and aspirations of the sort of protest movements which, ten years before, had found a champion in the romantic military figure of General Boulanger. To the royalists, militarists, the League of Patriots and the innately conservative French working classes who had been attracted by Boulanger's Celtic magnetism[2] were now added the *anti-Drefusards* and all those who regarded politicians, the Jews, aesthetes, freemasons, intellectuals, and the English as jointly or severally the cause of France's present dishonour and disarray. Together these various elements added up to a potentially formidable opposition, and one which, if united and kindled by the right kind of leadership, could become a serious threat not only to the government but to the whole edifice of republican France. 'What hope is there', the right-wing journal *La Libre Parole* asked its readers in February 1899, 'for a country where it is men like Delcassé who give the orders, and men like Marchand merely obey?'

In this situation it was not surprising that the French government was reluctant to do anything which might add to Marchand's reputation and popular appeal. In the negotiations which preceded the agreement of 21 March it could be said by the cynics that it actually suited the government to be obliged to give up any territory or treaty which Marchand and his expedition had secured. For the same reason Marchand and his companions were kept as much away from the press and the public as could be unobtrusively arranged. A naval vessel, the *d'Assas*, was sent to Jibuti to bring them back to France as quickly and quietly as possible, and secret instructions were sent to the governor of Jibuti to do his best 'in the interests of France' to dissuade a particularly awkward representative of the French conservative press from exploiting the situation in his interviews and reports. It was an order which the governor, who was

---

[2] General Boulanger (1837–91) was the son of a Breton father and a Welsh mother. With his blue eyes and long blond beard this handsome fighting soldier on his huge black horse had for a short time great popular appeal in the eighteen eighties. He died, as he had lived, with great flair, shooting himself on the grave of his mistress in Brussels.

newly appointed by patronage and very anxious to please, was both ready and able to carry out, thanks, as he boasted in his reply, to his close personal relations with the journalist concerned. Similar pressures were applied when Marchand went through the Suez Canal. He and his party were finally disembarked in the security and obscurity of the naval base at Toulon on 30 May 1899. The colourful and appealing Senegalese soldiers and the Yakoma boatmen were ordered to remain there when Marchand and his fellow officers were put on the night train to Paris two days later. They arrived at the *gare de Lyon* early on the morning of 2 June.

The official reception accorded to Marchand and his men was a carefully blended mixture of ceremony and caution. Many of the individuals and organizations which had hoped to use Marchand's return for their own advantage were temporarily disarmed by the invitations sent to them to take part in the official welcome at the railway station and in the public speech-making, embracings and presentation of medals and swords of honour which followed. The crowd, estimated at ten thousand, which had gathered outside the station was kept at a distance by barriers put up by the police, and the cortège was taken through the streets of Paris at a brisk pace described by one aggrieved right-wing journal as *une allure folle* or breakneck speed.

Another reason for this careful management of Marchand's return to France was the fear that not only would it be exploited by the government's critics and opponents but that Marchand himself might agree to be their figurehead. Marchand was not, however, a man to allow himself to be used or exploited by anyone. Even in Cairo in November of the previous year, when he had come up from Fashoda and been so immoderate in his telegrams to Delcassé, he had been careful and responsible in what he had said to the press and at public meetings, a point which was duly noted and reported both when he had been at Jibuti and when he passed through Suez in the summer of 1899. Marchand was above all a soldier and a good Frenchman. He had a strong sense of duty and of discipline, and he applied it as much to himself as to others. A soldier's duty, as he saw it, was to obey orders, and in the last resort this meant the orders of the government and of the President of the Republic. As a good Frenchman he saw the dangers of division and disunity and the harm they had already done to his country. He had no wish to be used to further such divisions, particularly by the royalists and the rich and the ambitious. He was, and was proud to be, a man of the people, a carpenter's son who had risen from the ranks in an army in which it was said with pride that every soldier carried a field-marshal's baton in his knapsack.

So, as Colonel Marchand of the Marines faced the crowds outside the *gare de Lyon* and was driven in triumph through the streets of Paris, although he heard the occasional shouts and angry cries of *Vive l'armee!*, *À bas les traitres!*, *À bas les Juifs!*, *À bas les Drefusards!*, what touched him most was the crowd's simple good humour and the warmth of the welcome given to him by people of his own kind, and above all by the cries of *Vive la France!* That night at a reception given to Marchand and his fellow officers, and attended by many ambitious and self-seeking men of the right, generals, royalists, politicians, business men and journalists, and by delegations from bodies like *La Jeunesse Coloniale*, *La Jeunesse Nationaliste* and *La Ligue des Patriotes*, Marchand publically rejected the role offered to him. His answer was clear, simple and strong: 'Restons unis. Vive la France! C'est ce que je peux vous dire'.

Soon afterwards the French government fell, for reasons not connected with Marchand's expedition, but in the customary reshuffle which followed Delcassé again survived and continued as foreign minister. Waldeck-Rousseau, the new prime minister, decided that Marchand's continued exemplary unpolitical behaviour made the advantages of putting him and his men on public display outweigh the risks. On 14 July 1899 Marchand and his whole company of officers, non-commissioned officers, Senegalese soldiers and Yakoma boatmen paraded together for the last time on the racecourse at Longchamps. It was not destined or intended to be more than a gesture. A month later the Senegalese soldiers and the boatmen were sent back to Africa while Marchand and Baratier were subjected to a tiresome, long drawn-out and humiliating process of inquiry into the costs and the accounts of the expedition. The original allocation of money for the venture had been 600,000 francs. When all the unpaid bills, forgotten claims, and unauthorized items of expenditure had been unearthed and added up the total expenditure came, according to the investigators, to 1,114,110 francs. Marchand and Baratier refused to accept this figure and many of the details on which it was based, and they often expressed their dissent and disgust in very terse and military terms.

As France and England gradually drifted into alliance, so relations between the people of the two countries slowly improved. Although the Press and the public utterances of posturing politicians had sometimes given the impression that England and France were on the brink of hostilities in 1898, there is really no evidence in the archives in London and Paris that either government seriously considered going to war over Fashoda. There is no doubt however that feelings ran high on both sides of the Channel, and that relations between the parliaments, the Press and the people were at a very low ebb. There was therefore considerable scope for improvement, and it took many forms. One was a desire to slither the Fashoda affair under the carpet and to pretend, as far as could be, that it had never happened. To save France from the awkwardness of defeat and humiliation at Fashoda, and to save Britain from the equally awkward embarrassment of having won and got her own way, an undefined but perceptible conspiracy of polite silence settled like a fog on the usual channels of communication. It affected both countries but it was, if anything, more noticeable in England, partly perhaps because of the realization that victory at Fashoda had only been achieved at the cost of the public humiliation of a band of particularly brave and honourable men. So it was that when the time came in 1908 for Cromer to publish his classic *Modern Egypt*, which was widely read on both sides of the Channel, he added the footnote saying he had 'purposely omitted any account of what is known as the "Fashoda incident" from this work.' 'I should', he continued, 'be most unwilling to do anything which might contribute to revive public interest in an affair which is now, happily for all concerned, well-nigh forgotten.' Even the word 'Fashoda' was erased from the map, and the place was known henceforth by its Shilluk name of Kodok.

A short time afterwards Marchand was sent to China on a military mission. It was not an important mission, and China was a conveniently long way away. When he returned he found the army had nothing more to offer him and he was retired on half pay. The war in 1914 came as a relief to a man who had found it difficult to adjust to civilian life and to marriage. He was recalled to the colours and, restored to his true *métier*, he rose to be a general of distinction and courage. He died, still a bitter and disappointed man, in 1934 when he was 68.

Baratier never returned to Africa but he remained in the army, and had a successful career as a cavalry commander. During the great war he too rose to be a general and was still a serving officer when he died in the field of a heart attack in 1917. But of all the officers of the expedition Mangin had the most distinguished, the most colourful and the most tempestuous career. He acquired a reputation as a courageous and obstinate soldier, and earned the nickname of 'The Butcher' because of the number of men who were killed, on both sides, whenever he was in command. He was finally relieved of his command of the French army 10th corps for throwing his divisions again and again, regardless of cost, against entrenched German positions on the western front.

Germain, who also went to China with Marchand, became a colonel and died suddenly in Paris in 1906. Largeau went back to Africa but he returned to France on the outbreak of war and was killed at Verdun in 1916. Dr Emily became a general in the French army medical corps and lived to a ripe old age. It was he who, in his still vigorous eighties, delivered the funeral oration at Marchand's public funeral in 1934. The longest survivor of all however was Landeroin, the Arabic interpreter. He went back to Africa and joined the French colonial service, and had a long and mediocre career. When one looks now at the archaic steel engravings in old copies of the *Illustrated London News* and *L'Illustration* it comes as a surprise and a shock to discover that Landeroin, who had cooked elephant trunk *à la bordelaise* for Marchand and his companions in the Bahr el Ghazal, and had planted *haricots verts* in the Nile mud at Fashoda in 1898, was still alive in 1966. He died on 3 July of that year when he was a few days short of his ninety-fifth birthday.

Bibliography

A. Manuscript and other unpublished material

Public Record Office, London.

Foreign Office papers
  FO 1 (Abyssinia)
  FO 27 (France)
  FO 78 (Turkey) includes papers relating to Egypt.
  FO 97 (treaties) contains details of Anglo-French Agreement of 21 March 1899.
  FO 141 (Cairo Agency archives)
  FO 146 (Paris Embassy archives)

Confidential Prints
  FO 881/7042x Bahr el Ghazal: Precis of Events 1878–98.
  FO 881/7042xx Correspondence with French Government: Valley of Upper Nile 1890–97

Other papers
  PRO 30/40 Ardagh papers.
  PRO 30/57 Kitchener papers.
  PRO 633 Cromer papers. vols VI and VII

Hatfield House, Hertfordshire.
  Papers of the third Marquess of Salisbury: series A correspondence: vols 83–4, 92–3, 96, 109–13, 116–19.
University of Durham Library: Oriental Section.
  Sudan Archive: Papers of General Sir Reginald Wingate.
Archives Nationales, Paris.
  99 AP 1–3. Papiers Baratier.[1]
Archives nationales: section Outre-mer.
  Missions 42–44
  Afrique III. 32–36

B. Official publications

British Library
White Papers and Blue Books
  Africa no. 2 (1892) Papers respecting the Proposed Railway from Mombasa to Lake Victoria Nyanza.

[1] Includes Baratier's unpublished account of the final stages of the expedition's journey from Fashoda to Jibuti. (See also under Printed Books and Articles.)

Africa no. 4 (1894) Papers relating to the Anglo-Congolese Agreement.
Africa no. 5 (1894) Further Papers.
Africa no. 10 (1898) Report on the Mutiny of the Soudanese Troops in Uganda.
Egypt no. 2 (1898) Correspondence with the French Government respecting the Valley of the Upper Nile.
Egypt no. 3 (1898) Further Correspondence
British Documents on the Origins of the War 1898–1914: edited by G. P. Gooch and H. W. V. Temperley. London 1927 et seq.
Documents diplomatiques français 1871–1914. First Series. Paris 1929 et seq.
Documents diplomatiques: Affaires du Haut Nil et du Bahr-el-Ghazal 1897–98.

C. Printed books and articles

Andrew, C., *Théophile Delcassé and the Making of the* Entente Cordiale (London, 1968).
Austin, H. W., *With Macdonald in Uganda* (London, 1903).
Baratier, A. E. A., *Souvenirs de la Mission Marchand*
   I Au Congo: de Loango à Brazzaville (Paris, undated).
   II Vers le Nil: de Brazzaville à Fort Desaix (Paris, 1912).
   III Fachoda (Paris, 1941).
Bobichon, H., *Contribution à l'histoire de la Mission Marchand* (Paris, 1936).
Brown, R. G., *Fashoda Reconsidered* (John Hopkins Press, 1969).
Brunschwig, H., *Mythes et réalités de l'impérialisme colonial français 1871–1914* (Paris, 1960).
Castellani, C., *Vers le Nil français avec la Mission Marchand* (Paris, 1898).
Cecil, Lady Gwendolen, *Life of Robert, Marquis of Salisbury* (London, 1932).
Collins, R. O., *The Southern Sudan* (New Haven and London, 1962).
Cromer, Earl of, *Modern Egypt* (London, 1908).
Delbeque, J., *Vie de Général Marchand* (Paris, 1936).
Émily, Dr J. M., *Fachoda* (Paris, 1935).
Evans-Pritchard, E. E., *The Nuer* (Oxford, 1940).
   Witchcraft among the Azande (Oxford, 1937).
Grey, Viscount, *Twenty-Five Years* (London, 1925).
Hill, R. L., *A Biographical Dictionary of the Sudan* (London, 1967).
Jackson, Sir H. W., 'Fashoda', *Sudan Notes and Records* (1920).
Jesman, C., *The Russians in Ethiopia* (London, 1958).
Lebon, A., 'La Mission Marchand et le Cabinet Méline', (*Revue des Deux Mondes* 1900).
Magnus, P., *Kitchener: Portrait of an Imperialist* (London, 1958).

Mangin, C., 'Lettres de la Mission Marchand' *Revue des Deux Mondes* (1931).
Souvenirs d'Afrique (Paris, 1936).
Marchand, J. B., *Le Figaro* (26 August 1904) and *L'Illustration* (27 January 1934) [Origins of his expedition].
Le Matin (20 and 24 June 1905) [Accounts of his meeting with Kitchener at Fashoda].
Menier, M. A., Une lettre inédite de Marchand à Guillame Grandidier, *Revue d'Histoire des Colonies* (1953).
Michel, C., *Mission de Bonchamps: vers Fachoda à la rencontre de la Mission Marchand* (Paris, 1900).
Michel, M., *La Mission Marchand, 1895–99* (Paris, 1972).
Monteil, P-L., *Souvenirs Vécus, quelques feuillets de l'histoire coloniale. Les rivalités internationales* (Paris, 1924).
Perham, M., *Lugard: The Years of Adventure* (London, 1956).
Prat, O. de, 'Impressions d'un Lillois au Centre de l'Afrique', *Bulletin de la Societé de Géographie de Lille* (1897).
Prompt, V., 'Soudan Nilotique', *Bulletin de l'Institut Égyptien* (1893).
Renouvin, P., 'Les Origines de l'Expédition de Fachoda', *Revue Historique* (1948).
Sanderson, G. N., *England, Europe and the Upper Nile* (Edinburgh, 1965).
'Contribution from African Sources to the History of European Competition in the Upper Valley of the Nile', *Journal of African History* (1962).
Smith-Dorrien, H., *Memories of Forty-Eight Years Service* (London, 1925).
Stengers, J., 'Aux Origines de Fachoda: L'Expédition Monteil', *Revue Belge de Philologie et d'Histoire* (1958 and 1960).
Taylor., A. J. P., 'Prelude to Fashoda: The Question of the Upper Nile', *English Historical Review* (1950).
Wauters, A-J., 'Souvenirs de Fachoda et de l'Expédition Dhanis', *Mouvement Géographique* (1910).
Wright, P., *Conflict on the Nile* (London, 1972).

D. Other Sources

For the evidence of contemporary opinions and feelings provided in parliament and the Press I have, on the British side, made use of Hansard, *The Times*, the *Illustrated London News*, and the *Pall Mall Gazette*; on the French side I have leant heavily on the work of Mc Marc Michel.

*   *   *

Index